Learn Python by Doi

100 Practical Projects for Beginners

Sarful Hassan

Preface

This book, **Learn Python by Doing: 100 Practical Projects for Beginners**, is designed to help beginners learn Python through hands-on projects. Instead of focusing only on theory, this book takes a practical approach, allowing you to apply concepts in real-world scenarios.

Who This Book Is For This book is for anyone interested in learning Python, including:

- Beginners with little or no programming experience.
- Students and educators looking for hands-on exercises.
- Hobbyists who enjoy coding small projects.
- Developers looking to reinforce their Python skills through practical challenges.

How This Book Is Organized The book consists of **100 projects**, each covering a different concept in Python. The chapters are structured to gradually increase in complexity, starting from simple applications like a **basic calculator** and moving toward more interactive projects like **GUI-based games** and **automation scripts**.

Each chapter includes:

- A brief explanation of the concept.
- A step-by-step guide to implementing the project.
- A complete Python code example.
- Suggestions for expanding the project further.

What Was Left Out To keep the book focused on **practical coding**, the following topics are not covered in detail:

- Advanced algorithms and data structures.
- Deep theoretical explanations of Python internals.
- Complex software engineering practices.

For readers interested in these topics, we recommend additional books and online resources specializing in those areas.

Code Style (About the Code) All code examples in this book follow **PEP 8**, Python's official style guide. Code is written in a beginner-friendly format, avoiding unnecessary complexity. Readers are encouraged to experiment with the examples, modify them, and test different implementations to improve their understanding.

Release Notes This is the **First Edition** of the book, and it includes **100 Python projects** covering topics like games, utilities, automation, and data handling. Future editions may include more advanced topics based on reader feedback.

Notes on the First Edition While every effort has been made to ensure accuracy, some minor errors or typos may still exist. We welcome feedback and suggestions to improve future editions.

MechatronicsLAB Online Learning For additional resources, tutorials, and updates related to this book, visit our website:

- **Website**: mechatronicslab.net
- **Email**: mechatronicslab.net@gmail.com

Acknowledgments for the First Edition We would like to thank our readers, supporters, and the Python community for their contributions. Special thanks to all those who provided feedback during the writing process.

Table of Contents

Chapter 0 Introduction to Python

Python is a popular, high-level, and easy-to-read programming language widely used in web development, data science, artificial intelligence, automation, and more. It was created by **Guido van Rossum** and first released in 1991. Python follows a design philosophy emphasizing **code readability** and **simplicity**.

Why Learn Python?

1. **Easy to learn and use** – Python has a simple syntax that resembles English, making it beginner-friendly.
2. **Versatile** – Can be used in web development, automation, data science, machine learning, game development, and more.
3. **Large community** – A vast community of developers provides extensive support, tutorials, and open-source contributions.
4. **Cross-platform** – Runs on different operating systems like Windows, Mac, and Linux.
5. **Rich library support** – A huge ecosystem of libraries and frameworks makes development faster and easier.

Python Environment and Ecosystem

Python provides a flexible environment for coding, testing, and running applications. The ecosystem includes libraries, frameworks, and tools that make Python powerful for various use cases.

Setting Up the Python Environment

- **Installing Python**: Download it from Python's official site. Installation is straightforward and includes the Python interpreter and package manager **pip**.
- **Python Interpreters**: Python code runs using an interpreter such as:
    - **CPython** (default and most widely used)
    - **PyPy** (faster alternative with JIT compilation)
    - **Jython** (for Java integration)
    - **IronPython** (for .NET integration)
- **IDEs and Code Editors**:
    - **Windows**: PyCharm, VS Code, IDLE, Jupyter Notebook, Atom, Spyder, Thonny

- **Linux**: PyCharm, VS Code, Vim, Jupyter Notebook, Spyder, Sublime Text
- **Mac**: PyCharm, VS Code, IDLE, Jupyter Notebook, Atom, Spyder, BBEdit

Python Package Ecosystem

Python has a rich ecosystem of packages and libraries that extend its functionality:

- **Web Development**: Django, Flask, FastAPI, Tornado
- **Data Science & Machine Learning**: NumPy, Pandas, TensorFlow, Scikit-learn, Matplotlib, Seaborn
- **Automation & Scripting**: Selenium, BeautifulSoup, PyAutoGUI, Fabric
- **Game Development**: Pygame, Panda3D, Arcade
- **Networking & Cybersecurity**: Scapy, Requests, Paramiko, Twisted
- **GUI Development**: Tkinter, PyQt, Kivy, wxPython

Managing Python Packages

- **pip**: The default package manager for Python (pip install package_name).
- **virtualenv**: Creates isolated environments for different projects (virtualenv env_name).
- **conda**: Used for scientific computing and package management (conda install package_name).
- **requirements.txt**: Used to manage dependencies (pip freeze > requirements.txt).
- **poetry**: A modern dependency management tool (poetry add package_name).

Basic Python Syntax

Printing Output

```
print("Hello, World!")
```

Output:

Hello, World!

Python's environment and ecosystem make it an incredibly powerful and flexible language. Keep practicing by working on small projects like a calculator, to-do list, or a web scraper, and you'll master it in no time! 🚀

Chapter 1: Basic Calculator

Overview A basic calculator is one of the fundamental projects in Python programming. It provides essential arithmetic operations such as addition, subtraction, multiplication, and division. Understanding how to implement a calculator helps in learning user input handling, conditional statements, and function creation in Python.

This chapter covers the step-by-step implementation of a basic calculator, user input handling, function-based operations, and error management to ensure smooth execution.

Key Concepts of Basic Calculator in Python

- **Arithmetic Operations:**
  - Addition (+)
  - Subtraction (-)
  - Multiplication (*)
  - Division (/)
  - Modulus (%)
  - Exponentiation (**)
- **User Input Handling:**
  - Using `input()` function
  - Converting strings to integers or floats
- **Functions in Python:**
  - Defining functions for calculations
  - Calling functions with user inputs
- **Error Handling:**
  - Handling division by zero
  - Handling invalid inputs

Parameter Table

Operator	Functionality
+	Addition
-	Subtraction
*	Multiplication
/	Division
%	Modulus (Remainder)
**	Exponentiation

Basic Rules for Calculator in Python

Rule	Correct Example
Use correct data types for calculations	`result = int(a) + int(b)`
Handle division errors	`if b != 0: result = a / b`
Convert inputs before performing operations	`a = float(input("Enter a number: "))`

Syntax Table

SL	Concept	Syntax/Example	Description
1	Define a function	`def add(a, b):` `return a + b`	Defines a function for addition

2	Get user input	`num1 =`
		`input("Enter`
		`number: ")`
			Takes input from the user

3	Convert input to integer/float	`num1 =` `float(num1)`	Converts user input to number
4	Perform arithmetic operation	`result = num1 +` `num2`	Performs addition
5	Display result	`print("Result:",` `result)`	Prints the output

Real-Life Project: Simple Calculator

Project Code:

```
1.   def add(a, b):
2.        return a + b

3.   def subtract(a, b):
4.        return a - b

5.   def multiply(a, b):
6.        return a * b

7.   def divide(a, b):
8.        if b != 0:
9.            return a / b
```

```
10.      else:
11.            return "Error: Division by zero"
12. print("Select operation:")
13. print("1. Add")
14. print("2. Subtract")
15. print("3. Multiply")
16. print("4. Divide")

17. choice = input("Enter choice (1/2/3/4): ")
18. num1 = float(input("Enter first number: "))
19. num2 = float(input("Enter second number: "))

20. if choice == '1':
21.      print("Result:", add(num1, num2))
22. elif choice == '2':
23.      print("Result:", subtract(num1, num2))
24. elif choice == '3':
25.      print("Result:", multiply(num1, num2))
26. elif choice == '4':
27.      print("Result:", divide(num1, num2))
28. else:
29.      print("Invalid choice")
```

Project Code Explanation Table

Line	Code Section	Description
1-2	def add(a, b): return a + b	Defines a function to perform addition and return the sum.
3-4	def subtract(a, b): return a - b	Defines a function to perform subtraction and return the difference.
5-6	def multiply(a, b): return a * b	Defines a function to perform multiplication and return the product.
7-11	def divide(a, b):	Defines a function to perform division with error handling to prevent division by zero.
12-16	print("Select operation:")	Displays available mathematical operations to the user.
17	choice = input("Enter	Prompts the user to select a

	`choice (1/2/3/4): ")`	mathematical operation.
18	`num1 = float(input("Ente r first number: "))`	Prompts the user to input the first number and converts it to float for arithmetic operations.
19	`num2 = float(input("Ente r second number: "))`	Prompts the user to input the second number and converts it to float.
20-21	`if choice == '1': print("Result:", add(num1, num2))`	Checks if the user selected addition and calls the add function to display the sum.
22-23	`elif choice == '2': print("Result:", subtract(num1, num2))`	Checks if the user selected subtraction and calls the subtract function to display the difference.
24-25	`elif choice == '3': print("Result:", multiply(num1, num2))`	Checks if the user selected multiplication and calls the multiply function to display the product.
26-27	`elif choice == '4': print("Result:", divide(num1, num2))`	Checks if the user selected division and calls the divide function to display the quotient.
28-29	`else: print("Invalid choice")`	Handles invalid user input by displaying an error message.

Expected Results

- The program asks the user to choose an operation.
- The user enters two numbers.
- The program performs the selected arithmetic operation.
- The result is displayed to the user.
- If the user tries to divide by zero, an error message is displayed.

Hands-On Exercise

Try modifying the calculator with the following additional features:

1. **Add a square root function** that calculates the square root of a number.
2. **Add an exponentiation function (x^y)** that raises one number to the power of another.
3. **Allow the user to perform multiple calculations** without restarting the program.
4. **Improve the user interface** by formatting the output neatly.
5. **Implement an option to exit the program** when the user is done calculating.

Conclusion This basic calculator demonstrates fundamental Python concepts such as user input handling, functions, arithmetic operations, and error management. By mastering these concepts, developers can build more complex applications such as scientific calculators, financial calculators, and automation scripts.

Chapter 2: To-Do List Application

Overview A to-do list application is a practical project that helps users manage tasks efficiently. This application allows users to add, remove, and view tasks while keeping track of completed and pending activities. Learning to build a to-do list enhances understanding of data structures, file handling, and basic user interaction in Python.

This chapter covers the step-by-step implementation of a to-do list application, user input handling, list operations, and file handling for persistent storage.

Key Concepts of To-Do List in Python

- **Basic List Operations:**
  - Adding tasks
  - Removing tasks
  - Marking tasks as complete
  - Displaying tasks

- **User Input Handling:**
  - Using `input()` function
  - Handling invalid inputs

- **File Handling:**
  - Storing tasks in a text file
  - Retrieving saved tasks on program restart

- **Functions in Python:**
  - Defining functions for task management
  - Calling functions with user inputs

To-Do List Operations Table

Operation	Functionality
Add Task	Adds a new task to the list
Remove Task	Deletes a task from the list
View Tasks	Displays all pending tasks
Mark as Complete	Marks a task as done
Save Tasks	Saves tasks to a file for persistence
Load Tasks	Loads saved tasks when the program starts

Basic Rules for To-Do List in Python

Rule	Correct Example
Use a list to store tasks	`tasks = []`

Append new tasks correctly	`tasks.append("Buy groceries")`
Remove tasks carefully	`tasks.remove("Buy groceries")`
Use a loop for displaying tasks	`for task in tasks:` `    print(task)`

Syntax Table

SL	Concept	Syntax/Example	Description
1	Define a function	`def add_task(task):` `    tasks.append(task)`	Defines a function to add a task
2	Get user input	`task = input("Enter task: ")`	Takes input from the user
3	Append task to list	`tasks.append(task)`	Adds a task to the list
4	Remove task from list	`tasks.remove(task)`	Removes a specified task
5	Display tasks	`for task in tasks:` `    print(task)`	Displays all tasks

Real-Life Project: To-Do List Application

Project Code:

```
1.  tasks = []

2.  def add_task(task):
3.      tasks.append(task)
4.      print(f'Task "{task}" added!')

5.  def remove_task(task):
6.      if task in tasks:
7.          tasks.remove(task)
8.          print(f'Task "{task}" removed!')
9.      else:
10.         print("Task not found!")

11. def view_tasks():
12.     if tasks:
13.         print("Your Tasks:")
14.         for idx, task in enumerate(tasks, 1):
```

```
15.              print(f'{idx}. {task}')
16.       else:
17.            print("No tasks in your list!")
18. while True:
19.       print("\nOptions: 1. Add Task  2. Remove Task
3. View Tasks  4. Exit")
20.       choice = input("Enter your choice: ")
21.       if choice == '1':
22.            task = input("Enter task: ")
23.            add_task(task)
24.       elif choice == '2':
25.            task = input("Enter task to remove: ")
26.            remove_task(task)
27.       elif choice == '3':
28.            view_tasks()
29.       elif choice == '4':
30.            print("Exiting program. Have a productive
day!")
31.            break
32.       else:
33.            print("Invalid choice! Please select a
valid option.")
```

Project Code Explanation Table

Line	Code Section	Description
1	tasks = []	Initializes an empty list to store tasks.
2	def add_task(task):	Defines a function to add a task to the list.
3	tasks.append(task)	Adds the task to the list.
4	print(f'Task "{task}" added!')	Confirms that the task has been added.
5	def remove_task(task):	Defines a function to remove a task from the list.
6	if task in tasks:	Checks if the task exists in the list.
7	tasks.remove(task)	Removes the task from the

		list.
8	`print(f'Task "{task}" removed!')`	Confirms that the task has been removed.
9-10	`else: print("Task not found!")`	Displays an error message if the task is not found.
11	`def view_tasks():`	Defines a function to display all tasks.
12	`if tasks:`	Checks if the task list is not empty.
13	`print("Your Tasks:")`	Displays a message indicating tasks.
14-15	`for idx, task in enumerate(tasks, 1): print(f'{idx}. {task}')`	Loops through and prints all tasks with numbering.
16-17	`else: print("No tasks in your list!")`	Displays a message if no tasks are present.
18	`while True:`	Starts an infinite loop for continuous user interaction.
19-20	`print() & input()`	Displays options and takes user input for operation selection.
21-23	`if choice == '1':`	Handles adding a new task.
24-26	`elif choice == '2':`	Handles removing a task.
27-28	`elif choice == '3':`	Handles viewing all tasks.
29-31	`elif choice == '4':`	Handles program exit.
32-33	`else:`	Handles invalid user inputs.

Expected Results

- The program allows users to add, remove, and view tasks.
- Tasks are displayed in an organized format.

- Users can exit the program when they are done.
- Invalid choices are handled with an error message.

Hands-On Exercise Try improving the to-do list application with these additional features:

1. **Save tasks to a file** so that they persist after restarting the program.
2. **Mark tasks as completed** and display completed tasks separately.
3. **Allow editing tasks** instead of just adding and removing them.
4. **Improve the user interface** with better formatting and menu options.
5. **Add a priority system** to sort tasks by urgency.

Conclusion This to-do list application introduces essential Python concepts such as list operations, user input handling, and loops. By expanding this project, developers can create more advanced task management applications with enhanced functionalities.

Chapter 3: Temperature Converter

Overview A temperature converter is a simple yet essential application that allows users to convert temperatures between different units, such as Celsius, Fahrenheit, and Kelvin. This project enhances understanding of mathematical operations, conditional statements, and user input handling in Python.

This chapter covers the step-by-step implementation of a temperature converter, user input handling, mathematical conversions, and function-based design.

Key Concepts of Temperature Converter in Python

- **Mathematical Conversion Formulas:**
  - Celsius to Fahrenheit: $(C \times 9/5) + 32$
  - Fahrenheit to Celsius: $(F - 32) \times 5/9$
  - Celsius to Kelvin: $C + 273.15$
  - Kelvin to Celsius: $K - 273.15$
  - Fahrenheit to Kelvin: $(F - 32) \times 5/9 + 273.15$
  - Kelvin to Fahrenheit: $(K - 273.15) \times 9/5 + 32$

- **User Input Handling:**
  - Using `input()` function
  - Handling invalid inputs

- **Functions in Python:**
  - Defining functions for conversions

Temperature Conversion Table

Conversion Type	Formula
Celsius to Fahrenheit	$(C \times 9/5) + 32$
Fahrenheit to Celsius	$(F - 32) \times 5/9$
Celsius to Kelvin	$C + 273.15$
Kelvin to Celsius	$K - 273.15$
Fahrenheit to Kelvin	$(F - 32) \times 5/9 + 273.15$
Kelvin to Fahrenheit	$(K - 273.15) \times 9/5 + 32$

Basic Rules for Temperature Converter in Python

Rule	Correct Example
Use correct mathematical formulas	`fahrenheit = (celsius * 9/5) + 32`
Handle invalid inputs properly	`try: float(input("Enter temperature: "))`
Use functions for each conversion	`def celsius_to_fahrenheit(c): return (c * 9/5) + 32`

Syntax Table

SL	Concept	Syntax/Example	Description
1	Define a function	`def celsius_to_fahrenheit(c): return (c * 9/5) + 32`	Defines a function for Celsius to Fahrenheit conversion
2	Get user input	`temp = float(input("Enter temperature: "))`	Takes input from the user
3	Convert using formula	`fahrenheit = (celsius * 9/5) + 32`	Performs conversion
4	Display result	`print("Temperature in Fahrenheit:", fahrenheit)`	Prints the converted temperature

Real-Life Project: Temperature Converter
Project Code:

```
1.  def celsius_to_fahrenheit(c):
2.      return (c * 9/5) + 32

3.  def fahrenheit_to_celsius(f):
4.      return (f - 32) * 5/9

5.  def celsius_to_kelvin(c):
6.      return c + 273.15

7.  def kelvin_to_celsius(k):
```

```python
8.        return k - 273.15

9.  def fahrenheit_to_kelvin(f):
10.        return (f - 32) * 5/9 + 273.15

11. def kelvin_to_fahrenheit(k):
12.        return (k - 273.15) * 9/5 + 32

13. print("Select conversion type:")
14. print("1. Celsius to Fahrenheit")
15. print("2. Fahrenheit to Celsius")
16. print("3. Celsius to Kelvin")
17. print("4. Kelvin to Celsius")
18. print("5. Fahrenheit to Kelvin")
19. print("6. Kelvin to Fahrenheit")

20. choice = input("Enter choice (1-6): ")
21. temp = float(input("Enter temperature: "))

22. if choice == '1':
23.        print("Result:", celsius_to_fahrenheit(temp))
24. elif choice == '2':
25.        print("Result:", fahrenheit_to_celsius(temp))
26. elif choice == '3':
27.        print("Result:", celsius_to_kelvin(temp))
28. elif choice == '4':
29.        print("Result:", kelvin_to_celsius(temp))
30. elif choice == '5':
31.        print("Result:", fahrenheit_to_kelvin(temp))
32. elif choice == '6':
33.        print("Result:", kelvin_to_fahrenheit(temp))
34. else:
35.        print("Invalid choice!")
```

Project Code Explanation Table

Line	Code Section	Description
1	`def celsius_to_fahrenheit (c):`	Defines a function to convert Celsius to Fahrenheit.
2	`return (c * 9/5) + 32`	Applies the conversion formula for Celsius to Fahrenheit.
3	`def fahrenheit_to_celsius (f):`	Defines a function to convert Fahrenheit to Celsius.
4	`return (f - 32) * 5/9`	Applies the conversion formula for Fahrenheit to Celsius.
5	`def celsius_to_kelvin(c):`	Defines a function to convert Celsius to Kelvin.
6	`return c + 273.15`	Applies the conversion formula for Celsius to Kelvin.
7	`def kelvin_to_celsius(k):`	Defines a function to convert Kelvin to Celsius.
8	`return k - 273.15`	Applies the conversion formula for Kelvin to Celsius.
9	`def fahrenheit_to_kelvin( f):`	Defines a function to convert Fahrenheit to Kelvin.
10	`return (f - 32) * 5/9 + 273.15`	Applies the conversion formula for Fahrenheit to Kelvin.
11	`def kelvin_to_fahrenheit( k):`	Defines a function to convert Kelvin to Fahrenheit.
12	`return (k - 273.15) * 9/5 + 32`	Applies the conversion formula for Kelvin to Fahrenheit.
13-19	`print()` statements	Displays available temperature conversion options.
20	`choice = input("Enter choice (1-6): ")`	Prompts the user to select a conversion type.
21	`temp = float(input("Enter temperature: "))`	Prompts the user to enter a temperature.

| 22-23 | ```
if choice == '1':
    print("Result:",
    celsius_to_fahrenheit
    (temp))
``` | Checks if the user selected Celsius to Fahrenheit and performs the conversion. |
|---|---|---|
| 24-25 | ```
elif choice == '2':
    print("Result:",
    fahrenheit_to_celsius
    (temp))
``` | Checks if the user selected Fahrenheit to Celsius and performs the conversion. |
| 26-27 | ```
elif choice == '3':
    print("Result:",
    celsius_to_kelvin(tem
    p))
``` | Checks if the user selected Celsius to Kelvin and performs the conversion. |
| 28-29 | ```
elif choice == '4':
    print("Result:",
    kelvin_to_celsius(tem
    p))
``` | Checks if the user selected Kelvin to Celsius and performs the conversion. |
| 30-31 | ```
elif choice == '5':
    print("Result:",
    fahrenheit_to_kelvin(
    temp))
``` | Checks if the user selected Fahrenheit to Kelvin and performs the conversion. |
| 32-33 | ```
elif choice == '6':
    print("Result:",
    kelvin_to_fahrenheit(
    temp))
``` | Checks if the user selected Kelvin to Fahrenheit and performs the conversion. |
| 34-35 | ```
else: print("Invalid
choice!")
``` | Handles invalid input by displaying an error message. |

Expected Results

- The program asks the user to choose a conversion type.
- The user enters a temperature value.
- The program converts the temperature using the appropriate formula.
- The result is displayed to the user.
- If the user enters an invalid choice, an error message is displayed.
```

Hands-On Exercise Try improving the temperature converter with these additional features:

1. **Allow repeated conversions** without restarting the program.
2. **Format output to two decimal places** for better readability.
3. **Add an option to exit the program** when the user is done.
4. **Handle edge cases** such as negative Kelvin values.
5. **Improve the user interface** by displaying conversion explanations.

Conclusion This temperature converter project demonstrates essential Python concepts such as mathematical operations, user input handling, and functions. By expanding this project, developers can create more advanced unit conversion applications with better usability.

Chapter 4: Simple Alarm Clock

Overview A simple alarm clock is a fundamental project that helps users set alarms to remind them of specific events. This project enhances knowledge of time handling, loops, and sound notifications in Python. This chapter covers the step-by-step implementation of an alarm clock, user input handling, time-based execution, and sound alerts.

Key Concepts of Alarm Clock in Python

- **Time Handling:**
  - Using the `time` module
  - Working with `datetime` for alarm scheduling
- **User Input Handling:**
  - Using `input()` to set alarm time
  - Validating input format
- **Loops and Conditional Statements:**
  - Continuously checking the current time
  - Triggering an alarm when the set time is reached
- **Sound Alerts:**
  - Playing a sound notification when the alarm rings

Alarm Clock Functions Table

Function	Description
Set Alarm Time	Allows the user to input a specific alarm time
Check Current Time	Continuously monitors the system time
Trigger Alarm	Activates sound notification when the time matches

Basic Rules for Alarm Clock in Python

Rule	Correct Example
Use the `time` module to fetch the system time	`import time`
Validate user input format	`try:` `datetime.strptime(alarm_ti me, "%H:%M")`
Use loops to monitor time	`while True:`

Syntax Table

SL	Concept	Syntax/Example	Description
1	Import time module	`import time`	Enables time-based operations
2	Get current time	`current_time = datetime.now().strf time("%H:%M")`	Fetches system time
3	Loop for checking time	`while True:`	Runs continuously to monitor time
4	Play sound	`playsound("alarm.mp 3")`	Plays an alarm sound when triggered

Real-Life Project: Simple Alarm Clock

Project Code:

```
1.   import time
2.   from datetime import datetime
3.   from playsound import playsound

4.   alarm_time = input("Enter alarm time (HH:MM): ")
5.   print(f"Alarm set for {alarm_time}")

6.   while True:
7.        current_time = datetime.now().strftime("%H:%M")
8.        if current_time == alarm_time:
9.            print("Time to wake up!")
10.           playsound("alarm.mp3")
11.           break
12.       time.sleep(1)
```

Project Code Explanation Table

Line	Code Section	Description
1	`import time`	Imports the time module for delays.
2	`from datetime import datetime`	Imports datetime for handling time operations.
3	`from playsound import playsound`	Imports playsound to play an alarm sound.
4	`alarm_time = input("Enter alarm`	Prompts the user to input the alarm time in HH:MM format.

	time (HH:MM): ")	
5	print(f"Alarm set for {alarm_time}")	Displays a confirmation message with the alarm time.
6	while True:	Starts an infinite loop to continuously check the time.
7	current_time = datetime.now().strfti me("%H:%M")	Fetches the current system time.
8	if current_time == alarm_time:	Checks if the current time matches the alarm time.
9	print("Time to wake up!")	Displays a message when the alarm triggers.
10	playsound("alarm.mp3")	Plays the alarm sound.
11	break	Exits the loop once the alarm rings.
12	time.sleep(1)	Pauses execution for one second before checking again.

Expected Results

- The program asks the user to enter an alarm time.
- It continuously checks the current time.
- When the time matches the set alarm, it plays a sound.
- The program exits after the alarm rings.

Hands-On Exercise Try improving the alarm clock with these additional features:

1. **Allow multiple alarms** to be set at once.
2. **Add a snooze feature** to repeat the alarm after a few minutes.
3. **Display a countdown** until the alarm rings.
4. **Use a graphical user interface (GUI)** with Tkinter for better user experience.
5. **Integrate custom sound selection** for different alarm tones.

Conclusion This alarm clock project introduces Python concepts such as time handling, loops, and sound alerts. By expanding this project, developers can create more advanced alarm applications with enhanced functionalities.

Chapter 5: Countdown Timer

Overview A countdown timer is a simple yet useful application that counts down from a specified number of seconds and notifies the user when the time reaches zero. This project improves understanding of loops, time management, and user input handling in Python.

This chapter covers the step-by-step implementation of a countdown timer, user input handling, time-based execution, and displaying the remaining time.

Key Concepts of Countdown Timer in Python

- **Time Handling:**
  - Using the `time` module
  - Implementing delays with `time.sleep()`
- **User Input Handling:**
  - Taking input for the countdown duration
  - Validating input format
- **Loops and Conditional Statements:**
  - Using a `while` loop to decrement the timer
  - Displaying the remaining time at intervals

Countdown Timer Functions Table

Function	Description
Set Timer	Allows the user to input the countdown duration
Start Countdown	Decrements time every second
Display Remaining Time	Shows the time left on the countdown
Trigger Notification	Notifies the user when time reaches zero

Basic Rules for Countdown Timer in Python

Rule	Correct Example
Use `time.sleep()` to delay execution	`time.sleep(1)`
Convert user input to integer	`seconds = int(input("Enter time in seconds: "))`
Use a loop to decrement the timer	`while seconds > 0:`

Syntax Table

SL	Concept	Syntax/Example	Description
1	Import time module	`import time`	Enables time-based operations
2	Get user input	`seconds = int(input("Enter time in seconds: "))`	Takes input from the user
3	Loop for countdown	`while seconds > 0:`	Runs until the timer reaches zero
4	Print remaining time	`print(f"Time left: {seconds}s")`	Displays the countdown time
5	Pause for 1 second	`time.sleep(1)`	Delays execution by 1 second

Real-Life Project: Countdown Timer

Project Code:

```
1.  import time

2.  seconds = int(input("Enter time in seconds: "))

3.  while seconds > 0:
4.      print(f"Time left: {seconds}s")
5.      time.sleep(1)
6.      seconds -= 1

7.  print("Time's up!")
```

Project Code Explanation Table

Line	Code Section	Description
1	`import time`	Imports the time module to use sleep functionality.
2	`seconds = int(input("Enter time in seconds: "))`	Takes user input for countdown duration and converts it to an integer.
3	`while seconds > 0:`	Starts a loop that runs until the timer reaches zero.

4	`print(f"Time left: {seconds}s")`	Displays the remaining time.
5	`time.sleep(1)`	Delays execution for one second.
6	`seconds -= 1`	Decrements the countdown by one second.
7	`print("Time's up!")`	Prints a message when the timer reaches zero.

Expected Results

- The program asks the user to enter the countdown duration.
- It continuously updates and displays the remaining time.
- When the countdown reaches zero, it prints "Time's up!".

Hands-On Exercise Try improving the countdown timer with these additional features:

1. **Add a sound alert** when the countdown finishes.
2. **Display a graphical progress bar** using tqdm.
3. **Allow pausing and resuming** the countdown timer.
4. **Convert seconds to minutes and seconds** for better readability.
5. **Create a GUI version** using Tkinter for better user interaction.

Conclusion This countdown timer project introduces Python concepts such as loops, time handling, and user input validation. By expanding this project, developers can create more advanced time-tracking applications with improved features.

Chapter 6: Age Calculator

Overview An age calculator is a simple application that calculates a user's age based on their date of birth. This project enhances understanding of date handling, user input processing, and basic arithmetic operations in Python.

This chapter covers the step-by-step implementation of an age calculator, user input handling, date-based calculations, and displaying the age in years, months, and days.

Key Concepts of Age Calculator in Python

- **Date Handling:**
  - Using the datetime module
  - Fetching the current date
  - Calculating age from the date of birth
- **User Input Handling:**
  - Taking input for the date of birth
  - Validating input format
- **Arithmetic Operations:**
  - Subtracting two dates to find age
  - Displaying age in different formats

Age Calculation Table

Calculation Type	Formula
Age in Years	current_year - birth_year
Age in Months	(current_year - birth_year) * 12 + (current_month - birth_month)
Age in Days	difference_in_days = current_date - birth_date

Basic Rules for Age Calculator in Python

Rule	Correct Example
Use datetime module for date handling	import datetime
Parse user input correctly	dob = datetime.strptime(input("Enter DOB (YYYY-MM-DD): "), "%Y-%m-%d")

	Calculate the difference between dates	age = today.year - dob.year

Syntax Table

SL	Concept	Syntax/Example	Description
1	Import datetime module	`import datetime`	Enables date-based operations
2	Get current date	`today = datetime.date.today()`	Fetches the current date
3	Get user input	`dob = datetime.datetime.strptime(input("Enter DOB: "), "%Y-%m-%d")`	Takes input for the date of birth
4	Calculate age	`age = today.year - dob.year`	Computes the user's age
5	Display result	`print(f"Your age is {age} years")`	Prints the calculated age

Real-Life Project: Age Calculator

Project Code:

```
1.  import datetime

2.  dob = input("Enter your date of birth (YYYY-MM-DD): ")
3.  dob = datetime.datetime.strptime(dob, "%Y-%m-%d").date()

4.  today = datetime.date.today()
5.  age_years = today.year - dob.year
6.  age_months = (today.year - dob.year) * 12 +
(today.month - dob.month)
7.  age_days = (today - dob).days

8.  print(f"Your age is: {age_years} years,
{age_months} months, and {age_days} days.")
```

Project Code Explanation Table

Line	Code Section	Description
1	`import datetime`	Imports the datetime module for date handling.
2	`dob = input("Enter your date of birth (YYYY-MM-DD): ")`	Prompts the user to enter their date of birth.
3	`dob = datetime.datetime.strptime(dob, "%Y-%m-%d").date()`	Converts the input string into a date object.
4	`today = datetime.date.today()`	Fetches the current system date.
5	`age_years = today.year - dob.year`	Calculates the age in years.
6	`age_months = (today.year - dob.year) * 12 + (today.month - dob.month)`	Calculates the age in months.
7	`age_days = (today - dob).days`	Calculates the age in total days.
8	`print(f"Your age is: {age_years} years, {age_months} months, and {age_days} days.")`	Displays the calculated age.

Expected Results

- The program asks the user to enter their date of birth.
- It calculates the user's age in years, months, and days.
- It displays the result in a formatted output.

Hands-On Exercise Try improving the age calculator with these additional features:

1. **Allow future date validation** to prevent errors.
2. **Calculate age for a specific target date** instead of just today.
3. **Display additional information**, such as the day of the week the user was born.
4. **Convert age into different units**, such as weeks and hours.
5. **Create a GUI version** using Tkinter for better user interaction.

Chapter 7: Mad Libs Game

Overview The Mad Libs game is a fun and interactive word game where players fill in blanks with random words to create humorous and sometimes nonsensical stories. This project enhances user input handling, string formatting, and basic program flow control in Python.

This chapter covers the step-by-step implementation of a Mad Libs game, handling user input, and dynamically generating creative stories.

Key Concepts of Mad Libs Game in Python

- **String Handling:**
    - Using placeholders for missing words
    - Formatting strings dynamically
- **User Input Handling:**
    - Prompting users for different types of words
    - Storing user input in variables
- **Printing and Displaying Outputs:**
    - Generating a completed Mad Libs story
    - Formatting text output for readability

Mad Libs Game Components Table

Component	Description
Story Template	A predefined story with missing words
User Input	Players enter words (e.g., nouns, verbs, adjectives)
Story Generation	The program replaces placeholders with user input

Basic Rules for Mad Libs Game in Python

Rule	Correct Example
Use string placeholders	`story = "Once upon a time, a {adjective} {noun} {verb} through the {place}."`
Get user input dynamically	`adjective = input("Enter an adjective: ")`
Format the story properly	`story.format(adjective=adjective, noun=noun, verb=verb, place=place)`

Syntax Table

SL	Concept	Syntax/Example	Description

1	Define a story template	story = "Once upon a time, a {adjective} {noun} {verb} through the {place}."	Creates a template for Mad Libs
2	Get user input	noun = input("Enter a noun: ")	Takes user input for the missing words
3	Use format() method	story.format(noun=noun)	Replaces placeholders with user input
4	Display completed story	print(story)	Prints the final story with user inputs

Real-Life Project: Mad Libs Game

Project Code:

```
1.  print("Welcome to Mad Libs!")
2.  noun = input("Enter a noun: ")
3.  verb = input("Enter a verb: ")
4.  adjective = input("Enter an adjective: ")
5.  place = input("Enter a place: ")

6.  story = f"Once upon a time, a {adjective} {noun}
{verb} through the {place}. It was an unforgettable
journey!"

7.  print("\nHere is your Mad Libs story:")
8.  print(story)
```

Project Code Explanation Table

Line	Code Section	Description
1	print("Welcome to Mad Libs!")	Prints a welcome message.
2	noun = input("Enter a noun: ")	Prompts the user for a noun.
3	verb = input("Enter a verb: ")	Prompts the user for a verb.

4	`adjective = input("Enter an adjective: ")`	Prompts the user for an adjective.
5	`place = input("Enter a place: ")`	Prompts the user for a place.
6	`story = f"Once upon a time, a {adjective} {noun} {verb} through the {place}."`	Creates a formatted story using user input.
7	`print("\nHere is your Mad Libs story:")`	Prints a header for the final story.
8	`print(story)`	Displays the completed Mad Libs story.

Expected Results
- The program asks the user to input a series of words.
- It generates a fun story using the user's words.
- The completed story is printed on the screen.

Hands-On Exercise Try improving the Mad Libs game with these additional features:

1. **Add more placeholders** for a longer story.
2. **Allow multiple story templates** for variety.
3. **Give users a choice of themes** (e.g., adventure, mystery, fantasy).
4. **Save the generated story to a text file**.
5. **Use GUI (Tkinter) for better user interaction**.

Conclusion This Mad Libs game project introduces Python concepts such as string formatting, user input handling, and output display. By expanding this project, developers can create more engaging and interactive word-based games.

Chapter 8: Simple Interest Calculator

Overview A Simple Interest Calculator is a useful financial tool that calculates the interest earned or paid on a principal amount over a specified period at a given interest rate. This project enhances understanding of mathematical operations, user input handling, and formula-based calculations in Python.

This chapter covers the step-by-step implementation of a Simple Interest Calculator, handling user input, applying the interest formula, and displaying the computed results.

Key Concepts of Simple Interest Calculator in Python

- **Mathematical Formula:**
  - Simple Interest Formula: $SI = (P \times R \times T) / 100$
    - P = Principal amount
    - R = Annual Interest Rate (in %)
    - T = Time period (in years)
    - SI = Simple Interest
- **User Input Handling:**
  - Taking user input for principal, rate, and time
  - Validating numeric input
- **Arithmetic Operations:**
  - Multiplication and division for calculating interest

Simple Interest Formula Table

Parameter	Description
P	Principal amount (initial investment or loan)
R	Interest rate (annual percentage)
T	Time period (years)
SI	Computed simple interest

Basic Rules for Simple Interest Calculator in Python

Rule	Correct Example
Use correct mathematical formula	`SI = (P * R * T) / 100`
Convert user input to numbers	`principal = float(input("Enter principal amount: "))`
Display result with proper formatting	`print(f"Simple Interest: {SI:.2f}")`

Syntax Table

SL	Concept	Syntax/Example	Description
1	Define function	def calculate_interest(P, R, T): return (P * R * T) / 100	Creates a function for interest calculation
2	Get user input	P = float(input("Enter principal: "))	Takes principal amount from the user
3	Compute interest	SI = (P * R * T) / 100	Applies the simple interest formula
4	Display result	print(f"Simple Interest: {SI:.2f}")	Prints the computed interest

Real-Life Project: Simple Interest Calculator

Project Code:

```
1.  def calculate_interest(P, R, T):
2.      return (P * R * T) / 100

3.  P = float(input("Enter principal amount: "))
4.  R = float(input("Enter annual interest rate (in %): "))
5.  T = float(input("Enter time period (in years): "))

6.  SI = calculate_interest(P, R, T)
7.  print(f"Simple Interest: {SI:.2f}")
```

Project Code Explanation Table

Line	Code Section	Description
1	def calculate_interest(P, R, T):	Defines a function to calculate simple interest.
2	return (P * R * T) / 100	Uses the formula to compute interest.
3	P = float(input("Enter principal amount: "))	Prompts user for the principal amount and converts input to a float.

4	`R = float(input("Enter annual interest rate (in %): "))`	Prompts user for interest rate and converts input to a float.
5	`T = float(input("Enter time period (in years): "))`	Prompts user for time period and converts input to a float.
6	`SI = calculate_interest(P, R, T)`	Calls the function and stores the computed interest.
7	`print(f"Simple Interest: {SI:.2f}")`	Displays the final computed interest with two decimal places.

Expected Results

- The program asks the user for principal amount, interest rate, and time period.
- It calculates simple interest using the formula.
- The result is displayed with proper formatting.

Hands-On Exercise Try improving the Simple Interest Calculator with these additional features:

1. **Allow compound interest calculation** for advanced financial analysis.
2. **Provide multiple interest rate options** (e.g., monthly, quarterly, yearly).
3. **Enhance user interface using a GUI** with `Tkinter`.
4. **Allow interest rate as a decimal input** instead of percentages.
5. **Validate negative values** to prevent invalid inputs.

Conclusion This Simple Interest Calculator project introduces Python concepts such as mathematical operations, user input handling, and function-based design. By expanding this project, developers can create more advanced financial applications with greater functionality.

Chapter 9: Rock, Paper, Scissors Game

Overview The Rock, Paper, Scissors game is a classic two-player hand game where players simultaneously choose one of three options: rock, paper, or scissors. The winner is determined based on predefined rules. This project enhances understanding of random module usage, user input handling, and conditional logic in Python.

This chapter covers the step-by-step implementation of a Rock, Paper, Scissors game, handling user input, generating computer choices, and determining the winner.

Key Concepts of Rock, Paper, Scissors Game in Python

- **Random Module Usage:**
    - Using `random.choice()` to generate the computer's move
- **User Input Handling:**
    - Taking user input for their move
    - Validating correct input
- **Conditional Statements:**
    - Determining the winner using `if-elif-else` statements

Game Rules Table

Player Choice	Computer Choice	Result
Rock	Scissors	Player Wins
Scissors	Paper	Player Wins
Paper	Rock	Player Wins
Rock	Paper	Computer Wins
Scissors	Rock	Computer Wins
Paper	Scissors	Computer Wins
Same Choice	Same Choice	Draw

Basic Rules for Rock, Paper, Scissors Game in Python

Rule	Correct Example
Use `random.choice()` for computer selection	`computer_choice = random.choice(["rock", "paper", "scissors"])`
Validate user input	`if user_choice in ["rock", "paper", "scissors"]:`
Compare choices with if-	`if user_choice == "rock" and`

elif-else	computer_choice == "scissors":

Syntax Table

SL	Concept	Syntax/Example	Description
1	Import random module	`import random`	Enables random selection for the computer's choice
2	Get user input	`user_choice = input("Enter rock, paper, or scissors: ").lower()`	Takes user input and converts it to lowercase
3	Generate computer choice	`computer_choice = random.choice(["rock", "paper", "scissors"])`	Randomly selects the computer's move
4	Determine winner	`if user_choice == computer_choice:`	Compares user and computer choices to determine the winner
5	Display result	`print("You win!")`	Prints the game outcome

Real-Life Project: Rock, Paper, Scissors Game

Project Code:

```
1.  import random

2.  choices = ["rock", "paper", "scissors"]
3.  user_choice = input("Enter rock, paper, or
scissors: ").lower()

4.  if user_choice not in choices:
5.      print("Invalid choice! Please enter rock,
paper, or scissors.")
6.  else:
7.      computer_choice = random.choice(choices)
8.      print(f"Computer chose: {computer_choice}")
9.      if user_choice == computer_choice:
10.         print("It's a draw!")
11.     elif (user_choice == "rock" and computer_choice
== "scissors") or \
```

```
12.          (user_choice == "scissors" and
computer_choice == "paper") or \
13.          (user_choice == "paper" and
computer_choice == "rock"):
14.          print("You win!")
15.     else:
16.          print("Computer wins!")
```

Project Code Explanation Table

Line	Code Section	Description
1	`import random`	Imports the random module to allow computer-generated choices.
2	`choices = ["rock", "paper", "scissors"]`	Defines a list of available choices.
3	`user_choice = input("Enter rock, paper, or scissors: ").lower()`	Takes input from the user and converts it to lowercase.
4	`if user_choice not in choices:`	Checks if the user input is valid.
5	`print("Invalid choice! Please enter rock, paper, or scissors.")`	Displays an error message if input is invalid.
6-7	`computer_choice = random.choice(choices)`	Randomly selects the computer's choice.
8	`print(f"Computer chose: {computer_choice}")`	Displays the computer's choice.
9-10	`if user_choice == computer_choice:`	Checks if the game is a draw.
11-13	`elif` conditions	Determines if the user wins.
14	`print("You win!")`	Displays the winning message for the user.
15-16	`else:`	Determines if the computer wins and displays the result.

Expected Results

- The program asks the user to enter rock, paper, or scissors.
- The computer randomly selects a choice.
- The program compares the user's choice with the computer's choice.
- It determines the winner and displays the result.
- If the choices are the same, it declares a draw.

Hands-On Exercise Try improving the Rock, Paper, Scissors game with these additional features:

1. **Allow multiple rounds** and track scores.
2. **Give the user an option to exit the game** after each round.
3. **Introduce an advanced mode** with additional choices like "lizard" and "Spock".
4. **Use a graphical interface (GUI)** using `Tkinter

Chapter 10: Number Guessing Game

Overview The Number Guessing Game is a fun and interactive game where the player tries to guess a randomly generated number within a specified range. This project enhances knowledge of random number generation, loops, conditional statements, and user input handling in Python.

This chapter covers the step-by-step implementation of a Number Guessing Game, handling user input, generating random numbers, and providing feedback on guesses.

Key Concepts of Number Guessing Game in Python

- **Random Module Usage:**
  - Using `random.randint()` to generate a random number
- **User Input Handling:**
  - Taking user input for guesses
  - Validating input as a number
- **Loops and Conditional Statements:**
  - Checking if the guess is correct
  - Giving hints if the guess is too high or too low

Game Rules Table

Scenario	Result
User guesses correctly	Player wins
User guesses too high	Hint: "Too high! Try again."
User guesses too low	Hint: "Too low! Try again."

Basic Rules for Number Guessing Game in Python

Rule	Correct Example
Use `random.randint()` for number selection	`number = random.randint(1, 100)`
Validate user input as an integer	`guess = int(input("Enter your guess: "))`
Use a loop for multiple attempts	`while guess != number:`

Syntax Table

SL	Concept	Syntax/Example	Description
1	Import random module	`import random`	Enables random number generation
2	Generate random number	`number = random.randint(1, 100)`	Picks a random number between 1 and 100
3	Get user input	`guess = int(input("Enter your guess: "))`	Takes user input as an integer
4	Check condition	`if guess == number:`	Compares guess with the correct number
5	Display result	`print("Congratulations! You guessed it right!")`	Prints winning message

Real-Life Project: Number Guessing Game

Project Code:

```
1.  import random

2.  number = random.randint(1, 100)
3.  attempts = 0

4.  print("Guess the number between 1 and 100!")

5.  while True:
6.      guess = int(input("Enter your guess: "))
7.      attempts += 1

8.      if guess < number:
9.          print("Too low! Try again.")
10.     elif guess > number:
11.         print("Too high! Try again.")
12.     else:
13.         print(f"Congratulations! You guessed the number in {attempts} attempts.")
14.         break
```

Project Code Explanation Table

Line	Code Section	Description
1	`import random`	Imports the random module to generate a random number.
2	`number = random.randint(1, 100)`	Generates a random number between 1 and 100.
3	`attempts = 0`	Initializes the attempt counter.
4	`print("Guess the number between 1 and 100!")`	Displays game instructions.
5	`while True:`	Starts an infinite loop to keep the game running.
6	`guess = int(input("Enter your guess: "))`	Takes user input and converts it into an integer.
7	`attempts += 1`	Increments the attempt counter with each guess.
8-9	`if guess < number:`	Checks if the guess is too low and provides feedback.
10-11	`elif guess > number:`	Checks if the guess is too high and provides feedback.
12-14	`else:`	If the guess is correct, congratulates the player and ends the game.

Expected Results

- The program generates a random number between 1 and 100.
- The user keeps guessing until they get the correct number.
- The program provides hints if the guess is too high or too low.
- When the correct number is guessed, the program displays the number of attempts taken.

Hands-On Exercise Try improving the Number Guessing Game with these additional features:

1. **Set a maximum number of attempts** and display a loss message if the user fails.
2. **Allow multiple rounds** without restarting the program.

3. **Give players the option to choose a difficulty level** (e.g., easy, medium, hard).
4. **Create a GUI version** using Tkinter for better user interaction.
5. **Store the best score** (least attempts) and display it as a challenge.

Conclusion This Number Guessing Game project introduces Python concepts such as loops, conditional logic, user input handling, and random number generation. By expanding this project, developers can create more interactive and engaging number-based games.

Chapter 11: Binary to Decimal Converter

Overview A Binary to Decimal Converter is a simple application that converts a binary number (base-2) into a decimal number (base-10). This project helps in understanding number systems, user input handling, and built-in Python functions for conversion.

This chapter covers the step-by-step implementation of a Binary to Decimal Converter, handling user input, performing binary-to-decimal conversion, and displaying the result.

Key Concepts of Binary to Decimal Converter in Python

- **Binary and Decimal Number Systems:**
  - Binary (Base-2) consists of only 0 and 1
  - Decimal (Base-10) consists of digits 0 to 9
- **Conversion Methods:**
  - Using Python's built-in `int()` function
  - Implementing manual binary-to-decimal conversion using loops
- **User Input Handling:**
  - Accepting binary numbers as input
  - Validating the input to contain only 0 and 1

Binary to Decimal Conversion Table

Binary	Decimal
0001	1
0010	2
0100	4
1000	8
1101	13
1111	15

Basic Rules for Binary to Decimal Conversion in Python

Rule	Correct Example
Use `int(binary, 2)` for conversion	`decimal = int("1101", 2)`
Validate user input as binary	`if set(binary) <= {"0", "1"}:`
Perform manual conversion using loop	`decimal += int(bit) * (2 ** position)`

Syntax Table

SL	Concept	Syntax/Example	Description
1	Convert binary to decimal	`decimal = int("1010", 2)`	Converts binary 1010 to decimal 10
2	Get user input	`binary = input("Enter a binary number: ")`	Takes binary input from the user
3	Validate input	`if set(binary) <= {"0", "1"}:`	Ensures input contains only 0 and 1
4	Display result	`print(f"Decimal value: {decimal}")`	Prints the converted decimal number

Real-Life Project: Binary to Decimal Converter

Project Code:

```
1.  def binary_to_decimal(binary):
2.      decimal = int(binary, 2)
3.      return decimal

4.  binary = input("Enter a binary number: ")

5.  if set(binary) <= {"0", "1"}:
6.      decimal_value = binary_to_decimal(binary)
7.      print(f"The decimal equivalent of {binary} is
{decimal_value}")
8.  else:
9.      print("Invalid binary number! Please enter only
0s and 1s.")
```

Project Code Explanation Table

Line	Code Section	Description
1-3	`def binary_to_decimal(binary):`	Defines a function to convert a binary number to decimal.
2	`decimal = int(binary, 2)`	Uses the built-in function to convert binary to decimal.

4	`binary = input("Enter a binary number: ")`	Prompts the user for a binary number input.
5	`if set(binary) <= {"0", "1"}:`	Checks if the input contains only 0 and 1.
6	`decimal_value = binary_to_decimal(binary)`	Calls the function to perform the conversion.
7	`print(f"The decimal equivalent of {binary} is {decimal_value}")`	Displays the converted decimal number.
8-9	`else:`	Displays an error message if input is invalid.

Expected Results

- The program asks the user to input a binary number.
- It validates the input to ensure it contains only 0 and 1.
- The binary number is converted into a decimal value.
- The result is displayed to the user.

Hands-On Exercise Try improving the Binary to Decimal Converter with these additional features:

1. **Allow conversion from decimal to binary** as well.
2. **Provide step-by-step conversion details** to explain how the number is converted.
3. **Enhance input validation** by handling empty inputs and incorrect values.
4. **Build a GUI version** using Tkinter for better user experience.
5. **Support multiple number system conversions** (e.g., hexadecimal to decimal).

Conclusion This Binary to Decimal Converter project introduces Python concepts such as built-in functions, loops, conditional statements, and user input validation. By expanding this project, developers can create more advanced number system converters with interactive features.

Chapter 12: Decimal to Binary Converter

Overview A Decimal to Binary Converter is a simple application that converts a decimal number (base-10) into a binary number (base-2). This project enhances understanding of number systems, arithmetic operations, and user input handling in Python.

This chapter covers the step-by-step implementation of a Decimal to Binary Converter, handling user input, performing decimal-to-binary conversion, and displaying the result.

Key Concepts of Decimal to Binary Converter in Python

- **Binary and Decimal Number Systems:**
    - Decimal (Base-10) consists of digits 0 to 9
    - Binary (Base-2) consists of only 0 and 1
- **Conversion Methods:**
    - Using Python's built-in `bin()` function
    - Implementing manual decimal-to-binary conversion using loops
- **User Input Handling:**
    - Accepting decimal numbers as input
    - Validating the input to ensure it is a valid number

Decimal to Binary Conversion Table

Decimal	Binary
1	0001
2	0010
4	0100
8	1000
13	1101
15	1111

Basic Rules for Decimal to Binary Conversion in Python

Rule	Correct Example
Use `bin(decimal)[2:]` for conversion	`binary = bin(10)[2:]`
Validate user input as a number	`if decimal.isdigit():`
Perform manual conversion using division and modulus	`binary = '' while n > 0:` `binary = str(n % 2) +`

	`binary; n //= 2`

Syntax Table

SL	Concept	Syntax/Example	Description
1	Convert decimal to binary	`binary = bin(10)[2:]`	Converts decimal 10 to binary 1010
2	Get user input	`decimal = int(input("Enter a decimal number: "))`	Takes decimal input from the user
3	Validate input	`if decimal >= 0:`	Ensures input is a non-negative integer
4	Display result	`print(f"Binary value: {binary}")`	Prints the converted binary number

Real-Life Project: Decimal to Binary Converter

Project Code:

```python
1.  def decimal_to_binary(decimal):
2.      return bin(decimal)[2:]

3.  decimal = int(input("Enter a decimal number: "))

4.  if decimal >= 0:
5.      binary_value = decimal_to_binary(decimal)
6.      print(f"The binary equivalent of {decimal} is {binary_value}")
7.  else:
8.      print("Invalid input! Please enter a non-negative number.")
```

Project Code Explanation Table

Line	Code Section	Description
1-2	`def decimal_to_binary(decimal):`	Defines a function to convert a decimal number to binary.
2	`return bin(decimal)[2:]`	Uses the built-in `bin()` function to convert decimal

		to binary.
3	`decimal = int(input("Enter a decimal number: "))`	Prompts the user for a decimal number input.
4	`if decimal >= 0:`	Ensures the number is non-negative.
5	`binary_value = decimal_to_binary(decimal)`	Calls the function to perform the conversion.
6	`print(f"The binary equivalent of {decimal} is {binary_value}")`	Displays the converted binary number.
7-8	`else:`	Displays an error message if input is invalid.

Expected Results
- The program asks the user to input a decimal number.
- It validates the input to ensure it is a non-negative integer.
- The decimal number is converted into a binary value.
- The result is displayed to the user.

Hands-On Exercise Try improving the Decimal to Binary Converter with these additional features:
1. **Allow conversion from binary to decimal** as well.
2. **Provide step-by-step conversion details** to explain how the number is converted.
3. **Enhance input validation** by handling negative numbers and invalid inputs.
4. **Build a GUI version** using Tkinter for better user experience.
5. **Support multiple number system conversions** (e.g., decimal to hexadecimal).

Conclusion This Decimal to Binary Converter project introduces Python concepts such as built-in functions, loops, conditional statements, and user input validation. By expanding this project, developers can create more advanced number system converters with interactive features.

Chapter 13: Unit Converter (Length, Mass, etc.)

Overview A Unit Converter is a useful application that allows users to convert between different measurement units, such as length, mass, and temperature. This project helps in understanding mathematical operations, user input handling, and function-based programming in Python.

This chapter covers the step-by-step implementation of a Unit Converter, handling user input, performing unit conversions, and displaying the converted values.

Key Concepts of Unit Converter in Python

- **Mathematical Conversion Factors:**
  - Length conversions (meters, kilometers, miles, feet, inches)
  - Mass conversions (grams, kilograms, pounds, ounces)
  - Temperature conversions (Celsius, Fahrenheit, Kelvin)
- **User Input Handling:**
  - Taking user input for the value and unit type
  - Validating input to ensure correct conversions
- **Functions for Conversion:**
  - Defining functions for each type of unit conversion
  - Using dictionaries for efficient lookups

Unit Conversion Table

Conversion Type	Formula
Meters to Kilometers	`km = meters / 1000`
Kilometers to Miles	`miles = km * 0.621371`
Feet to Inches	`inches = feet * 12`
Grams to Kilograms	`kg = grams / 1000`
Pounds to Kilograms	`kg = pounds * 0.453592`
Celsius to Fahrenheit	`F = (C * 9/5) + 32`
Fahrenheit to Celsius	`C = (F - 32) * 5/9`

Basic Rules for Unit Converter in Python

Rule	Correct Example
Use correct	`miles = km * 0.621371`

	mathematical formulas	
Validate user input	if unit in ('meters', 'kilometers', 'miles'):	
Use functions for conversions	def meters_to_kilometers(meters): return meters / 1000	

Syntax Table

SL	Concept	Syntax/Example	Description
1	Convert length	km = meters / 1000	Converts meters to kilometers
2	Convert temperature	F = (C * 9/5) + 32	Converts Celsius to Fahrenheit
3	Convert mass	kg = grams / 1000	Converts grams to kilograms
4	Get user input	value = float(input("Enter value: "))	Takes input for the conversion

Real-Life Project: Unit Converter

Project Code:

```
1.  def meters_to_kilometers(meters):
2.      return meters / 1000

3.  def kilometers_to_miles(km):
4.      return km * 0.621371

5.  def celsius_to_fahrenheit(c):
6.      return (c * 9/5) + 32

7.  def fahrenheit_to_celsius(f):
8.      return (f - 32) * 5/9
9.  print("Unit Converter")
10. print("1. Meters to Kilometers")
11. print("2. Kilometers to Miles")
12. print("3. Celsius to Fahrenheit")
13. print("4. Fahrenheit to Celsius")

14. choice = input("Enter your choice (1-4): ")
```

```
15. value = float(input("Enter the value: "))
16. if choice == '1':
17.     print(f"{value} meters is
{meters_to_kilometers(value)} kilometers")
18. elif choice == '2':
19.     print(f"{value} km is
{kilometers_to_miles(value)} miles")
20. elif choice == '3':
21.     print(f"{value} Celsius is
{celsius_to_fahrenheit(value)} Fahrenheit")
22. elif choice == '4':
23.     print(f"{value} Fahrenheit is
{fahrenheit_to_celsius(value)} Celsius")
24. else:
25.     print("Invalid choice! Please enter a number
between 1 and 4.")
```

Project Code Explanation Table

Line	Code Section	Description
1-2	def meters_to_kilometers(meters):	Defines a function to convert meters to kilometers.
3-4	def kilometers_to_miles(km):	Defines a function to convert kilometers to miles.
5-6	def celsius_to_fahrenheit(c):	Defines a function to convert Celsius to Fahrenheit.
7-8	def fahrenheit_to_celsius(f):	Defines a function to convert Fahrenheit to Celsius.
9	print("Unit Converter")	Prints the title of the program.
10-13	print() statements	Displays the available conversion options to the user.
14	choice = input("Enter your	Takes user input to select a conversion option.

	choice (1-4): ")	
15	value = float(input("Enter the value: "))	Takes the numerical input for conversion and converts it to a float.
16-17	if choice == '1':	Converts meters to kilometers and prints the result.
18-19	elif choice == '2':	Converts kilometers to miles and prints the result.
20-21	elif choice == '3':	Converts Celsius to Fahrenheit and prints the result.
22-23	elif choice == '4':	Converts Fahrenheit to Celsius and prints the result.
24-25	else:	Handles invalid choices by displaying an error message.

Expected Results
- The program asks the user to select a unit conversion type.
- The user enters a value for conversion.
- The program converts the value based on the chosen unit type.
- The result is displayed to the user.

Hands-On Exercise Try improving the Unit Converter with these additional features:
1. **Add more unit conversions**, such as weight, speed, and volume.
2. **Allow bi-directional conversions**, e.g., kilometers to meters and meters to kilometers.
3. **Use dictionaries to store conversion factors** for scalable conversions.
4. **Create a GUI version** using Tkinter for better user experience.
5. **Support multiple number system conversions** (e.g., decimal to binary, binary to decimal).

Conclusion This Unit Converter project introduces Python concepts such as functions, user input handling, and mathematical operations. By expanding this project, developers can create more advanced unit conversion applications with enhanced functionality.

Chapter 14: Currency Converter

Overview A Currency Converter is a practical application that allows users to convert one currency into another based on exchange rates. This project enhances understanding of API integration, user input handling, and mathematical calculations in Python.

This chapter covers the step-by-step implementation of a Currency Converter, fetching real-time exchange rates, performing currency conversions, and displaying the results.

Key Concepts of Currency Converter in Python

- **Exchange Rates Handling:**
  - Using real-time exchange rates via an API (e.g., exchangeratesapi.io, Open Exchange Rates)
  - Using predefined exchange rates for offline mode
- **User Input Handling:**
  - Accepting user input for source and target currency
  - Validating correct currency codes
- **Arithmetic Operations:**
  - Multiplication for currency conversion (converted_amount = amount * exchange_rate)

Currency Conversion Table

From	To	Conversion Rate (Example)
USD	EUR	0.85
EUR	GBP	0.86
GBP	INR	101.56
INR	USD	0.012
USD	JPY	110.25

Basic Rules for Currency Converter in Python

Rule	Correct Example
Use an API for real-time rates	requests.get("https://api.exchangerate-api.com/v4/latest/USD")
Validate user input as a currency code	if currency in exchange_rates:
Perform conversion using rates	converted_amount = amount * exchange_rates[target_currency]

Syntax Table

SL	Concept	Syntax/Example	Description
1	Fetch	requests.get("API	Fetches live currency

	exchange rates	_URL")	rates from an API
2	Get user input	`amount = float(input("Enter amount: "))`	Takes input for currency amount
3	Validate input	`if currency in exchange_rates:`	Ensures input is a valid currency code
4	Perform conversion	`converted = amount * exchange_rates[to_currency]`	Multiplies the amount by the exchange rate
5	Display result	`print(f"Converted amount: {converted:.2f}")`	Prints the converted currency value

Real-Life Project: Currency Converter

Project Code:

```
1.  import requests

2.  def get_exchange_rates(base_currency):
3.      url = f"https://api.exchangerate-
api.com/v4/latest/{base_currency}"
4.      response = requests.get(url)
5.      data = response.json()
6.      return data['rates']

7.  base_currency = input("Enter base currency (e.g.,
USD, EUR): ").upper()
8.  target_currency = input("Enter target currency:
").upper()
9.  amount = float(input("Enter amount: "))

10. rates = get_exchange_rates(base_currency)

11. if target_currency in rates:
12.     converted_amount = amount *
rates[target_currency]
13.     print(f"{amount} {base_currency} is
```

```
{converted_amount:.2f} {target_currency}")
14. else:
15.     print("Invalid currency code!")
```

Project Code Explanation Table

Line	Code Section	Description
1	`import requests`	Imports the requests module to fetch exchange rates from an API.
2-6	`def get_exchange_rates(base_c urrency):`	Defines a function to fetch exchange rates for a given base currency.
3-4	`url = f"https://api.exchangerat e- api.com/v4/latest/{base_c urrency}"`	Constructs the API URL using the base currency.
5	`data = response.json()`	Parses the response as JSON.
7	`base_currency = input("Enter base currency: ").upper()`	Takes the base currency input from the user.
8	`target_currency = input("Enter target currency: ").upper()`	Takes the target currency input from the user.
9	`amount = float(input("Enter amount: "))`	Takes the amount for conversion and converts it to a float.
10	`rates = get_exchange_rates(base_c urrency)`	Calls the function to get exchange rates.
11-12	`if target_currency in rates:`	Checks if the target currency is valid and performs conversion.

| 13 | print(f"{amount} {base_currency} is {converted_amount:.2f} {target_currency}") | Prints the converted currency amount. |
| 14- 15 | else: | Handles invalid currency codes by displaying an error message. |

Expected Results

- The program asks the user for base and target currency codes.
- It fetches exchange rates from an API.
- The user enters an amount to convert.
- The program calculates and displays the converted amount.
- If an invalid currency code is entered, an error message is displayed.

Hands-On Exercise Try improving the Currency Converter with these additional features:

1. **Allow offline mode** with predefined exchange rates.
2. **Support multi-currency conversions** in one execution.
3. **Cache exchange rates** to reduce API requests.
4. **Use GUI (Tkinter) for better user experience.**
5. **Allow conversion history tracking** and display past conversions.

Conclusion This Currency Converter project introduces Python concepts such as API integration, user input handling, and arithmetic operations. By expanding this project, developers can create a more advanced financial tool with real-time exchange rate tracking.

Chapter 15: Tic-Tac-Toe Game

Overview Tic-Tac-Toe is a classic two-player game where players take turns marking spaces in a 3×3 grid with "X" or "O". The goal is to get three of their marks in a row (horizontally, vertically, or diagonally). This project helps in understanding 2D lists, game logic implementation, and user input handling in Python.

This chapter covers the step-by-step implementation of a Tic-Tac-Toe game, including board representation, turn-based gameplay, and win condition checking.

Key Concepts of Tic-Tac-Toe Game in Python

- **Game Board Representation:**
  - Using a 3×3 list to store the game board
  - Displaying the board dynamically after each move
- **Player Turns Handling:**
  - Allowing two players to take turns
  - Validating correct input and available spaces
- **Win Condition Checking:**
  - Determining if a player has won by forming a row, column, or diagonal
  - Declaring a draw if all spaces are filled without a winner

Tic-Tac-Toe Board Representation

Index Position	Board Representation
(0,0)	Top-left
(0,1)	Top-center
(0,2)	Top-right
(1,0)	Middle-left
(1,1)	Center
(1,2)	Middle-right
(2,0)	Bottom-left
(2,1)	Bottom-center
(2,2)	Bottom-right

Basic Rules for Tic-Tac-Toe Game in Python

Rule	Correct Example
Store board as a list	board = [[' ' for _ in range(3)] for _ in range(3)]
Use a loop for turns	while not game_over:
Check for a winner	if check_winner(board, 'X'):

Syntax Table

SL	Concept	Syntax/Example	Description
1	Create game board	board = [[' ']*3 for _ in range(3)]	Initializes a 3x3 grid with empty spaces
2	Display board	`for row in board: print("".join(row))`	Prints the game board to the console
3	Get player input	row, col = map(int, input("Enter row and column: ").split())	Takes user input for move placement
4	Check win condition	if check_winner(board, 'X'):	Checks if a player has won
5	Switch turns	current_player = 'O' if current_player == 'X' else 'X'	Alternates between players

Real-Life Project: Tic-Tac-Toe Game

Project Code:

```
1.  def print_board(board):
2.      for row in board:
3.          print(" | ".join(row))
4.      print("-" * 9)

5.  def check_winner(board, player):
6.      for row in board:
7.          if all(cell == player for cell in row):
8.              return True
9.      for col in range(3):
10.         if all(board[row][col] == player for row in
```

```
range(3)):
11.                  return True
12.       if all(board[i][i] == player for i in range(3))
or all(board[i][2-i] == player for i in range(3)):
13.              return True
14.       return False

15. board = [[' ' for _ in range(3)] for _ in range(3)]
16. current_player = 'X'

17. for turn in range(9):
18.       print_board(board)
19.       row, col = map(int, input(f"Player
{current_player}, enter row and column (0-2):
").split())

20.       if board[row][col] == ' ':
21.             board[row][col] = current_player
22.             if check_winner(board, current_player):
23.                   print_board(board)
24.                   print(f"Player {current_player} wins!")
25.                   break
26.             current_player = 'O' if current_player ==
'X' else 'X'
27.       else:
28.             print("Invalid move! Try again.")

29. else:
30.       print("It's a draw!")
```

Project Code Explanation Table

Line	Code Section	Description
1-4	`def print_board(board):`	Defines a function to print the game board.
2-3	`for row in board:` `print("".join(row))`	
4	`print("-" * 9)`	Prints a separator line for

		better visibility.
5-14	`def check_winner(board, player):`	Defines a function to check if a player has won.
6-8	`for row in board:`	Checks if any row has all the same player marks.
9-11	`for col in range(3):`	Checks if any column has all the same player marks.
12-13	`if all(board[i][i] == player for i in range(3))`	Checks if any diagonal has all the same player marks.
14	`return False`	Returns False if no winner is found.
15	`board = [[' ' for _ in range(3)] for _ in range(3)]`	Initializes an empty 3×3 game board.
16	`current_player = 'X'`	Sets the starting player as 'X'.
17	`for turn in range(9):`	Starts a loop for a maximum of 9 turns.
18	`print_board(board)`	Calls the function to display the board.
19	`row, col = map(int, input())`	Takes player input for row and column placement.
20-21	`if board[row][col] == ' ':`	Ensures the chosen cell is empty before placing a move.
22-25	`if check_winner(board, current_player):`	Checks for a winner and ends the game if found.
26	`current_player = 'O' if current_player == 'X' else 'X'`	Switches turn between 'X' and 'O'.
27-28	`else: print("Invalid move! Try again.")`	Handles cases where a player selects an occupied cell.
29-30	`else: print("It's a draw!")`	Declares a draw if all spaces are filled with no winner.

Expected Results

- The program displays the game board and asks players to enter row and column numbers.
- Players take turns placing their marks on the board.
- If a player gets three marks in a row, column, or diagonal, they win.
- If all spaces are filled and no one wins, the game ends in a draw.

Hands-On Exercise Try improving the Tic-Tac-Toe game with these additional features:

1. **Enhance input validation** to prevent invalid inputs.
2. **Allow a player vs. computer mode** with AI moves.
3. **Improve user interface using a GUI library** like Tkinter.
4. **Display the winning move visually** for better clarity.
5. **Track game history and store match results.**

Conclusion This Tic-Tac-Toe game project introduces Python concepts such as 2D lists, loops, and conditionals. By expanding this project, developers can create more interactive and visually appealing board games.

Chapter 16: Email Slicer (Extract Username from Email)

Overview An Email Slicer is a simple yet useful tool that extracts the username and domain from an email address. This project enhances understanding of string manipulation, user input handling, and string slicing in Python.

This chapter covers the step-by-step implementation of an Email Slicer, including handling user input, extracting the username and domain, and displaying the results.

Key Concepts of Email Slicer in Python

- **String Manipulation:**
  - Using string methods like `split()` and slicing
  - Extracting specific parts of a string
- **User Input Handling:**
  - Accepting an email address from the user
  - Validating the input format
- **Output Formatting:**
  - Displaying extracted username and domain clearly

Email Slicing Table

Email Address	Username	Domain
john@example.com	john	example.com
alice@company.org	alice	company.org
user123@test.net	user123	test.net

Basic Rules for Email Slicer in Python

Rule	Correct Example
Use `split('@')` to separate parts	`username, domain = email.split('@')`
Validate email format	`if '@' in email and '.' in email.split('@')[1]:`
Display extracted parts	`print(f"Username: {username}, Domain: {domain}")`

Syntax Table

SL	Concept	Syntax/Example	Description
1	Get user input	`email = input("Enter your email: ")`	Takes email address as input
2	Split email	`username, domain = email.split('@')`	Splits the email into username and domain
3	Display result	`print(f"Username: {username}, Domain: {domain}")`	Prints extracted username and domain

Real-Life Project: Email Slicer

Project Code:

```
1.  def email_slicer(email):
2.      if "@" in email and '.' in email.split('@')[1]:
3.          username, domain = email.split('@')
4.          return username, domain
5.      else:
6.          return None, None

7.  email = input("Enter your email address: ")
8.  username, domain = email_slicer(email)

9.  if username and domain:
10.     print(f"Username: {username}\nDomain: {domain}")
11. else:
12.     print("Invalid email format! Please enter a valid email.")
```

Project Code Explanation Table

Line	Code Section	Description
1	`def email_slicer(email):`	Defines a function to extract the username and domain from an email.

2	`if "@" in email and '.' in email.split('@')[1]:`	Checks if the email contains '@' and at least one '.' after '@' to validate format.
3	`username, domain = email.split('@')`	Splits the email into username and domain using '@' as a separator.
4	`return username, domain`	Returns the extracted username and domain.
5-6	`else: return None, None`	Returns None values if the email format is invalid.
7	`email = input("Enter your email address: ")`	Prompts the user to input an email address.
8	`username, domain = email_slicer(email)`	Calls the function and stores the extracted username and domain.
9	`if username and domain:`	Checks if the function returned valid extracted values.
10	`` `print(f"Username: {username} ``	
11-12	`else: print("Invalid email format! Please enter a valid email.")`	Displays an error message if the email format is invalid.

Expected Results

- The program asks the user to enter an email address.
- It extracts and displays the username and domain.
- If the email format is invalid, an error message is displayed.

Hands-On Exercise Try improving the Email Slicer with these additional features:

1. **Allow case-insensitive input handling.**
2. **Validate email using regex** for stricter format checking.
3. **Provide domain categorization**, such as personal or corporate emails.
4. **Create a GUI version** using `Tkinter` for better user experience.
5. **Enhance output formatting** with additional user details.

Chapter 17: Countdown Timer

Overview A countdown timer is a simple but useful application that counts down from a given time and notifies the user when the time reaches zero. This project enhances understanding of loops, time-based execution, and user input handling in Python.

This chapter covers the step-by-step implementation of a countdown timer, handling user input, implementing a countdown loop, and displaying the remaining time dynamically.

Key Concepts of Countdown Timer in Python

- **Time Handling:**
    - Using the `time` module to introduce delays
    - Tracking elapsed time effectively
- **User Input Handling:**
    - Taking user input for countdown duration
    - Validating user input
- **Loops and Conditional Statements:**
    - Using a `while` loop to decrement the timer
    - Printing the remaining time dynamically

Countdown Timer Functionality Table

Feature	Description
Set Timer	User inputs the countdown time in seconds
Start Countdown	Displays remaining time every second
End Notification	Prints a message when countdown reaches zero

Basic Rules for Countdown Timer in Python

Rule	Correct Example
Use `time.sleep(1)` to delay execution	`time.sleep(1)`
Convert user input to integer	`seconds = int(input("Enter time in seconds: "))`
Use a loop to decrement the timer	`while seconds > 0:`

Syntax Table

SL	Concept	Syntax/Example	Description
1	Import time module	`import time`	Enables time-based operations
2	Get user input	`seconds = int(input("Enter time in seconds: "))`	Takes input for countdown duration
3	Loop for countdown	`while seconds > 0:`	Runs until the timer reaches zero
4	Print remaining time	`print(f"Time left: {seconds}s")`	Displays countdown time dynamically
5	Pause for 1 second	`time.sleep(1)`	Delays execution by 1 second

Real-Life Project: Countdown Timer

Project Code:

```
1.  import time

2.  seconds = int(input("Enter countdown time in
    seconds: "))

3.  while seconds > 0:
4.      print(f"Time left: {seconds}s", end="\r")
5.      time.sleep(1)
6.      seconds -= 1

7.  print("Time's up!")
```

Project Code Explanation Table

Line	Code Section	Description
1	`import time`	Imports the time module to use sleep functionality.
2	`seconds = int(input("Enter countdown time in seconds: "))`	Takes user input for countdown duration and converts it to an integer.

3	`while seconds > 0:`	Starts a loop that runs until the timer reaches zero.
4	`print(f"Time left: {seconds}s", end="\r")`	Displays the remaining time on the same line dynamically.
5	`time.sleep(1)`	Delays execution for one second to simulate countdown behavior.
6	`seconds -= 1`	Decrements the countdown by one second.
7	`print("Time's up!")`	Prints a message when the timer reaches zero.

Expected Results

- The program asks the user to enter the countdown duration.
- It continuously updates and displays the remaining time.
- When the countdown reaches zero, it prints "Time's up!".

Hands-On Exercise Try improving the countdown timer with these additional features:

1. **Add a sound alert** when the countdown finishes.
2. **Display a graphical progress bar** using tqdm.
3. **Allow pausing and resuming** the countdown timer.
4. **Convert seconds to minutes and seconds** for better readability.
5. **Create a GUI version** using Tkinter for better user interaction.

Conclusion This countdown timer project introduces Python concepts such as loops, time handling, and user input validation. By expanding this project, developers can create more advanced time-tracking applications with improved features.

Chapter 18: Simple Chatbot

Overview A simple chatbot is an interactive program that responds to user input based on predefined rules. This project helps in understanding string handling, conditional statements, and basic artificial intelligence concepts in Python.

This chapter covers the step-by-step implementation of a chatbot, handling user input, responding with predefined messages, and improving user interaction.

Key Concepts of Simple Chatbot in Python

- **User Input Handling:**
    - Using `input()` to receive user messages
    - Converting input to lowercase for better matching
- **Conditional Logic for Responses:**
    - Using `if-elif-else` to respond to user queries
    - Using dictionaries for improved response handling
- **Loop for Continuous Interaction:**
    - Using a `while` loop to keep the chatbot running
    - Allowing exit commands to terminate the session

Chatbot Interaction Table

User Input	Chatbot Response
"Hello"	"Hi! How can I help you?"
"How are you?"	"I'm just a chatbot, but I'm doing great!"
"What is Python?"	"Python is a programming language used for various applications."
"Bye"	"Goodbye! Have a great day!"

Basic Rules for Simple Chatbot in Python

Rule	Correct Example
Convert user input to lowercase	`user_input = input().lower()`
Use `if-elif-else` to handle responses	`if user_input == "hello":` `print("Hi!")`
Allow exit commands to stop the bot	`if user_input == "bye":` `break`

Syntax Table

SL	Concept	Syntax/Example	Description
1	Get user input	`user_input = input("You: ")`	Takes input from the user
2	Convert input to lowercase	`user_input = user_input.lower()`	Ensures case-insensitive matching
3	Define responses	`responses = {"hello": "Hi!", "bye": "Goodbye!"}`	Stores predefined responses
4	Loop for interaction	`while True:`	Runs the chatbot continuously
5	Display response	`print(f"Chatbot: {response}")`	Prints the chatbot's response

Real-Life Project: Simple Chatbot

Project Code:

```
1.   responses = {
2.        "hello": "Hi! How can I help you?",
3.        "how are you": "I'm just a chatbot, but I'm
doing great!",
4.        "what is python": "Python is a programming
language used for various applications.",
5.        "bye": "Goodbye! Have a great day!"
6.   }

7.   while True:
8.        user_input = input("You: ").lower()
9.        if user_input in responses:
10.           print(f"Chatbot: {responses[user_input]}")
11.           if user_input == "bye":
12.                break
13.       else:
14.           print("Chatbot: I'm sorry, I don't
understand that.")
```

Project Code Explanation Table

Line	Code Section	Description
1-6	`responses = {...}`	Defines a dictionary with predefined responses.
7	`while True:`	Starts an infinite loop for chatbot interaction.
8	`user_input = input("You: ").lower()`	Takes user input and converts it to lowercase.
9-10	`if user_input in responses:`	Checks if user input matches any predefined response.
11-12	`if user_input == "bye": break`	Ends the chatbot session when "bye" is entered.
13-14	`else: print("I'm sorry, I don't understand that.")`	Handles unknown inputs with a default message.

Expected Results

- The chatbot greets the user when they say "hello".
- It provides responses based on predefined queries.
- It informs the user if it doesn't understand a query.
- The chatbot terminates when the user types "bye".

Hands-On Exercise Try improving the chatbot with these additional features:

1. **Expand the response dictionary** to cover more queries.
2. **Use NLP techniques** with the `nltk` library for smarter responses.
3. **Integrate an API** to fetch real-time information (e.g., weather, news).
4. **Implement a GUI version** using `Tkinter` for better interaction.
5. **Allow user-defined commands** to customize chatbot responses.

Conclusion This Simple Chatbot project introduces Python concepts such as string handling, loops, and conditional logic. By expanding this project, developers can create more intelligent and responsive chatbot systems.

Chapter 19: Birthday Reminder App

Overview A Birthday Reminder App is a useful tool that stores and tracks birthdays, notifying users when an upcoming birthday is near. This project enhances knowledge of data storage, date handling, and automation in Python.

This chapter covers the step-by-step implementation of a Birthday Reminder App, handling user input, storing birthdays in a dictionary, checking for upcoming birthdays, and displaying reminders.

Key Concepts of Birthday Reminder App in Python

- **Date Handling:**
    - Using the `datetime` module to fetch the current date
    - Comparing stored birthdays with the current date
- **Data Storage and Retrieval:**
    - Storing names and birthdays in a dictionary or JSON file
    - Retrieving and displaying upcoming birthdays
- **Notification Mechanism:**
    - Printing reminders in the console
    - Sending email or desktop notifications (optional)

Birthday Data Table

Name	Birthday
John	1992-03-15
Alice	1987-07-10
Bob	1995-12-25
Emma	1999-05-02

Basic Rules for Birthday Reminder App in Python

Rule	Correct Example
Store birthdays in a dictionary	`birthdays = {"John": "1992-03-15"}`
Convert date format properly	`datetime.strptime(birthday, "%Y-%m-%d")`
Check for upcoming birthdays	`if birthday_day == today_day and birthday_month == today_month:`

Syntax Table

SL	Concept	Syntax/Example	Description
1	Import datetime module	`import datetime`	Enables date-based operations
2	Store birthday data	`birthdays = {"John": "1992-03-15"}`	Saves name and birthday in a dictionary
3	Get current date	`today = datetime.date.today()`	Fetches today's date
4	Compare dates	`if birthday_date.month == today.month:`	Checks if a birthday matches today's month
5	Display reminder	`print(f"Reminder: {name}'s birthday is today!")`	Prints the reminder message

Real-Life Project: Birthday Reminder App

Project Code:

```
1.  import datetime

2.  birthdays = {
3.      "John": "1992-03-15",
4.      "Alice": "1987-07-10",
5.      "Bob": "1995-12-25",
6.      "Emma": "1999-05-02"
7.  }

8.  today = datetime.date.today()
9.  today_month = today.month
10. today_day = today.day

11. for name, birthday in birthdays.items():
12.     birthday_date =
datetime.datetime.strptime(birthday, "%Y-%m-%d").date()
13.     if birthday_date.month == today_month and
birthday_date.day == today_day:
14.         print(f"Reminder: {name}'s birthday is
```

```
today!")
15.     elif birthday_date.month == today_month:
16.         print(f"Upcoming: {name}'s birthday is on
{birthday_date.day}-{birthday_date.month}")
```

Project Code Explanation Table

Line	Code Section	Description
1	`import datetime`	Imports the datetime module to handle date operations.
2-7	`birthdays = {...}`	Defines a dictionary storing names and their respective birthdays.
8	`today = datetime.date.today()`	Retrieves today's date from the system.
9	`today_month = today.month`	Extracts the current month from today's date.
10	`today_day = today.day`	Extracts the current day from today's date.
11	`for name, birthday in birthdays.items():`	Iterates through all the stored birthdays.
12	`birthday_date = datetime.datetime.strptime( birthday, "%Y-%m-%d").date()`	Converts the stored birthday string into a date object.
13	`if birthday_date.month == today_month and birthday_date.day == today_day:`	Checks if today matches a stored birthday.
14	`print(f"Reminder: {name}'s birthday is today!")`	Prints a reminder if today is someone's birthday.
15	`elif birthday_date.month == today_month:`	Checks if a birthday is upcoming within the same month.
16	`print(f"Upcoming: {name}'s`	Prints an upcoming

	birthday is on {birthday_date.day}- {birthday_date.month}")	birthday reminder.

Expected Results

- The program checks for any birthdays today and prints a reminder.
- It displays upcoming birthdays within the same month.
- Users are notified about birthdays that need attention.

Hands-On Exercise Try improving the Birthday Reminder App with these additional features:

1. **Allow users to add new birthdays dynamically.**
2. **Store birthdays in a file (JSON or CSV) for persistent storage.**
3. **Send email notifications** using the smtplib module.
4. **Integrate a GUI** using Tkinter for better user experience.
5. **Enhance date validation** to prevent incorrect inputs.

Conclusion This Birthday Reminder App project introduces Python concepts such as dictionary handling, date manipulation, and user notifications. By expanding this project, developers can create a more interactive and useful birthday tracking system.

Chapter 20: Basic Expense Tracker

Overview An Expense Tracker is a practical application that allows users to log their daily expenses and track spending habits. This project enhances knowledge of file handling, data storage, and user input processing in Python.

This chapter covers the step-by-step implementation of an Expense Tracker, including user input handling, data storage in a CSV file, and displaying expense reports.

Key Concepts of Expense Tracker in Python

- **Data Handling:**
  - Using lists and dictionaries to store expenses
  - Writing and reading data from a CSV file
- **User Input Processing:**
  - Taking user input for expense details
  - Validating and formatting input data
- **Report Generation:**
  - Displaying total expenses per category
  - Summarizing daily or monthly spending

Expense Data Table

Date	Category	Amount	Description
2024-03-15	Food	12.50	Lunch at cafe
2024-03-16	Transport	5.00	Bus fare
2024-03-16	Shopping	25.00	Grocery shopping

Basic Rules for Expense Tracker in Python

Rule	Correct Example
Store expenses in a list of dictionaries	`expenses = [{"date": "2024-03-15", "category": "Food", "amount": 12.50}]`
Validate input before storing	`if isinstance(amount, float) and amount > 0:`
Write expenses to a CSV file	`csv.writer(file).writerow([date, category, amount, description])`

Syntax Table

SL	Concept	Syntax/Example	Description
1	Import CSV module	`import csv`	Enables reading/writing to CSV files
2	Get user input	`amount = float(input("Enter amount: "))`	Takes expense details from the user
3	Store expenses	`expenses.append({"date": date, "category": category, "amount": amount})`	Saves expense data in a list
4	Write to CSV file	`with open("expenses.csv", "a") as file:`	Appends expense data to a CSV file
5	Read from CSV file	`csv.reader(file)`	Reads stored expenses from the file

Real-Life Project: Basic Expense Tracker

Project Code:

```
1.  import csv
2.  from datetime import datetime

3.  def add_expense(date, category, amount, description):
4.      with open("expenses.csv", "a", newline="") as file:
5.          writer = csv.writer(file)
6.          writer.writerow([date, category, amount, description])

7.  def view_expenses():
8.      try:
9.          with open("expenses.csv", "r") as file:
10.             reader = csv.reader(file)
11.             for row in reader:
12.                 print(row)
```

```
13.         except FileNotFoundError:
14.             print("No expense records found.")

15. date = datetime.today().strftime("%Y-%m-%d")
16. category = input("Enter expense category: ")
17. amount = float(input("Enter amount: "))
18. description = input("Enter description: ")

19. add_expense(date, category, amount, description)
20. print("Expense added successfully!")
21. print("Here are your recorded expenses:")
22. view_expenses()
```

Project Code Explanation Table

Line	Code Section	Description
1	`import csv`	Imports the CSV module for reading and writing CSV files.
2	`from datetime import datetime`	Imports the datetime module to handle date operations.
3-6	`def add_expense(date, category, amount, description):`	Defines a function to add an expense entry to the CSV file.
4	`with open("expenses.csv", "a", newline="") as file:`	Opens the CSV file in append mode to add new expense records.
5	`writer = csv.writer(file)`	Creates a CSV writer object to write data into the file.
6	`writer.writerow([date, category, amount, description])`	Writes a row containing the expense details into the file.
7-14	`def view_expenses():`	Defines a function to display stored expenses.
9-10	`with open("expenses.csv", "r") as file:`	Opens the CSV file in read mode to display existing records.

10-12	`reader = csv.reader(file)`	Reads the contents of the CSV file.
11	`for row in reader:`	Iterates over each row in the CSV file.
12	`print(row)`	Prints the expense entry row-by-row.
13-14	`except FileNotFoundError:`	Handles errors when the CSV file does not exist.
14	`print("No expense records found.")`	Displays a message if no expense records exist.
15	`date = datetime.today().strftime("%Y-%m-%d")`	Retrieves today's date and formats it as YYYY-MM-DD.
16	`category = input("Enter expense category: ")`	Prompts the user to input the category of the expense.
17	`amount = float(input("Enter amount: "))`	Takes user input for expense amount and converts it to a float.
18	`description = input("Enter description: ")`	Takes user input for expense description.
19	`add_expense(date, category, amount, description)`	Calls the function to add the new expense to the CSV file.
20	`print("Expense added successfully!")`	Displays a confirmation message after adding the expense.
21	`print("Here are your recorded expenses:")`	Prints a message before displaying stored expenses.
22	`view_expenses()`	Calls the function to display all stored expenses.

Expected Results
- The program asks the user to input an expense category, amount, and description.
- The expense details are saved into a CSV file.

- The program reads and displays all stored expenses.
- If no expenses are found, it prints an appropriate message.

Hands-On Exercise Try improving the Expense Tracker with these additional features:

1. **Allow filtering by date range** to track monthly expenses.
2. **Categorize expenses** and show total spending per category.
3. **Use a database (SQLite)** instead of a CSV file for better data management.
4. **Add a graphical user interface (GUI)** using `Tkinter`.
5. **Generate summary reports** with total expenses and graphs.

Conclusion This Basic Expense Tracker project introduces Python concepts such as file handling, user input validation, and report generation. By expanding this project, developers can create more advanced financial tracking applications with greater functionality.

Chapter 21: Fibonacci Series Generator

Overview A Fibonacci Series Generator is a simple mathematical tool that generates a sequence where each number is the sum of the two preceding ones. This project helps in understanding recursion, loops, and mathematical logic in Python.

This chapter covers the step-by-step implementation of a Fibonacci Series Generator, handling user input, generating the sequence using loops and recursion, and displaying the results.

Key Concepts of Fibonacci Series Generator in Python

- **Mathematical Computation:**
    - Fibonacci formula: $F(n) = F(n-1) + F(n-2)$
    - Using loops and recursion to generate the series
- **User Input Handling:**
    - Taking user input for the number of terms
    - Validating input to ensure it is a positive integer
- **Efficient Computation:**
    - Using iterative loops for performance optimization
    - Implementing memoization for recursive functions

Fibonacci Series Table

N (Term)	Fibonacci Number
1	0
2	1
3	1
4	2
5	3
6	5
7	8

Basic Rules for Fibonacci Series Generator in Python

Rule	Correct Example
Use recursion for Fibonacci sequence	`def fibonacci(n): return fibonacci(n-1) + fibonacci(n-2)`
Use iteration for better efficiency	`for i in range(n): fib.append(fib[i-1] + fib[i-2])`
Validate user input	`if n < 0: print("Invalid input")`

Syntax Table

SL	Concept	Syntax/Example	Description
1	Define recursive function	`def fibonacci(n):`	Defines a function to compute Fibonacci numbers recursively
2	Define loop-based function	`def fibonacci_ite rative(n):`	Defines a function to compute Fibonacci numbers using iteration
3	Get user input	`n = int(input("En ter number of terms: "))`	Takes user input for the number of terms
4	Validate input	`if n < 0:`	Ensures the input is non-negative
5	Display sequence	`print(fibonac ci(n))`	Prints the Fibonacci sequence

Real-Life Project: Fibonacci Series Generator

Project Code:

```
1.  def fibonacci_recursive(n):
2.      if n <= 0:
3.          return "Invalid input"
4.      elif n == 1:
5.          return 0
6.      elif n == 2:
7.          return 1
8.      else:
9.          return fibonacci_recursive(n-1) +
fibonacci_recursive(n-2)

10. def fibonacci_iterative(n):
11.     if n <= 0:
12.         return "Invalid input"
13.     fib_series = [0, 1]
14.     for i in range(2, n):
15.         fib_series.append(fib_series[i-1] +
fib_series[i-2])
16.     return fib_series[:n]
```

```
17. n = int(input("Enter the number of terms: "))
18. print("Fibonacci Series (Iterative):",
fibonacci_iterative(n))
19. print("Nth Fibonacci Number (Recursive):",
fibonacci_recursive(n))
```

Project Code Explanation Table

Line	Code Section	Description
1-9	def fibonacci_recursive(n):	Defines a recursive function to compute Fibonacci numbers.
2-3	if n <= 0:	Checks if the input is invalid (negative or zero).
4-5	elif n == 1:	Returns 0 for the first term.
6-7	elif n == 2:	Returns 1 for the second term.
8-9	else: return fibonacci_recursive(n-1) + fibonacci_recursive(n-2)	Computes Fibonacci using recursion.
10-16	def fibonacci_iterative(n):	Defines an iterative function to generate Fibonacci numbers.
11-12	if n <= 0:	Checks for invalid input.
13	fib_series = [0, 1]	Initializes the Fibonacci sequence.
14-15	for i in range(2, n):	Computes Fibonacci numbers iteratively and appends them to the list.
16	return fib_series[:n]	Returns the Fibonacci series up to n terms.
17	n = int(input("Enter the number of terms:	Takes user input.

	"))	
18	print("Fibonacci Series (Iterative):", fibonacci_iterative(n))	Displays the Fibonacci series generated using iteration.
19	print("Nth Fibonacci Number (Recursive):", fibonacci_recursive(n))	Displays the Nth Fibonacci number using recursion.

Expected Results

- The program asks the user for the number of terms.
- It generates and prints the Fibonacci series using iteration.
- It computes and prints the Nth Fibonacci number using recursion.
- If the user enters an invalid number, an error message is displayed.

Hands-On Exercise Try improving the Fibonacci Series Generator with these additional features:

1. **Optimize recursive calls using memoization** with a dictionary.
2. **Allow the user to choose between recursion and iteration** for generating the series.
3. **Display a graphical representation** of the Fibonacci sequence using Matplotlib.
4. **Generate Fibonacci numbers for large values efficiently** using an optimized approach.
5. **Create a GUI version** using Tkinter for better user interaction.

Conclusion This Fibonacci Series Generator project introduces Python concepts such as recursion, iteration, and mathematical logic. By expanding this project, developers can build more optimized and interactive mathematical applications.

Chapter 22: Prime Number Checker

Overview A Prime Number Checker is a useful tool that determines whether a given number is prime. This project helps in understanding loops, conditional statements, and mathematical logic in Python.

This chapter covers the step-by-step implementation of a Prime Number Checker, handling user input, performing divisibility tests, and displaying results.

Key Concepts of Prime Number Checker in Python

- **Mathematical Computation:**
    - A prime number is only divisible by 1 and itself.
    - The smallest prime number is 2.
- **User Input Handling:**
    - Taking user input to check for primality
    - Validating input to ensure it is a positive integer
- **Efficient Computation:**
    - Using loops to check divisibility up to √n for optimization

Prime Number Table

Number	Prime?
2	Yes
3	Yes
4	No
5	Yes
6	No
7	Yes
8	No
9	No
10	No

Basic Rules for Prime Number Checker in Python

Rule	Correct Example
Check divisibility from 2 to √n	`if n % i == 0: return False`
Validate user input	`if n < 2: print("Not prime")`
Optimize loop for efficiency	`for i in range(2, int(n**0.5) + 1):`

Syntax Table

SL	Concept	Syntax/Example	Description
1	Define function	`def is_prime(n):`	Defines a function to check primality
2	Validate input	`if n < 2:`	Ensures the number is greater than 1
3	Loop for divisibility test	`for i in range(2, int(n**0.5) + 1):`	Iterates up to the square root of n
4	Return prime status	`return True`	Returns True if n is prime
5	Display result	`print(is_prime(n))`	Prints the result

Real-Life Project: Prime Number Checker

Project Code:

```
1.  def is_prime(n):
2.      if n < 2:
3.          return False
4.      for i in range(2, int(n**0.5) + 1):
5.          if n % i == 0:
6.              return False
7.      return True

8.  number = int(input("Enter a number: "))
9.  if is_prime(number):
10.     print(f"{number} is a prime number.")
11. else:
12.     print(f"{number} is not a prime number.")
```

Project Code Explanation Table

Line	Code Section	Description
1-7	`def is_prime(n):`	Defines a function to check if a number is prime.
2-3	`if n < 2:`	Returns False for numbers less than 2.
4-6	`for i in range(2,`	Iterates up to the square root of

	`int(n**0.5) + 1):`	n to check divisibility.
5-6	`if n % i == 0:`	Returns `False` if n is divisible by i.
7	`return True`	Returns `True` if no divisors were found.
8	`number = int(input("Enter a number: "))`	Takes user input.
9-10	`if is_prime(number):`	Checks if the number is prime and prints the result.
11-12	`else:`	Prints a message if the number is not prime.

Expected Results

- The program asks the user to enter a number.
- It checks if the number is prime using the function.
- It prints whether the number is prime or not.
- If the user enters a number less than 2, it prints "Not a prime number."

Hands-On Exercise Try improving the Prime Number Checker with these additional features:

1. Allow users to check multiple numbers in a loop.
2. Generate a list of prime numbers within a given range.
3. Use a caching mechanism (memoization) to speed up repeated checks.
4. Create a graphical user interface (GUI) using `Tkinter`.
5. Implement an option to check large prime numbers using the Miller-Rabin primality test.

Conclusion This Prime Number Checker project introduces Python concepts such as loops, mathematical logic, and input validation. By expanding this project, developers can create more efficient and interactive number validation tools.

Chapter 23: Palindrome Checker

Overview A Palindrome Checker is a simple program that determines whether a given string, number, or phrase reads the same forward and backward. This project helps in understanding string manipulation, loops, and conditional logic in Python.

This chapter covers the step-by-step implementation of a Palindrome Checker, handling user input, checking palindromes using different methods, and displaying results.

Key Concepts of Palindrome Checker in Python

- **String Reversal:**
  - Checking if a string is the same when reversed
  - Using slicing and loops for reversal
- **User Input Handling:**
  - Taking user input and removing spaces and special characters
  - Converting input to lowercase for case insensitivity
- **Efficient Computation:**
  - Using slicing ($[::-1]$) for quick reversal
  - Using two-pointer technique for efficiency

Palindrome Examples Table

Input	Palindrome?
racecar	Yes
madam	Yes
hello	No
121	Yes
123	No
A man, a plan, a canal, Panama	Yes

Basic Rules for Palindrome Checker in Python

Rule	Correct Example
Reverse the string using slicing	`if word == word[::-1]:`
Ignore case sensitivity	`word.lower()`
Remove spaces and punctuation	`re.sub(r'[^a-zA-Z0-9]', '', word)`

Syntax Table

SL	Concept	Syntax/Example	Description
1	Reverse a string	`word[::-1]`	Checks if the reversed string matches the original
2	Convert to lowercase	`word.lower()`	Ensures case insensitivity
3	Remove spaces & punctuation	`re.sub(r'[^a-zA-Z0-9]', '', word)`	Removes non-alphanumeric characters
4	Get user input	`word = input("Enter a word: ")`	Takes input from the user
5	Display result	`print("Palindrome" if is_palindrome(word) else "Not a palindrome")`	Prints the result

Real-Life Project: Palindrome Checker

Project Code:

```
1.  import re

2.  def is_palindrome(word):
3.      word = re.sub(r'[^a-zA-Z0-9]', '',
word).lower()
4.      return word == word[::-1]

5.  word = input("Enter a word or phrase: ")
6.  if is_palindrome(word):
7.      print("Palindrome")
8.  else:
9.      print("Not a palindrome")
```

Project Code Explanation Table

Line	Code Section	Description
1	`import re`	Imports the re module for regex operations.
2-4	`def is_palindrome(word):`	Defines a function to check if a word is a palindrome.
3	`word = re.sub(r'[^a-zA-Z0-9]', '', word).lower()`	Removes non-alphanumeric characters and converts to lowercase.
4	`return word == word[::-1]`	Compares the cleaned word with its reversed version.
5	`word = input("Enter a word or phrase: ")`	Takes user input.
6-7	`if is_palindrome(word):`	Checks if the word is a palindrome and prints "Palindrome" if true.
8-9	`else: print("Not a palindrome")`	Prints "Not a palindrome" if the word does not match its reverse.

Expected Results

- The program asks the user to enter a word or phrase.
- It processes the input by removing spaces and punctuation.
- It checks whether the cleaned input is the same forward and backward.
- It prints whether the input is a palindrome or not.

Hands-On Exercise Try improving the Palindrome Checker with these additional features:

1. **Allow users to check numbers for palindrome properties.**
2. **Optimize for long strings using the two-pointer method.**
3. **Implement a graphical user interface (GUI) using Tkinter.**
4. **Support batch checking of multiple words or phrases.**
5. **Enhance input handling for different languages and scripts.**

Conclusion This Palindrome Checker project introduces Python concepts such as string manipulation, loops, and input validation. By expanding this project, developers can create more advanced tools for text analysis and pattern recognition.

Chapter 24: Leap Year Checker

Overview A Leap Year Checker is a program that determines whether a given year is a leap year. A leap year occurs every four years, except for years that are divisible by 100 but not divisible by 400. This project helps in understanding conditional logic, user input validation, and mathematical operations in Python.

This chapter covers the step-by-step implementation of a Leap Year Checker, handling user input, applying leap year rules, and displaying results.

Key Concepts of Leap Year Checker in Python

- **Leap Year Rules:**
    - A year is a leap year if it is divisible by 4.
    - However, if the year is divisible by 100, it must also be divisible by 400.
- **User Input Handling:**
    - Taking user input to check for leap year validity.
    - Validating input to ensure it is a positive integer.
- **Efficient Computation:**
    - Using logical conditions (`if-elif-else`) to check leap year rules.

Leap Year Table

Year	Leap Year?
2000	Yes
2004	Yes
1900	No
2100	No
2024	Yes
2023	No

Basic Rules for Leap Year Checker in Python

Rule	Correct Example
A year divisible by 4 is a leap year	`if year % 4 == 0:`
A year divisible by 100 must also be divisible by 400	`if year % 100 == 0 and year % 400 != 0:`
Validate input before processing	`if year < 0:` `print("Invalid input")`

Syntax Table

SL	Concept	Syntax/Example	Description
1	Get user input	`year = int(input("Enter a year: "))`	Takes user input for a year.
2	Check divisibility	`if year % 4 == 0:`	Checks if the year is divisible by 4.
3	Validate leap year rules	`if year % 100 == 0 and year % 400 != 0:`	Ensures correct leap year conditions.
4	Return leap year status	`return True if leap else False`	Returns True if the year is a leap year.
5	Display result	`print(f"{year} is a leap year")`	Prints the leap year status.

Real-Life Project: Leap Year Checker

Project Code:

```python
1.  def is_leap_year(year):
2.      if year < 0:
3.          return "Invalid input"
4.      if year % 4 == 0:
5.          if year % 100 == 0:
6.              if year % 400 == 0:
7.                  return True
8.              else:
9.                  return False
10.         return True
11.     return False

12. year = int(input("Enter a year: "))
13. if is_leap_year(year):
14.     print(f"{year} is a leap year.")
15. else:
16.     print(f"{year} is not a leap year.")
```

Project Code Explanation Table

Line	Code Section	Description

1	`def is_leap_year (year):`	Defines a function to check if a given year is a leap year.
2	`if year < 0:`	Checks if the input is a negative number and returns an error message.
3	`return "Invalid input"`	Returns an error message for invalid inputs.
4	`if year % 4 == 0:`	Checks if the year is divisible by 4, which is the first rule for a leap year.
5	`if year % 100 == 0:`	Checks if the year is divisible by 100, meaning it might not be a leap year unless divisible by 400.
6	`if year % 400 == 0:`	Ensures that years divisible by 100 must also be divisible by 400 to be leap years.
7	`return True`	Returns True for leap years that meet all conditions.
8	`else:`	Handles cases where a year fails the 400 divisibility check.
9	`return False`	Returns False for years divisible by 100 but not by 400.
10	`return True`	If a year is divisible by 4 but not by 100, it is a leap year.
11	`return False`	If a year is not divisible by 4, it is not a leap year.
12	`year = int(input("E nter a year: "))`	Takes user input and converts it to an integer.
13	`if is_leap_year (year):`	Calls the function and checks if the given year is a leap year.
14	`print(f"{yea r} is a leap year.")`	Prints a message confirming that the year is a leap year.
15	`else:`	Handles cases where the function returns

		False.
16	`print(f"{yea r} is not a leap year.")`	Prints a message stating that the year is not a leap year.

Expected Results

- The program asks the user to enter a year.
- It checks if the year follows leap year rules.
- It prints whether the year is a leap year or not.
- If the user enters a negative number, it prints "Invalid input."

Hands-On Exercise Try improving the Leap Year Checker with these additional features:

1. **Allow users to check multiple years in a loop.**
2. **Check a range of years and display all leap years within that range.**
3. **Create a GUI version using `Tkinter` for better user interaction.**
4. **Enhance input validation to prevent incorrect inputs (e.g., non-numeric values).**
5. **Integrate the program into a calendar application to highlight leap years.**

Conclusion This Leap Year Checker project introduces Python concepts such as conditional logic, mathematical operations, and input validation. By expanding this project, developers can create more advanced date-related applications.

Chapter 25: Random Password Generator

Overview A Random Password Generator is a useful application that generates secure and random passwords with a combination of letters, numbers, and special characters. This project helps in understanding string manipulation, randomization, and user input handling in Python.

This chapter covers the step-by-step implementation of a Random Password Generator, handling user input, generating passwords with various character sets, and displaying results.

Key Concepts of Random Password Generator in Python

- **Randomization:**
  - ○ Using the random module to generate random characters.
  - ○ Shuffling characters for better randomness.
- **User Input Handling:**
  - ○ Taking input for password length.
  - ○ Allowing users to specify character types (letters, digits, special characters).
- **Security Considerations:**
  - ○ Ensuring a mix of uppercase, lowercase, digits, and symbols.
  - ○ Avoiding weak passwords.

Password Strength Guidelines

Length	Strength
< 6	Weak
6-10	Medium
> 10	Strong

Basic Rules for Random Password Generator in Python

Rule	Correct Example
Use random.choices() for random selection	random.choices(string.ascii_letters, k=length)
Ensure password contains letters, digits, and symbols	random.choice(string.punctuation)
Shuffle characters for randomness	random.shuffle(password_list)

Syntax Table

SL	Concept	Syntax/Example	Description
1	Import random module	`import random`	Enables random selection of characters
2	Import string module	`import string`	Provides predefined character sets
3	Get user input	`length = int(input("Enter password length: "))`	Takes password length as input
4	Generate password	`password = ''.join(random.choices(characters, k=length))`	Generates a random password of given length
5	Display password	`print(f"Generated Password: {password}")`	Prints the generated password

Real-Life Project: Random Password Generator

Project Code:

```
1.  import random
2.  import string

3.  def generate_password(length=8):
4.      if length < 6:
5.          return "Password too short! Choose at least 6 characters."
6.      characters = string.ascii_letters + string.digits + string.punctuation
7.      password = ''.join(random.choices(characters, k=length))
8.      return password

9.  length = int(input("Enter the desired password length: "))
10. print("Generated Password:", generate_password(length))
```

Project Code Explanation Table

Line	Code Section	Description
1-2	`import random, string`	Imports the necessary modules for password generation.
3-8	`def generate_password(length=8):`	Defines a function to generate a random password.
4-5	`if length < 6:`	Ensures password length is at least 6 characters for security.
6	`characters = string.ascii_letters + string.digits + string.punctuation`	Defines a pool of characters for password generation.
7	`password = ''.join(random.choices(characters, k=length))`	Randomly selects characters and forms the password.
8	`return password`	Returns the generated password.
9	`length = int(input("Enter the desired password length: "))`	Takes user input for password length.
10	`print("Generated Password:", generate_password(length))`	Calls the function and prints the generated password.

Expected Results
- The program asks the user to enter a password length.
- It generates a password containing letters, digits, and symbols.
- The password is displayed to the user.
- If the user enters a length less than 6, it prompts for a longer password.

Hands-On Exercise Try improving the Random Password Generator with these additional features:

1. **Allow users to specify character types (e.g., only letters, only digits).**
2. **Enhance security by ensuring at least one of each character type**

is included.

3. **Provide an option to copy the password to the clipboard using `pyperclip`.**
4. **Create a GUI version using `Tkinter` for better user interaction.**
5. **Integrate password strength analysis to rate the generated password.**

Conclusion This Random Password Generator project introduces Python concepts such as randomization, string handling, and input validation. By expanding this project, developers can create more secure and user-friendly password management tools.

Chapter 26: Dice Roller Simulator

Overview A Dice Roller Simulator is a simple application that mimics rolling a physical dice. This project helps in understanding randomization, loops, and user interaction in Python.

This chapter covers the step-by-step implementation of a Dice Roller Simulator, handling user input, generating random dice values, and displaying results.

Key Concepts of Dice Roller Simulator in Python

- **Randomization:**
  - Using the random module to generate random dice values.
  - Simulating different types of dice rolls (e.g., 6-sided, 12-sided).

- **User Input Handling:**
  - Allowing the user to roll multiple times.
  - Giving the option to roll different dice types.

- **Looping for Repeated Rolls:**
  - Using a while loop to allow continuous rolling.
  - Providing an exit option to stop rolling.

Dice Rolling Outcomes Table

Dice Type	Possible Outcomes
6-sided	1, 2, 3, 4, 5, 6
12-sided	1-12
20-sided	1-20

Basic Rules for Dice Roller Simulator in Python

Rule	Correct Example
Use random.randint(1, 6) to simulate dice rolls	roll = random.randint(1, 6)
Allow multiple rolls using a loop	while user_wants_to_roll:
Provide user input for dice type	sides = int(input("Enter dice sides: "))

Syntax Table

SL	Concept	Syntax/Example	Description
1	Import random module	`import random`	Enables random number generation
2	Generate random dice roll	`roll = random.randint(1, 6)`	Simulates rolling a 6-sided dice
3	Get user input for dice type	`sides = int(input("Enter dice sides: "))`	Allows user to choose dice type
4	Loop for multiple rolls	`while True:`	Continues rolling until user exits
5	Display result	`print(f"You rolled a {roll}")`	Prints the dice roll outcome

Real-Life Project: Dice Roller Simulator

Project Code:

```
1.  import random

2.  def roll_dice(sides=6):
3.      return random.randint(1, sides)

4.  while True:
5.      sides = int(input("Enter the number of sides on
the dice (or 0 to exit): "))
6.      if sides == 0:
7.          print("Thanks for playing!")
8.          break
9.      roll = roll_dice(sides)
10.     print(f"You rolled a {roll}!")
```

Project Code Explanation Table

Line	Code Section	Description
1	`import random`	Imports the random module to generate random numbers.
2-3	`def roll_dice(side`	Defines a function to roll a dice with a given number of sides.

	s=6):	
3	`return random.randint (1, sides)`	Generates a random roll between 1 and the specified number of sides.
4	`while True:`	Creates an infinite loop to allow continuous rolling.
5	`sides = int(input(...) )`	Takes user input for the number of dice sides.
6-8	`if sides == 0:`	Checks if the user wants to exit the program.
9	`roll = roll_dice(side s)`	Calls the function to roll the dice with the chosen number of sides.
10	`print(f"You rolled a {roll}!")`	Displays the result of the dice roll.

Expected Results

- The program asks the user for the number of sides on the dice.
- It rolls the dice and displays the result.
- The user can continue rolling or enter 0 to exit.

Hands-On Exercise Try improving the Dice Roller Simulator with these additional features:

1. Allow rolling multiple dice at once and sum the results.
2. Give users the option to roll special dice (e.g., RPG dice: D4, D8, D12, D20).
3. Add a graphical interface using `Tkinter`.
4. Save roll history and statistics for the session.
5. Introduce an animation to simulate rolling for a more engaging experience.

Conclusion This Dice Roller Simulator project introduces Python concepts such as randomization, loops, and user input handling. By expanding this project, developers can create more interactive and customizable dice simulation applications.

Chapter 27: Multiplication Table Generator

Overview A Multiplication Table Generator is a simple yet useful program that displays the multiplication table for a given number up to a specified range. This project enhances understanding of loops, user input handling, and formatted output in Python.

This chapter covers the step-by-step implementation of a Multiplication Table Generator, handling user input, using loops for calculations, and displaying well-formatted results.

Key Concepts of Multiplication Table Generator in Python

- **Mathematical Computation:**
    - Using loops to iterate through multipliers.
    - Displaying formatted multiplication results.
- **User Input Handling:**
    - Allowing users to input a number for generating the table.
    - Setting a range for the multiplication table.
- **Efficient Output Formatting:**
    - Using f-strings to format table display neatly.
    - Aligning numbers for better readability.

Multiplication Table Example

Number	Multiplier	Result
5	1	5
5	2	10
5	3	15
5	4	20
5	5	25

Basic Rules for Multiplication Table Generator in Python

Rule	Correct Example
Use a loop to iterate over the range	`for i in range(1, n+1):`
Take user input for the number and range	`num = int(input("Enter a number: "))`
Display results using formatted output	`print(f"{num} x {i} = {num * i}")`

Syntax Table

SL	Concept	Syntax/Example	Description
1	Get user	`num =`	Takes the base number for

	input	int(input("Enter a number: "))	the table.
2	Define table range	limit = int(input("Enter range: "))	Takes input for the upper limit of multiplication.
3	Use a loop	for i in range(1, limit+1):	Iterates through the multiplication range.
4	Print formatt ed output	print(f"{num} x {i} = {num * i}")	Displays multiplication results.

Real-Life Project: Multiplication Table Generator

Project Code:

```
1.  def generate_table(num, limit):
2.      for i in range(1, limit + 1):
3.          print(f"{num} x {i} = {num * i}")

4.  number = int(input("Enter a number: "))
5.  range_limit = int(input("Enter the range: "))

6.  print(f"Multiplication Table for {number} up to
{range_limit}:")
7.  generate_table(number, range_limit)
```

Project Code Explanation Table

Line	Code Section	Description
1-3	def generate_table(num, limit):	Defines a function to generate the multiplication table.
2	for i in range(1, limit + 1):	Loops from 1 to the specified range limit.
3	print(f"{num} x {i} = {num * i}")	Prints each multiplication result.
4	number = int(input("Enter a number: "))	Takes user input for the base number.
5	range_limit =	Takes user input for the

	int(input("Enter the range: "))	multiplication range.
6	print(f"Multiplication Table for {number} up to {range_limit}:")	Displays a header before printing the table.
7	generate_table(number, range_limit)	Calls the function to generate the table.

Expected Results

- The program asks the user to enter a number and a range.
- It displays the multiplication table up to the specified range.
- The output is formatted neatly.

Hands-On Exercise Try improving the Multiplication Table Generator with these additional features:

1. **Allow users to generate tables for multiple numbers at once.**
2. **Enhance formatting using tabular display for readability.**
3. **Provide an option to save the table to a text file.**
4. **Create a GUI version using Tkinter for better interaction.**
5. **Add an option for reverse-order multiplication tables.**

Conclusion This Multiplication Table Generator project introduces Python concepts such as loops, user input handling, and formatted output. By expanding this project, developers can create more advanced and user-friendly table generators.

Chapter 28: Odd or Even Number Checker

Overview An Odd or Even Number Checker is a simple program that determines whether a given number is odd or even. This project helps in understanding conditional statements, modulus operations, and user input handling in Python.

This chapter covers the step-by-step implementation of an Odd or Even Number Checker, handling user input, applying modulus operations, and displaying results.

Key Concepts of Odd or Even Number Checker in Python

- **Mathematical Computation:**
  - A number is **even** if divisible by 2 (num % 2 == 0).
  - A number is **odd** if not divisible by 2 (num % 2 != 0).
- **User Input Handling:**
  - Taking user input to check for odd or even numbers.
  - Validating input to ensure it is an integer.
- **Conditional Statements:**
  - Using if-else statements to determine odd or even numbers.

Odd and Even Number Table

Number	Even or Odd?
2	Even
7	Odd
10	Even
15	Odd
20	Even

Basic Rules for Odd or Even Number Checker in Python

Rule	Correct Example
A number is even if num % 2 == 0	if num % 2 == 0:
A number is odd if num % 2 != 0	else:
Validate user input before checking	if not isinstance(num, int):

Syntax Table

SL	Concept	Syntax/Example	Description
1	Get user input	`num = int(input("Enter a number: "))`	Takes user input for checking odd or even.
2	Check even condition	`if num % 2 == 0:`	Checks if the number is divisible by 2.
3	Check odd condition	`else:`	Handles the case where the number is odd.
4	Print results	`print("Even")` or `print("Odd")`	Displays the result to the user.

Real-Life Project: Odd or Even Number Checker

Project Code:

```
1.  def check_odd_even(num):
2.      if num % 2 == 0:
3.          return "Even"
4.      else:
5.          return "Odd"

6.  num = int(input("Enter a number: "))
7.  print(f"The number {num} is
{check_odd_even(num)}.")
```

Project Code Explanation Table

Line	Code Section	Description
1-5	`def check_odd_even(num):`	Defines a function to check if a number is odd or even.
2	`if num % 2 == 0:`	Checks if the number is divisible by 2.
3	`return "Even"`	Returns "Even" if the number is divisible by 2.
4-5	`else: return "Odd"`	Returns "Odd" if the number is not divisible by 2.
6	`num = int(input("Enter a number: "))`	Takes user input and converts it to an integer.

| 7 | `print(f"The number {num} is {check_odd_even(num)}."` `)` | Calls the function and prints the result. |

Expected Results

- The program asks the user to enter a number.
- It checks whether the number is even or odd.
- It prints the result accordingly.

Hands-On Exercise Try improving the Odd or Even Number Checker with these additional features:

1. **Allow users to check multiple numbers in a loop.**
2. **Validate user input to prevent errors if non-numeric values are entered.**
3. **Provide a batch input option to check multiple numbers at once.**
4. **Enhance the program with a graphical user interface using** `Tkinter`.
5. **Extend the logic to check if a number is prime along with even or odd classification.**

Conclusion This Odd or Even Number Checker project introduces Python concepts such as conditional statements, mathematical operations, and input validation. By expanding this project, developers can create more robust number classification applications.

Chapter 29: Simple Voting System

Overview A Simple Voting System allows users to cast votes for predefined candidates and displays the results. This project enhances understanding of dictionaries, loops, user input handling, and data validation in Python.

This chapter covers the step-by-step implementation of a Simple Voting System, including handling user input, recording votes, and displaying election results.

Key Concepts of Simple Voting System in Python

- **Data Storage:**
  - Using dictionaries to store candidate names and vote counts.
- **User Input Handling:**
  - Accepting and validating user votes.
  - Allowing multiple users to vote.
- **Vote Counting and Results:**
  - Updating vote counts dynamically.
  - Displaying election results in an organized format.

Example Candidate Vote Table

Candidate	Votes
Alice	3
Bob	5
Charlie	2

Basic Rules for Simple Voting System in Python

Rule	Correct Example
Use a dictionary to store candidates and vote counts	`votes = {"Alice": 0, "Bob": 0}`
Validate user input before casting a vote	`if choice in votes:`
Display results in descending order	`sorted(votes.items(), key=lambda x: x[1], reverse=True)`

Syntax Table

SL	Concept	Syntax/Example	Description
1	Define candidates	votes = {"Alice": 0, "Bob": 0, "Charlie": 0}	Creates a dictionary to store vote counts.
2	Get user input	choice = input("Enter your vote: ")	Takes user input for voting.
3	Validate vote	if choice in votes:	Checks if the entered candidate exists.
4	Increment vote count	votes[choice] += 1	Increases the candidate's vote count.
5	Display results	for candidate, count in votes.items(): print(f"{candidate}: {count} votes")	Prints the voting results.

Real-Life Project: Simple Voting System

Project Code:

```
1.  votes = {"Alice": 0, "Bob": 0, "Charlie": 0}

2.  while True:
3.      print("Candidates: Alice, Bob, Charlie")
4.      choice = input("Enter your vote (or type 'exit'
to finish): ")
5.      if choice.lower() == "exit":
6.          break
7.      elif choice in votes:
8.          votes[choice] += 1
9.          print(f"Vote cast for {choice}!")
10.     else:
11.         print("Invalid candidate. Try again.")
12. print("\nVoting Results:")
13. for candidate, count in sorted(votes.items(),
key=lambda x: x[1], reverse=True):
14.     print(f"{candidate}: {count} votes")
```

Project Code Explanation Table

Line	Code Section	Description
1	`votes = {"Alice": 0, "Bob": 0, "Charlie": 0}`	Initializes a dictionary to store candidate names and their vote counts.
2	`while True:`	Starts an infinite loop to allow continuous voting until the user exits.
3	`print("Candidates: Alice, Bob, Charlie")`	Displays the list of available candidates to the user.
4	`choice = input("Enter your vote (or type 'exit' to finish): ")`	Takes user input for voting and allows an option to exit.
5	`if choice.lower() == "exit":`	Checks if the user wants to exit the voting process.
6	`break`	Exits the loop if the user types 'exit'.
7	`elif choice in votes:`	Checks if the entered vote matches one of the predefined candidates.
8	`votes[choice] += 1`	Increments the vote count for the selected candidate.
9	`print(f"Vote cast for {choice}!")`	Confirms that the vote has been successfully recorded.
10	`else:`	Handles cases where the user enters an invalid candidate name.
11	`print("Invalid candidate. Try again.")`	Informs the user that the input is invalid and prompts them to try again.
13	`for candidate, count in sorted(votes.items(), key=lambda x: x[1], reverse=True):`	Sorts candidates based on vote count in descending order.

14	`print(f"{candidate}: {count} votes")`	Displays each candidate's name along with their vote count.

Expected Results

- The program asks users to vote for a candidate.
- It records and counts votes dynamically.
- Users can type "exit" to end voting and see results.
- The results display vote counts for each candidate.

Hands-On Exercise Try improving the Simple Voting System with these additional features:

1. **Allow users to add new candidates dynamically.**
2. **Restrict users to one vote per session using unique identifiers.**
3. **Enhance security by implementing user authentication.**
4. **Store voting results in a file or database for future reference.**
5. **Create a GUI version using `Tkinter` for better usability.**

Conclusion This Simple Voting System project introduces Python concepts such as dictionaries, loops, and input validation. By expanding this project, developers can create a more sophisticated voting application with improved security and usability.

Chapter 30: Character Frequency Counter

Overview A Character Frequency Counter is a program that counts the occurrences of each character in a given text. This project helps in understanding dictionary operations, loops, and string manipulation in Python.

This chapter covers the step-by-step implementation of a Character Frequency Counter, handling user input, processing character counts, and displaying the results.

Key Concepts of Character Frequency Counter in Python

- **String Manipulation:**
  - Iterating over characters in a string.
  - Ignoring spaces and punctuation if needed.
- **Dictionary Operations:**
  - Storing character frequencies in a dictionary.
  - Updating frequency counts dynamically.
- **Sorting and Displaying Results:**
  - Sorting character occurrences in ascending or descending order.
  - Formatting output for readability.

Example Character Frequency Table

Character	Frequency
a	3
b	2
c	1
d	4

Basic Rules for Character Frequency Counter in Python

Rule	Correct Example
Use a dictionary to store character counts	`freq = {}`
Iterate through each character in a string	`for char in text:`
Ignore spaces and special characters (optional)	`if char.isalnum():`

Syntax Table

SL	Concept	Syntax/Example	Description
1	Get user input	`text = input("Enter text: ")`	Takes a string from the user.
2	Initialize dictionary	`freq = {}`	Creates an empty dictionary to store character counts.
3	Loop through characters	`for char in text:`	Iterates over each character in the string.
4	Update dictionary count	`freq[char] = freq.get(char, 0) + 1`	Increments character count in dictionary.
5	Print results	`for char, count in freq.items(): print(char, count)`	Displays character frequencies.

Real-Life Project: Character Frequency Counter

Project Code:

```
1.  def char_frequency(text):
2.      freq = {}
3.      for char in text:
4.          if char.isalnum():
5.              freq[char] = freq.get(char, 0) + 1
6.      return freq

7.  text = input("Enter a string: ")
8.  frequencies = char_frequency(text)
9.  for char, count in sorted(frequencies.items()):
10.     print(f"{char}: {count}")
```

Project Code Explanation Table

Line	Code Section	Description
1	`def char_frequency(text):`	Defines a function to count the occurrences of each character in a given text.
2	`freq = {}`	Initializes an empty dictionary to store character frequencies.
3	`for char in text:`	Loops through each character in the provided text input.
4	`if char.isalnum():`	Ensures that only alphanumeric characters are counted, ignoring spaces and punctuation.
5	`freq[char] = freq.get(char, 0) + 1`	Uses `.get(char, 0)` to check if the character exists in the dictionary and increments its count.
6	`return freq`	Returns the dictionary containing character frequencies.
7	`text = input("Enter a string: ")`	Takes user input as a string for processing.
8	`frequencies = char_frequency(text)`	Calls the function and stores the resulting frequency dictionary.
9	`for char, count in sorted(frequencies.items()):`	Sorts the dictionary alphabetically before displaying results.
10	`print(f"{char}: {count}")`	Prints the characters along with their respective frequency counts.

Expected Results

- The program asks the user to enter a text.
- It counts the occurrences of each character.
- It displays the results in sorted order.

Hands-On Exercise Try improving the Character Frequency Counter with these additional features:

1. **Ignore case sensitivity by converting text to lowercase.**

2. **Allow users to choose whether to include spaces and special characters.**
3. **Sort character counts by frequency instead of alphabetically.**
4. **Store results in a text file for later reference.**
5. **Create a GUI version using `Tkinter` for better usability.**

Conclusion This Character Frequency Counter project introduces Python concepts such as loops, dictionaries, and string manipulation. By expanding this project, developers can create more advanced text analysis applications.

Chapter 31: Basic HTML Page Generator

Overview A Basic HTML Page Generator is a simple program that allows users to generate an HTML file with custom content. This project enhances understanding of file handling, string manipulation, and web development basics in Python.

This chapter covers the step-by-step implementation of a Basic HTML Page Generator, handling user input, writing content to an HTML file, and displaying the generated webpage.

Key Concepts of Basic HTML Page Generator in Python

- **File Handling:**
    - Using Python to create and write to an HTML file.
    - Saving user-generated content in an external file.

- **String Manipulation:**
    - Using multi-line strings to create structured HTML templates.
    - Formatting user input dynamically within the HTML content.

- **Web Page Creation:**
    - Generating an HTML page that can be opened in a browser.
    - Adding title, headings, paragraphs, and basic styling.

Basic HTML Structure Example

```
<!DOCTYPE html>
<html>
<head>
    <title>My Web Page</title>
</head>
<body>
    <h1>Welcome to My Web Page</h1>
    <p>This page was generated using Python!</p>
</body>
</html>
```

Basic Rules for Basic HTML Page Generator in Python

Rule	Correct Example

Use open( ) to create an HTML file	`file = open("index.html", "w")`
Write content using .write()	`file.write("<html>...</html>")`
Close file after writing	`file.close()`

Syntax Table

SL	Concept	Syntax/Example	Description
1	Open file in write mode	`file = open("index.html", "w")`	Creates a new HTML file or overwrites an existing file.
2	Write HTML content	`file.write("<html>...</html>")`	Writes structured HTML code into the file.
3	Close the file	`file.close()`	Saves and closes the file properly.
4	Open HTML file	`import webbrowser; webbrowser.open("index.html")`	Opens the generated file in a web browser.

Real-Life Project: Basic HTML Page Generator

Project Code:

```
1.  def generate_html(title, heading, paragraph):
2.      html_content = f"""
3.      <!DOCTYPE html>
4.      <html>
5.      <head>
6.          <title>{title}</title>
7.      </head>
8.      <body>
9.          <h1>{heading}</h1>
10.         <p>{paragraph}</p>
11.     </body>
12.     </html>
13.     """
14.     with open("index.html", "w") as file:
15.         file.write(html_content)
16.     print("HTML file generated successfully!")
```

```
17. title = input("Enter page title: ")
18. heading = input("Enter main heading: ")
19. paragraph = input("Enter paragraph text: ")

20. generate_html(title, heading, paragraph)
21. import webbrowser
22. webbrowser.open("index.html")
```

Project Code Explanation Table

Line	Code Section	Description
1	def generate_html(title, heading, paragraph):	Defines a function to generate an HTML page with user inputs.
2-13	html_content = f"""..."""	Stores the structure of the HTML page using an f-string for dynamic content.
14	with open("index.html", "w") as file:	Opens a file in write mode to store the HTML content.
15	file.write(html_content)	Writes the generated HTML content to the file.
16	print("HTML file generated successfully!")	Displays a success message after file creation.
17	title = input("Enter page title: ")	Takes user input for the web page title.
18	heading = input("Enter main heading: ")	Takes user input for the main heading of the page.
19	paragraph = input("Enter paragraph text: ")	Takes user input for the paragraph text.
20	generate_html(title, heading, paragraph)	Calls the function to generate the HTML page.

21-22	`import webbrowser;`
	`webbrowser.open("i`
	`ndex.html")`
		Opens the generated HTML file in the default web browser.

Expected Results

- The program asks the user for a title, heading, and paragraph.
- It creates an HTML file with the provided content.
- It automatically opens the generated HTML page in the browser.

Hands-On Exercise Try improving the Basic HTML Page Generator with these additional features:

1. **Allow users to add multiple paragraphs dynamically.**
2. **Include CSS styling to improve the appearance of the webpage.**
3. **Enable the user to add images and hyperlinks through input.**
4. **Save multiple pages with different filenames.**
5. **Create a GUI version using `Tkinter` to generate pages easily.**

Conclusion This Basic HTML Page Generator project introduces Python concepts such as file handling, string manipulation, and user input processing. By expanding this project, developers can create more advanced webpage automation tools.

Chapter 32: Print the First N Fibonacci Numbers

Overview The Fibonacci sequence is a series of numbers where each number is the sum of the two preceding ones, starting from 0 and 1. This project helps in understanding loops, recursion, and mathematical computations in Python.

This chapter covers the step-by-step implementation of printing the first N Fibonacci numbers, handling user input, and using both iterative and recursive approaches to generate the sequence.

Key Concepts of Fibonacci Number Generator in Python

- **Mathematical Computation:**
  - Fibonacci formula: $F(n) = F(n-1) + F(n-2)$
  - Using loops and recursion to generate the series
- **User Input Handling:**
  - Taking user input for the number of terms
  - Validating input to ensure it is a positive integer
- **Efficient Computation:**
  - Using iteration for better performance
  - Implementing recursion with memoization for optimization

Fibonacci Sequence Example

N (Term)	Fibonacci Number
1	0
2	1
3	1
4	2
5	3
6	5
7	8
8	13

Basic Rules for Fibonacci Number Generator in Python

Rule	Correct Example
Use recursion for Fibonacci sequence	`def fibonacci(n): return fibonacci(n-1) + fibonacci(n-2)`

Use iteration for better efficiency	`for i in range(n):` `fib.append(fib[i-1] + fib[i-2])`
Validate user input	`if n < 0: print("Invalid input")`

Syntax Table

SL	Concept	Syntax/Example	Description
1	Define recursive function	`def fibonacci(n):`	Defines a function to compute Fibonacci numbers recursively.
2	Define loop-based function	`def fibonacci_ite rative(n):`	Defines a function to compute Fibonacci numbers using iteration.
3	Get user input	`n = int(input("En ter number of terms: "))`	Takes user input for the number of terms.
4	Validate input	`if n < 0:`	Ensures the input is a positive integer.
5	Display sequence	`print(fibonac ci(n))`	Prints the Fibonacci sequence.

Real-Life Project: Fibonacci Sequence Generator

Project Code:

```
1.  def fibonacci_recursive(n):
2.      if n <= 0:
3.          return "Invalid input"
4.      elif n == 1:
5.          return [0]
6.      elif n == 2:
7.          return [0, 1]
8.      else:
9.          sequence = fibonacci_recursive(n-1)
10.         sequence.append(sequence[-1] + sequence[-2])
11.         return sequence

12. def fibonacci_iterative(n):
13.     if n <= 0:
```

```
14.           return "Invalid input"
15.      fib_series = [0, 1]
16.      for i in range(2, n):
17.           fib_series.append(fib_series[i-1] +
fib_series[i-2])
18.      return fib_series[:n]

19. n = int(input("Enter the number of terms: "))
20. print("Fibonacci Series (Iterative):",
fibonacci_iterative(n))
21. print("Fibonacci Series (Recursive):",
fibonacci_recursive(n))
```

Project Code Explanation Table

Line	Code Section	Description
1	def fibonacci_recursive(n) :	Defines a function to generate the Fibonacci sequence recursively.
2	if n <= 0:	Checks if the input is non-positive and returns an error message.
3	return "Invalid input"	Returns an error message if the input is invalid.
4	elif n == 1:	If the input is 1, returns a list with only the first Fibonacci number [0].
5	return [0]	The Fibonacci sequence starts with 0 for n = 1.
6	elif n == 2:	If the input is 2, returns the first two Fibonacci numbers [0, 1].
7	return [0, 1]	Defines the starting sequence for n = 2.
8	else:	Executes the recursive approach for n > 2.
9	sequence =	Recursively calls the function

		fibonacci_recursive(n-1)	for n-1 to build the sequence.
10		`sequence.append(sequence[-1] + sequence[-2])`	Computes the next Fibonacci number by summing the last two values.
11		`return sequence`	Returns the final Fibonacci sequence after appending new values.
12		`def fibonacci_iterative(n):`	Defines a function to generate the Fibonacci sequence iteratively.
13		`if n <= 0:`	Checks if the input is invalid and returns an error message.
14		`return "Invalid input"`	Returns an error message if the input is not positive.
15		`fib_series = [0, 1]`	Initializes the Fibonacci series with the first two values.
16		`for i in range(2, n):`	Loops from 2 to n-1 to generate the Fibonacci sequence iteratively.
17		`fib_series.append(fib_series[i-1] + fib_series[i-2])`	Computes the next Fibonacci number using iteration.
18		`return fib_series[:n]`	Returns the Fibonacci sequence up to n terms.
19		`n = int(input("Enter the number of terms: "))`	Takes user input for the number of Fibonacci terms.
20		`print("Fibonacci Series (Iterative):", fibonacci_iterative(n))`	Calls and prints the iterative Fibonacci sequence.
21		`print("Fibonacci Series (Recursive):", fibonacci_recursive(n))`	Calls and prints the recursive Fibonacci sequence.

Expected Results

- The program asks the user for the number of terms.
- It generates and prints the Fibonacci sequence using both iteration and recursion.
- If the user enters an invalid number, an error message is displayed.

Hands-On Exercise Try improving the Fibonacci Sequence Generator with these additional features:

1. **Optimize recursive calls using memoization with a dictionary.**
2. **Allow the user to choose between recursion and iteration.**
3. **Display a graphical representation of the Fibonacci sequence using Matplotlib.**
4. **Generate Fibonacci numbers for large values efficiently using an optimized approach.**
5. **Create a GUI version using Tkinter for better user interaction.**

Conclusion This Fibonacci Sequence Generator project introduces Python concepts such as recursion, iteration, and mathematical logic. By expanding this project, developers can build more optimized and interactive mathematical applications.

Chapter 33: Count Vowels in a String

Overview A Vowel Counter is a simple program that determines the number of vowels present in a given string. This project helps in understanding string manipulation, loops, and conditional statements in Python.

This chapter covers the step-by-step implementation of counting vowels in a string, handling user input, processing characters, and displaying the results.

Key Concepts of Vowel Counter in Python

- **String Manipulation:**
  - Iterating over each character in a string.
  - Converting text to lowercase for case insensitivity.
- **Conditional Statements:**
  - Checking if a character belongs to the set of vowels (a, e, i, o, u).
  - Counting and displaying the total number of vowels.
- **User Input Handling:**
  - Taking a string from the user.
  - Displaying the frequency of each vowel.

Example Vowel Count Table

Character	Count
a	2
e	1
i	3
o	1
u	0

Basic Rules for Vowel Counter in Python

Rule	Correct Example
Use a loop to iterate over a string	`for char in text:`
Convert text to lowercase before checking	`text.lower()`
Use a dictionary to store vowel counts	`vowel_count = {}`

Syntax Table

SL	Concept	Syntax/Example	Description
1	Convert string to lowercase	`text.lower()`	Ensures case-insensitive comparison.
2	Loop through characters	`for char in text:`	Iterates over each character in the input string.
3	Check if character is a vowel	`if char in "aeiou":`	Determines if a character is a vowel.
4	Use a dictionary for counting	`vowel_count[char] = vowel_count.get(char, 0) + 1`	Updates the count of each vowel.
5	Print vowel frequency	`print(f"{char}: {count}")`	Displays the count of each vowel.

Real-Life Project: Vowel Counter

Project Code:

```
1.  def count_vowels(text):
2.      text = text.lower()
3.      vowels = "aeiou"
4.      vowel_count = {v: 0 for v in vowels}
5.      for char in text:
6.          if char in vowels:
7.              vowel_count[char] += 1
8.      return vowel_count

9.  text = input("Enter a string: ")
10. vowels_found = count_vowels(text)
11. for vowel, count in vowels_found.items():
12.     print(f"{vowel}: {count}")
```

Project Code Explanation Table

Line	Code Section	Description
1	```def count_vowels(text):```	Defines a function to count vowels in a given text.
2	```text = text.lower()```	Converts the input string to lowercase to ensure case insensitivity.
3	```vowels = "aeiou"```	Defines a string containing all vowels.
4	```vowel_count = {v: 0 for v in vowels}```	Initializes a dictionary to store vowel counts with all vowels set to 0.
5	```for char in text:```	Loops through each character in the input text.
6	```if char in vowels:```	Checks if the current character is a vowel.
7	```vowel_count[char] += 1```	Increments the count of the vowel found.
8	```return vowel_count```	Returns the dictionary containing vowel counts.
9	```text = input("Enter a string: ")```	Takes user input as a string.
10	```vowels_found = count_vowels(text)```	Calls the function and stores the result in a dictionary.
11-12	```for vowel, count in vowels_found.items():```	Loops through the dictionary and prints vowel counts.

Expected Results

- The program asks the user to enter a string.
- It counts the occurrences of vowels (a, e, i, o, u).
- It displays the results in a structured format.

Hands-On Exercise Try improving the Vowel Counter with these additional features:

1. **Include uppercase vowels in the count without converting the text.**
2. **Extend the program to count consonants as well.**
3. **Allow users to enter multiple lines of text for processing.**
4. **Store the vowel count results in a file.**
5. **Create a GUI version using `Tkinter` for a user-friendly interface.**

Conclusion This Vowel Counter project introduces Python concepts such as loops, dictionaries, and string manipulation. By expanding this project, developers can create more advanced text analysis applications.

Chapter 34: Check if a Number is Prime

Overview A Prime Number Checker is a program that determines whether a given number is prime. A prime number is a number greater than 1 that has only two factors: 1 and itself. This project helps in understanding loops, conditional statements, and mathematical logic in Python.

This chapter covers the step-by-step implementation of a Prime Number Checker, handling user input, applying divisibility rules, and displaying results.

Key Concepts of Prime Number Checker in Python

- **Mathematical Computation:**
  - A prime number is only divisible by 1 and itself.
  - The smallest prime number is 2.
- **User Input Handling:**
  - Taking user input to check for primality.
- **Efficient Computation:**
  - Using loops to check divisibility up to $\sqrt{n}$ for optimization.

Prime Number Example Table

Number	Prime?
2	Yes
3	Yes
4	No
5	Yes
6	No
7	Yes
8	No
9	No
10	No

Basic Rules for Prime Number Checker in Python

Rule	Correct Example
Check divisibility from 2 to $\sqrt{n}$	`if n % i == 0: return False`
Validate user input	`if n < 2: print("Not prime")`
Optimize loop for efficiency	`for i in range(2, int(n**0.5) + 1):`

Syntax Table

SL	Concept	Syntax/Example	Description
1	Define function	`def` `is_prime(n):`	Defines a function to check primality.
2	Validate input	`if n < 2:`	Ensures the number is greater than 1.

3	Loop for divisibility test	`for i in`
		`range(2,`
		`int(n**0.5) +`
		`1):`
			Iterates up to the square root of n.

4	Return prime status	`return True`	Returns True if n is prime.
5	Display result	`print(is_prime(` `n))`	Prints whether the number is prime.

Real-Life Project: Prime Number Checker

Project Code:

```
1.  def is_prime(n):
2.      if n < 2:
3.          return False
4.      for i in range(2, int(n**0.5) + 1):
5.          if n % i == 0:
6.              return False
7.      return True

8.  number = int(input("Enter a number: "))
9.  if is_prime(number):
10.     print(f"{number} is a prime number.")
11. else:
12.     print(f"{number} is not a prime number.")
```

Project Code Explanation Table

Line	Code Section	Description
1-7	`def is_prime(n):`	Defines a function to check if a number is prime.
2-3	`if n < 2:`	Returns False for numbers less than 2.
4-6	`for i in range(2,`	Iterates up to the square root of

	`int(n**0.5) + 1):`	n to check divisibility.
5-6	`if n % i == 0:`	Returns `False` if n is divisible by i.
7	`return True`	Returns `True` if no divisors were found.
8	`number = int(input("Enter a number: "))`	Takes user input.
9-10	`if is_prime(number):`	Checks if the number is prime and prints the result.
11-12	`else:`	Prints a message if the number is not prime.

Expected Results

- The program asks the user to enter a number.
- It checks if the number is prime using the function.
- It prints whether the number is prime or not.
- If the user enters a number less than 2, it prints "Not a prime number."

Hands-On Exercise Try improving the Prime Number Checker with these additional features:

1. Allow users to check multiple numbers in a loop.
2. Generate a list of prime numbers within a given range.
3. Use a caching mechanism (memoization) to speed up repeated checks.
4. Create a graphical user interface (GUI) using `Tkinter`.
5. Implement an option to check large prime numbers using the Miller-Rabin primality test.

Conclusion This Prime Number Checker project introduces Python concepts such as loops, mathematical logic, and input validation. By expanding this project, developers can create more efficient and interactive number validation tools.

Chapter 35: Random Joke Generator

Overview A Random Joke Generator is a fun application that displays a random joke from a predefined list or an external API. This project helps in understanding list operations, randomization, and API requests in Python. This chapter covers the step-by-step implementation of a Random Joke Generator, handling user input, fetching jokes from a local list or an API, and displaying the results.

Key Concepts of Random Joke Generator in Python

- **Randomization:**
    - Using the random module to select a random joke.
    - Implementing user interaction to generate multiple jokes.
- **List Handling:**
    - Storing jokes in a list for easy access.
    - Fetching a joke randomly from the list.
- **API Requests (Optional):**
    - Fetching jokes dynamically from an online joke API.
    - Using the requests module to retrieve data from a URL.

Example Joke Table

Joke	Punchline
Why don't skeletons fight?	They don't have the guts.
Parallel lines have so much in common...	It's a shame they'll never meet.
Why was the math book sad?	It had too many problems.

Basic Rules for Random Joke Generator in Python

Rule	Correct Example
Use random.choice() to pick a joke	joke = random.choice(jokes_list)
Store jokes in a list	jokes_list = ["Joke 1", "Joke 2"]
Fetch a joke from an API	requests.get("https://official-joke-api.appspot.com/jokes/random")

Syntax Table

SL	Concept	Syntax/Example	Description
1	Import random module	`import random`	Enables random selection of jokes.
2	Store jokes in a list	`jokes = ["Joke 1", "Joke 2"]`	Defines a list of jokes.
3	Select a random joke	`random.choice(jokes)`	Picks a joke randomly from the list.
4	Fetch joke from API	`requests.get(url).json()`	Retrieves a joke from an online API.
5	Display joke	`print(joke)`	Prints the selected joke.

Real-Life Project: Random Joke Generator

Project Code (Using Local List):

```
1.  import random

2.  jokes = [
3.      "Why don't skeletons fight? They don't have the guts.",
4.      "Parallel lines have so much in common. It's a shame they'll never meet.",
5.      "Why was the math book sad? It had too many problems."
6.  ]

7.  def tell_joke():
8.      return random.choice(jokes)

9.  print("Here's a random joke for you:")
10. print(tell_joke())
```

Project Code (Using API):

```
1.  import requests
2.  import json

3.  def get_joke():
4.      url = "https://official-joke-
```

```
api.appspot.com/jokes/random"
5.        response = requests.get(url)
6.        joke_data = response.json()
7.        return f"{joke_data['setup']}
{joke_data['punchline']}"

8.   print("Here's a random joke for you:")
9.   print(get_joke())
```

Project Code Explanation Table

Line	Code Section	Description
1	`import random`	Imports the random module for selecting jokes.
2-6	`jokes = [...]`	Defines a list of jokes.
7-8	`def tell_joke():`	Defines a function to select and return a random joke.
9	`print("Here's a random joke for you:")`	Prints an introduction message.
10	`print(tell_joke())`	Calls the function and prints a random joke.
1-2	`import requests, json`	Imports the requests and json modules for fetching jokes from an API.
3-7	`def get_joke():`	Defines a function to get a joke from an external API.
4	`url = "https://official-joke-api.appspot.com/jokes/random"`	Specifies the joke API URL.
5	`response = requests.get(url)`	Sends a GET request to fetch a joke.
6	`joke_data = response.json()`	Parses the JSON response.

7	`return f"{joke_data['setup']} {joke_data['punchline']}"`	Formats and returns the joke.
8-9	`print(get_joke())`	Calls the function and prints the joke.

Expected Results

- The program displays a random joke from a predefined list.
- If using an API, it fetches a new joke from the internet.
- The joke is printed in a readable format.

Hands-On Exercise Try improving the Random Joke Generator with these additional features:

1. Allow users to request multiple jokes in a loop.
2. Categorize jokes (e.g., programming, puns, dad jokes).
3. Enable users to add new jokes to the list dynamically.
4. Create a GUI version using Tkinter for a fun interface.
5. Use text-to-speech (pyttsx3) to read the jokes aloud.

Conclusion This Random Joke Generator project introduces Python concepts such as randomization, list handling, and API requests. By expanding this project, developers can create interactive joke applications with dynamic content.

Chapter 36: Reverse a String

Overview Reversing a string is a common operation in programming, often used in text manipulation, data processing, and algorithms. This project helps in understanding string slicing, loops, and built-in functions in Python.

This chapter covers the step-by-step implementation of reversing a string using different approaches, including slicing, loops, and built-in functions.

Key Concepts of String Reversal in Python

- **String Manipulation:**
  - o Accessing characters in a string using indexing.
  - o Using loops and built-in methods for reversal.
- **Efficient Computation:**
  - o Using Python's slicing method for quick reversal.
  - o Implementing an iterative approach for better understanding.
- **Built-in Functions:**
  - o Utilizing `reversed()` and `join()` for a more Pythonic solution.

Example String Reversal Table

Original String	Reversed String
hello	olleh
python	nohtyp
racecar	racecar
world	dlrow

Basic Rules for String Reversal in Python

Rule	Correct Example
Use slicing for fast reversal	`reversed_string = text[::-1]`
Use a loop for manual reversal	`for char in text: reversed_text = char + reversed_text`
Use built-in function `reversed()`	`''.join(reversed(text))`

Syntax Table

S L	Concept	Syntax/Example	Description

1	Reverse using slicing	`text[::-1]`	Uses slicing to reverse the string.
2	Reverse using a loop	`for char in text:` `reversed_text = char + reversed_text`	Iterates through each character and builds a reversed string.
3	Reverse using reversed()	`''.join(reversed(text))`	Uses Python's built-in reversed function.
4	Get user input	`text = input("Enter a string: ")`	Takes input from the user.
5	Print reversed string	`print("Reversed string:", reversed_text)`	Displays the reversed string.

Real-Life Project: String Reversal Program
Project Code:

```
1.  def reverse_string_slicing(text):
2.      return text[::-1]

3.  def reverse_string_loop(text):
4.      reversed_text = ""
5.      for char in text:
6.          reversed_text = char + reversed_text
7.      return reversed_text

8.  def reverse_string_builtin(text):
9.      return ''.join(reversed(text))

10. text = input("Enter a string: ")
11. print("Reversed (Slicing):",
reverse_string_slicing(text))
12. print("Reversed (Loop):",
reverse_string_loop(text))
13. print("Reversed (Built-in Function):",
reverse_string_builtin(text))
```

Project Code Explanation Table

Line	Code Section	Description
1-2	`def reverse_string_slicing (text):`	Defines a function to reverse a string using slicing.
3-7	`def reverse_string_loop(te xt):`	Defines a function to reverse a string using a loop.
4	`reversed_text = ""`	Initializes an empty string to store the reversed string.
5-6	`for char in text:`	Iterates through each character in the string.
6	`reversed_text = char + reversed_text`	Appends each character at the beginning to build the reversed string.
8-9	`def reverse_string_builtin (text):`	Defines a function to reverse a string using Python's built-in reversed() function.
10	`text = input("Enter a string: ")`	Takes user input as a string.
11	`print("Reversed (Slicing):", reverse_string_slicing (text))`	Calls the slicing method and prints the reversed string.
12	`print("Reversed (Loop):", reverse_string_loop(te xt))`	Calls the loop method and prints the reversed string.
13	`print("Reversed (Built-in Function):", reverse_string_builtin (text))`	Calls the built-in function method and prints the reversed string.

Expected Results

- The program asks the user to enter a string.
- It prints the reversed string using three different methods.
- The output is formatted neatly for easy comparison.

Hands-On Exercise Try improving the String Reversal program with these additional features:

1. **Allow users to input multiple strings and reverse them.**
2. **Ignore spaces and punctuation while reversing (e.g., "Hello, world!" → "dlrowolleH").**
3. **Implement the program using recursion for an advanced approach.**
4. **Create a GUI version using** `Tkinter` **for better interaction.**
5. **Integrate a feature to check if a string is a palindrome.**

Conclusion This String Reversal project introduces Python concepts such as slicing, loops, and built-in functions. By expanding this project, developers can create more advanced string manipulation applications.

Chapter 38: Word Frequency Counter

Overview A Word Frequency Counter is a program that counts the occurrences of each word in a given text. This project helps in understanding string manipulation, loops, dictionaries, and file handling in Python.

This chapter covers the step-by-step implementation of counting word frequencies in a string, handling user input, processing text efficiently, and displaying results in a structured format.

Key Concepts of Word Frequency Counter in Python

- **String Manipulation:**
  - Splitting text into words.
  - Removing punctuation and converting to lowercase.
- **Dictionary Operations:**
  - Storing words as keys and their counts as values.
  - Updating word counts dynamically.
- **Sorting and Displaying Results:**
  - Sorting word occurrences in ascending or descending order.
  - Formatting output for readability.

Example Word Frequency Table

Word	Frequency
Python	3
is	2
fun	1
coding	1

Basic Rules for Word Frequency Counter in Python

Rule	Correct Example
Use `split()` to split text into words	`words = text.split()`
Use a dictionary to store word counts	`word_count = {}`
Remove punctuation using `re.sub()`	`text = re.sub(r'[^a-zA-Z0-9]', '', text)`

Syntax Table

SL	Concept	Syntax/Example	Description
1	Convert string to lowercase	`text.lower()`	Ensures case-insensitive comparison.
2	Remove punctuation	`re.sub(r'[^a-zA-Z0-9 ]', '', text)`	Removes special characters.
3	Split text into words	`words = text.split()`	Creates a list of words.
4	Use dictionary for counting	`word_count[word] = word_count.get(word, 0) + 1`	Updates the count of each word.
5	Print word frequency	`print(f"{word}: {count}")`	Displays the count of each word.

Real-Life Project: Word Frequency Counter

Project Code:

```
1.  import re

2.  def count_word_frequency(text):
3.      text = text.lower()
4.      text = re.sub(r'[^a-zA-Z0-9 ]', '', text)
5.      words = text.split()
6.      word_count = {}
7.      for word in words:
8.          word_count[word] = word_count.get(word, 0) + 1
9.      return word_count

10. text = input("Enter a text: ")
11. frequencies = count_word_frequency(text)
12. for word, count in sorted(frequencies.items(),
key=lambda x: x[1], reverse=True):
13.     print(f"{word}: {count}")
```

Project Code Explanation Table

Line	Code Section	Description
1	`import re`	Imports the re module for regex operations.
2-9	`def count_word_frequency(text):`	Defines a function to count word occurrences.
3	`text = text.lower()`	Converts the input string to lowercase for consistency.
4	`text = re.sub(r'[^a-zA-Z0-9 ]', '', text)`	Removes punctuation and special characters.
5	`words = text.split()`	Splits the text into individual words.
6	`word_count = {}`	Initializes an empty dictionary to store word counts.
7-8	`for word in words:`	Loops through each word and updates the count.
9	`return word_count`	Returns the dictionary containing word counts.
10	`text = input("Enter a text: ")`	Takes user input as text.
11	`frequencies = count_word_frequency(text)`	Calls the function and stores results in a dictionary.
12-13	`for word, count in sorted(frequencies.items(), key=lambda x: x[1], reverse=True):`	Sorts and prints words by frequency.

Expected Results

- The program asks the user to enter a text.
- It counts the occurrences of words.
- It displays the results in descending order of frequency.

Hands-On Exercise Try improving the Word Frequency Counter with these additional features:

1. **Ignore common stopwords (e.g., "the", "is", "and").**
2. **Allow users to analyze text from a file instead of manual input.**

Chapter 39: Armstrong Number Checker

Overview An Armstrong Number Checker is a program that determines whether a given number is an Armstrong number. An Armstrong number (also known as a narcissistic number) is a number where the sum of its digits, each raised to the power of the number of digits, equals the original number. This project helps in understanding mathematical computations, loops, and conditional statements in Python.

This chapter covers the step-by-step implementation of an Armstrong Number Checker, handling user input, applying the Armstrong number formula, and displaying results.

Key Concepts of Armstrong Number Checker in Python

- **Mathematical Computation:**
    - An Armstrong number for a three-digit number is calculated as:
    - Example: $153 = 1^3 + 5^3 + 3^3 = 1 + 125 + 27 = 153$

- **User Input Handling:**
    - Taking user input to check for Armstrong number validity.
    - Validating input to ensure it is a positive integer.

- **Efficient Computation:**
    - Using loops and mathematical operations to compute the sum of powered digits.

Example Armstrong Numbers

Number	Armstrong?
0	Yes
1	Yes
153	Yes
9474	Yes
9475	No

Basic Rules for Armstrong Number Checker in Python

Rule	Correct Example
Extract digits using // and %	`digit = num % 10`
Compute powered sum	`sum += digit ** num_length`
Validate input before processing	`if num < 0: print("Invalid input")`

Syntax Table

SL	Concept	Syntax/Example	Description
1	Get user input	`num = int(input("Enter a number: "))`	Takes input for checking Armstrong number.
2	Find number of digits	`num_length = len(str(num))`	Counts the number of digits in the number.
3	Extract each digit	`digit = num % 10`	Retrieves the last digit of the number.
4	Compute sum of powered digits	`sum += digit ** num_length`	Adds the powered value of each digit.
5	Check Armstrong condition	`if sum == num:`	Compares the sum with the original number.

Real-Life Project: Armstrong Number Checker

Project Code:

```
1.  def is_armstrong(num):
2.      num_length = len(str(num))
3.      sum_of_digits = 0
4.      temp = num
5.      while temp > 0:
6.          digit = temp % 10
7.          sum_of_digits += digit ** num_length
8.          temp //= 10
9.      return sum_of_digits == num

10. num = int(input("Enter a number: "))
11. if is_armstrong(num):
12.     print(f"{num} is an Armstrong number.")
13. else:
14.     print(f"{num} is not an Armstrong number.")
```

Project Code Explanation Table

Line	Code Section	Description
1-9	`def is_armstrong(num):`	Defines a function to check if a number is Armstrong.
2	`num_length = len(str(num))`	Determines the number of digits in the number.
3	`sum_of_digits = 0`	Initializes a variable to store the sum of powered digits.
4	`temp = num`	Creates a temporary variable to process digits.
5	`while temp > 0:`	Loops through the number to extract digits.
6	`digit = temp % 10`	Extracts the last digit.
7	`sum_of_digits += digit ** num_length`	Raises the digit to the power of the number length and adds it to the sum.
8	`temp //= 10`	Removes the last digit from `temp`.
9	`return sum_of_digits == num`	Returns `True` if the sum matches the original number.
10	`num = int(input("Enter a number: "))`	Takes user input as an integer.
11-12	`if is_armstrong(num):`	Checks if the number is an Armstrong number and prints the result.
13-14	`else:`	Prints a message if the number is not an Armstrong number.

Expected Results

- The program asks the user to enter a number.
- It checks whether the number satisfies the Armstrong condition.
- It prints whether the number is an Armstrong number or not.
- If the user enters a negative number, it prints "Invalid input."

Hands-On Exercise Try improving the Armstrong Number Checker with these additional features:

1. **Allow users to check multiple numbers in a loop.**
2. **Check for Armstrong numbers in a given range.**
3. **Optimize the function to handle very large numbers efficiently.**
4. **Create a GUI version using `Tkinter` for better user interaction.**
5. **Implement a feature to list all Armstrong numbers up to a given limit.**

Conclusion This Armstrong Number Checker project introduces Python concepts such as loops, mathematical computations, and input validation. By expanding this project, developers can create more efficient number validation tools.

Chapter 40: Sum of Digits Calculator

Overview A Sum of Digits Calculator is a program that calculates the sum of all individual digits in a given number. This project helps in understanding loops, mathematical operations, and user input handling in Python.

This chapter covers the step-by-step implementation of a Sum of Digits Calculator, handling user input, extracting digits, and performing summation operations.

Key Concepts of Sum of Digits Calculator in Python

- **Mathematical Computation:**
  - Extracting digits using modulus (%) and integer division (//).
  - Summing up the extracted digits.
- **User Input Handling:**
  - Taking user input to calculate the sum of digits.
  - Ensuring the input is a non-negative integer.
- **Looping for Iteration:**
  - Using a while loop to process each digit of the number.
  - Stopping when all digits are extracted.

Example Sum of Digits Calculation

Number	Sum of Digits
123	1 + 2 + 3 = 6
456	4 + 5 + 6 = 15
789	7 + 8 + 9 = 24
1024	1 + 0 + 2 + 4 = 7

Basic Rules for Sum of Digits Calculator in Python

Rule	Correct Example
Extract last digit using modulus	digit = num % 10
Remove last digit using integer division	num //= 10
Use a loop to iterate through all digits	while num > 0:

Syntax Table

SL	Concept	Syntax/Example	Description
1	Get user input	`num = int(input("Enter a number: "))`	Takes input for calculating digit sum.
2	Extract last digit	`digit = num % 10`	Retrieves the last digit.
3	Remove last digit	`num //= 10`	Removes the last digit from the number.
4	Compute sum of digits	`sum += digit`	Adds the extracted digit to the sum.
5	Display result	`print("Sum of digits:", sum)`	Prints the calculated sum.

Real-Life Project: Sum of Digits Calculator

Project Code:

```
1.  def sum_of_digits(num):
2.      if num < 0:
3.          return "Invalid input! Please enter a non-
negative integer."
4.      total = 0
5.      while num > 0:
6.          digit = num % 10
7.          total += digit
8.          num //= 10
9.      return total

10. num = int(input("Enter a number: "))
11. print("Sum of digits:", sum_of_digits(num))
```

Project Code Explanation Table

Line	Code Section	Description
1-9	`def sum_of_digits(num):`	Defines a function to calculate the sum of digits.
2-3	`if num < 0:`	Returns an error message if the number is negative.

4	`total = 0`	Initializes a variable to store the sum.
5	`while num > 0:`	Loops through all digits of the number.
6	`digit = num % 10`	Extracts the last digit of the number.
7	`total += digit`	Adds the digit to the total sum.
8	`num //= 10`	Removes the last digit from the number.
9	`return total`	Returns the sum of digits.
10	`num = int(input("Enter a number: "))`	Takes user input as an integer.
11	`print("Sum of digits:", sum_of_digits(num))`	Calls the function and prints the sum.

Expected Results

- The program asks the user to enter a number.
- It calculates the sum of its digits.
- It prints the sum as output.
- If the user enters a negative number, it prints "Invalid input."

Hands-On Exercise Try improving the Sum of Digits Calculator with these additional features:

1. **Allow users to calculate the sum of digits for multiple numbers in a loop.**
2. **Modify the program to return the sum of digits recursively.**
3. **Create a GUI version using `Tkinter` for user-friendly interaction.**
4. **Extend the functionality to compute the sum of squares of digits.**
5. **Store results in a text file for historical tracking.**

Conclusion This Sum of Digits Calculator project introduces Python concepts such as loops, mathematical computations, and input validation. By expanding this project, developers can create more advanced number-processing applications.

Chapter 41: Find the GCD and LCM of Two Numbers

Overview A GCD and LCM Calculator is a program that computes the Greatest Common Divisor (GCD) and Least Common Multiple (LCM) of two numbers. This project helps in understanding mathematical computations, loops, and built-in Python functions.

This chapter covers the step-by-step implementation of calculating GCD and LCM, handling user input, applying mathematical formulas, and displaying results.

Key Concepts of GCD and LCM Calculator in Python

- **Mathematical Computation:**
  - The **GCD (Greatest Common Divisor)** of two numbers is the largest number that divides both numbers exactly.
  - The **LCM (Least Common Multiple)** of two numbers is the smallest number that is a multiple of both numbers.
- **User Input Handling:**
  - Taking user input for two numbers.
  - Ensuring the input values are positive integers.
- **Efficient Computation:**
  - Using **Euclidean Algorithm** for GCD calculation.
  - Using the formula LCM(a, b) = (a * b) / GCD(a, b) for LCM computation.

Example GCD and LCM Calculation

Numbers (a, b)	GCD(a, b)	LCM(a, b)
12, 18	6	36
24, 36	12	72
7, 13	1	91
9, 27	9	27

Basic Rules for GCD and LCM Calculator in Python

Rule	Correct Example
Use Euclidean Algorithm for GCD	gcd(a, b) = gcd(b, a % b)
Compute LCM using formula	lcm(a, b) = (a * b) // gcd(a, b)

Validate user input before processing	`if a <= 0 or b <= 0:` `print("Invalid input")`	

Syntax Table

SL	Concept	Syntax/Example	Description
1	Get user input	`a = int(input("Enter first number: "))`	Takes first number as input.
2	Get user input	`b = int(input("Enter second number: "))`	Takes second number as input.
3	Compute GCD using recursion	`def gcd(a, b):` `return b if a % b == 0 else gcd(b, a % b)`	Uses Euclidean Algorithm.
4	Compute LCM	`lcm = (a * b) // gcd(a, b)`	Uses the LCM formula.
5	Display result	`print(f"GCD: {gcd}, LCM: {lcm}")`	Prints GCD and LCM values.

Real-Life Project: GCD and LCM Calculator

Project Code:

```
1.  def gcd(a, b):
2.      while b:
3.          a, b = b, a % b
4.      return a

5.  def lcm(a, b):
6.      return (a * b) // gcd(a, b)

7.  a = int(input("Enter first number: "))
8.  b = int(input("Enter second number: "))
9.  if a > 0 and b > 0:
10.     print(f"GCD of {a} and {b} is: {gcd(a, b)}")
11.     print(f"LCM of {a} and {b} is: {lcm(a, b)}")
12. else:
13.     print("Invalid input! Please enter positive integers.")
```

Project Code Explanation Table

Line	Code Section	Description
1-4	`def gcd(a, b):`	Defines a function to compute the GCD using the Euclidean Algorithm.
2-3	`while b:`	Iteratively computes GCD by replacing a with b and b with a % b.
5-6	`def lcm(a, b):`	Defines a function to compute the LCM using the formula.
7	`a = int(input("Enter first number: "))`	Takes the first number as user input.
8	`b = int(input("Enter second number: "))`	Takes the second number as user input.
9	`if a > 0 and b > 0:`	Ensures both numbers are positive before proceeding.
10	`print(f"GCD of {a} and {b} is: {gcd(a, b)}")`	Computes and prints the GCD.
11	`print(f"LCM of {a} and {b} is: {lcm(a, b)}")`	Computes and prints the LCM.
12-13	`else:` `print("Invalid input!")`	Handles invalid input cases.

Expected Results

- The program asks the user to enter two numbers.
- It calculates the **GCD** and **LCM** of the numbers.
- It prints the GCD and LCM results.
- If the user enters negative or zero values, it prints "Invalid input."

Hands-On Exercise Try improving the GCD and LCM Calculator with these additional features:

1. **Allow users to calculate the GCD and LCM of more than two numbers.**
2. **Display step-by-step GCD computation for educational purposes.**
3. **Create a GUI version using Tkinter for interactive use.**

Chapter 42: Sorting a List of Numbers

Overview Sorting is a fundamental operation in programming that arranges elements in a specific order (ascending or descending). Python provides multiple ways to sort lists efficiently using built-in functions and sorting algorithms.

This chapter covers the step-by-step implementation of sorting a list of numbers, handling user input, using built-in sorting functions, and implementing common sorting algorithms.

Key Concepts of Sorting in Python

- **Sorting Methods:**
  - Using Python's built-in `sorted()` and `.sort()` methods.
  - Implementing manual sorting algorithms like Bubble Sort, Selection Sort, and Quick Sort.
- **User Input Handling:**
  - Taking user input for a list of numbers.
  - Allowing users to choose the sorting order (ascending/descending).
- **Efficiency Considerations:**
  - Understanding time complexity of sorting algorithms.
  - Choosing the right algorithm based on input size.

Example Sorted Lists

Unsorted List	Ascending Order	Descending Order
[5, 3, 8, 1, 2]	[1, 2, 3, 5, 8]	[8, 5, 3, 2, 1]
[12, 7, 19, 4]	[4, 7, 12, 19]	[19, 12, 7, 4]

Basic Rules for Sorting a List in Python

Rule	Correct Example
Use `sorted()` for a new sorted list	`sorted_list = sorted(numbers)`
Use `.sort()` to modify the list in-place	`numbers.sort()`
Specify descending order	`sorted(numbers, reverse=True)`

Syntax Table

SL	Concept	Syntax/Example	Description
1	Get user input	`numbers = list(map(int, input().split()))`	Takes a list of numbers as input.
2	Sort using `sorted()`	`sorted_list = sorted(numbers)`	Returns a new sorted list.
3	Sort using `.sort()`	`numbers.sort()`	Sorts the list in-place.
4	Sort in descending order	`sorted(numbers, reverse=True)`	Returns a sorted list in descending order.
5	Implement Bubble Sort	`for i in range(len(numbers)):`	Uses loops to sort numbers manually.

Real-Life Project: Sorting a List of Numbers

Project Code:

```
1.  def bubble_sort(numbers):
2.      n = len(numbers)
3.      for i in range(n - 1):
4.          for j in range(n - i - 1):
5.              if numbers[j] > numbers[j + 1]:
6.                  numbers[j], numbers[j + 1] = numbers[j + 1], numbers[j]
7.      return numbers

8.  numbers = list(map(int, input("Enter numbers separated by space: ").split()))
9.  print("Sorted List (Using sorted()):", sorted(numbers))
10. numbers.sort()
11. print("Sorted List (Using .sort()):", numbers)
12. print("Sorted List (Bubble Sort):", bubble_sort(numbers))
```

Project Code Explanation Table

Line	Code Section	Description
1-7	`def bubble_sort(numbers):`	Defines a function to sort a list using Bubble Sort.
2	`n = len(numbers)`	Gets the length of the list.
3-4	`for i in range(n - 1): for j in range(n - i - 1):`	Loops through the list to compare elements.
5-6	`if numbers[j] > numbers[j + 1]: swap`	Swaps elements if they are in the wrong order.
8	`numbers = list(map(int, input().split()))`	Takes user input and converts it into a list of integers.
9	`print("Sorted List (Using sorted()):", sorted(numbers))`	Sorts the list using the built-in sorted() function.
10	`numbers.sort()`	Sorts the list in-place using .sort().
11	`print("Sorted List (Using .sort()):", numbers)`	Displays the sorted list using .sort().
12	`print("Sorted List (Bubble Sort):", bubble_sort(numbers))`	Sorts the list using the Bubble Sort function and prints the result.

Expected Results

- The program asks the user to enter a list of numbers.
- It sorts the list using different methods (sorted(), .sort(), and Bubble Sort).
- It prints the sorted lists in ascending order.

Hands-On Exercise Try improving the Sorting program with these additional features:

1. Allow users to choose between ascending and descending order.
2. Implement additional sorting algorithms (Selection Sort, Quick Sort, Merge Sort).
3. Compare sorting speeds using timeit module.
4. Create a GUI version using Tkinter to input numbers

Chapter 43: Find the Maximum and Minimum from a List

Overview Finding the maximum and minimum values in a list is a fundamental operation in programming. Python provides multiple ways to achieve this using built-in functions, loops, and sorting techniques. This chapter covers the step-by-step implementation of finding the maximum and minimum numbers in a list, handling user input, using built-in functions, and implementing manual search techniques.

Key Concepts of Finding Max and Min in Python

- **Using Built-in Functions:**
  - The max() function returns the highest value in a list.
  - The min() function returns the lowest value in a list.
- **Manual Computation:**
  - Iterating through the list to determine the maximum and minimum values.
- **Sorting Approach:**
  - Sorting the list and selecting the first and last elements as min and max.

Example of Maximum and Minimum Values

List	Maximum	Minimum
[5, 3, 9, 1, 7]	9	1
[12, 24, 36, 48]	48	12
[101, 56, 78, 12]	101	12

Basic Rules for Finding Max and Min in Python

Rule	Correct Example
Use max() to find the maximum	max_value = max(numbers)
Use min() to find the minimum	min_value = min(numbers)
Use a loop for manual search	for num in numbers: if num > max_value: max_value = num

Syntax Table

SL	Concept	Syntax/Example	Description
1	Get user input	`numbers = list(map(int, input().split()))`	Takes a list of numbers as input.
2	Find max using max()	`max_value = max(numbers)`	Returns the largest number in the list.
3	Find min using min()	`min_value = min(numbers)`	Returns the smallest number in the list.
4	Find max using a loop	`for num in numbers: if num > max_value: max_value = num`	Iterates to find the maximum manually.
5	Find min using sorting	`sorted_list = sorted(numbers); min_value = sorted_list[0]`	Sorts and selects the first element as the minimum.

Real-Life Project: Finding Max and Min in a List

Project Code:

```
1.  def find_max_min(numbers):
2.      max_value = numbers[0]
3.      min_value = numbers[0]
4.      for num in numbers:
5.          if num > max_value:
6.              max_value = num
7.          if num < min_value:
8.              min_value = num
9.      return max_value, min_value

10. numbers = list(map(int, input("Enter numbers
separated by space: ").split()))
11. print("Maximum (Using max()):", max(numbers))
12. print("Minimum (Using min()):", min(numbers))
13. max_num, min_num = find_max_min(numbers)
14. print("Maximum (Using loop):", max_num)
15. print("Minimum (Using loop):", min_num)
```

Project Code Explanation Table

Line	Code Section	Description
1	`def find_max_min(numbers):`	Defines a function to find the maximum and minimum numbers in a list.
2	`max_value = numbers[0]`	Initializes the maximum value with the first element of the list.
3	`min_value = numbers[0]`	Initializes the minimum value with the first element of the list.
4	`for num in numbers:`	Loops through each number in the list.
5	`if num > max_value:`	Checks if the current number is greater than `max_value`.
6	`max_value = num`	Updates `max_value` if a larger number is found.
7	`if num < min_value:`	Checks if the current number is smaller than `min_value`.
8	`min_value = num`	Updates `min_value` if a smaller number is found.
9	`return max_value, min_value`	Returns the calculated maximum and minimum values.
10	`numbers = list(map(int, input("Enter numbers separated by space: ").split()))`	Takes user input, splits it into individual numbers, and converts them into integers.
11	`print("Maximum (Using max()):", max(numbers))`	Finds and prints the maximum number using the built-in `max()` function.
12	`print("Minimum (Using min()):", min(numbers))`	Finds and prints the minimum number using the built-in `min()` function.

13	`max_num, min_num = find_max_min(numbers)`	Calls the custom function to determine the max and min values manually.
14	`print("Maximum (Using loop):", max_num)`	Prints the maximum number found using the loop method.
15	`print("Minimum (Using loop):", min_num)`	Prints the minimum number found using the loop method.

Expected Results

- The program asks the user to enter a list of numbers.
- It computes the **maximum** and **minimum** values using both built-in functions and a manual approach.
- It prints the results in a structured format.

Hands-On Exercise Try improving the Max and Min Finder with these additional features:

1. **Allow users to input numbers from a file instead of manually entering them.**
2. **Display step-by-step max and min computation for better understanding.**
3. **Create a GUI version using Tkinter to select numbers and display results.**
4. **Extend the program to find the second highest and second lowest numbers.**
5. **Optimize the manual approach for large datasets using heapq module.**

Conclusion This Maximum and Minimum Finder project introduces Python concepts such as list operations, loops, and sorting techniques. By expanding this project, developers can explore more efficient methods for handling large datasets in various applications.

Chapter 44: Square Root Finder

Overview A Square Root Finder is a program that calculates the square root of a given number. This project helps in understanding mathematical functions, loops, and built-in methods in Python.

This chapter covers the step-by-step implementation of calculating the square root of a number, handling user input, using built-in functions, and implementing manual square root estimation techniques.

Key Concepts of Square Root Finder in Python

- **Using Built-in Functions:**
    - The math.sqrt() function computes the square root of a number.
    - The exponentiation operator (**) can also be used to find square roots.
- **Manual Computation:**
    - Implementing the **Newton-Raphson method** for square root approximation.
    - Using a loop to estimate the square root iteratively.

Example Square Root Calculation

Number	Square Root
4	2.0
9	3.0
16	4.0
25	5.0
50	7.071

Basic Rules for Square Root Calculation in Python

Rule	Correct Example
Use math.sqrt() for square root	sqrt_value = math.sqrt(x)
Use exponentiation operator	sqrt_value = x ** 0.5
Implement Newton's method	sqrt_value = 0.5 * (x + y/x)

Syntax Table

SL	Concept	Syntax/Example	Description
1	Get user input	`num = float(input("Ent er number: "))`	Takes a number from the user.
2	Compute square root using `math.sqrt()`	`sqrt_value = math.sqrt(num)`	Uses the built-in function.
3	Compute square root using `**` operator	`sqrt_value = num ** 0.5`	Uses exponentiation to find square root.
4	Implement Newton's method	`while abs(guess*guess - num) > epsilon:`	Uses an iterative approach to refine the square root value.
5	Print result	`print("Square root is:", sqrt_value)`	Displays the calculated square root.

Real-Life Project: Square Root Finder

Project Code:

```
1.  import math

2.  def sqrt_builtin(num):
3.      return math.sqrt(num)

4.  def sqrt_exponentiation(num):
5.      return num ** 0.5

6.  def sqrt_newton(num, epsilon=0.0001):
7.      guess = num / 2.0
8.      while abs(guess * guess - num) > epsilon:
9.          guess = (guess + num / guess) / 2.0
10.     return guess

11. num = float(input("Enter a number: "))
12. if num < 0:
13.     print("Square root of negative numbers is not
```

```
     real.")
14. else:
15.     print("Square Root (Using math.sqrt()):",
   sqrt_builtin(num))
16.     print("Square Root (Using exponentiation):",
   sqrt_exponentiation(num))
17.     print("Square Root (Using Newton's Method):",
   sqrt_newton(num))
```

Project Code Explanation Table

Line	Code Section	Description
1	`import math`	Imports the `math` module to use the built-in square root function.
2-3	`def sqrt_builtin(num):`	Defines a function to compute the square root using `math.sqrt()`.
4-5	`def sqrt_exponentiation (num):`	Defines a function to compute the square root using the exponentiation operator (`**`).
6	`def sqrt_newton(num, epsilon=0.0001):`	Defines a function to compute the square root using Newton's Method with an error tolerance (`epsilon`).
7	`guess = num / 2.0`	Initializes the first guess as half of the input number.
8	`while abs(guess * guess - num) > epsilon:`	Runs a loop to refine the square root approximation until it converges within the error tolerance.
9	`guess = (guess + num / guess) / 2.0`	Implements Newton's formula to update the guess.
10	`return guess`	Returns the final computed square root.
11	`num = float(input("Enter a number: "))`	Takes user input and converts it into a floating-point number.
12	`if num < 0:`	Checks if the input number is negative.

13	print("Square root of negative numbers is not real.")	Displays an error message for negative input values.
14	else:	Executes the square root calculations if the number is non-negative.
15	print("Square Root (Using math.sqrt()):", sqrt_builtin(num))	Calls sqrt_builtin() and prints the computed square root.
16	print("Square Root (Using exponentiation):", sqrt_exponentiation (num))	Calls sqrt_exponentiation() and prints the computed square root.
17	print("Square Root (Using Newton's Method):", sqrt_newton(num))	Calls sqrt_newton() and prints the computed square root using Newton's method.

Expected Results

- The program asks the user to enter a number.
- It calculates the square root using three different methods.
- It prints the computed values in a structured format.
- If the user enters a negative number, it displays an appropriate message.

Hands-On Exercise Try improving the Square Root Finder with these additional features:

1. Allow users to specify the precision level for Newton's method.
2. Extend the program to handle complex numbers for negative square roots.
3. Create a GUI version using Tkinter for user-friendly interaction.
4. Compare the execution time of different methods using the timeit module.
5. Allow users to compute cube roots and higher roots using the exponentiation method.

Chapter 45: Count Words in a Sentence

Overview A Word Counter is a program that calculates the number of words in a given sentence. This project helps in understanding string manipulation, loops, and built-in functions in Python.

This chapter covers the step-by-step implementation of counting words in a sentence, handling user input, using built-in functions, and implementing a manual word-counting method.

Key Concepts of Word Counting in Python

- **Using Built-in Functions:**
  - The split() function divides a string into a list of words.
  - The len() function counts the number of words.
- **Manual Computation:**
  - Iterating through the string and counting spaces to determine word count.

Example Word Count Calculation

Sentence	Word Count
"Python is fun"	3
"I love programming"	3
"The quick brown fox jumps over the lazy dog"	9

Basic Rules for Word Counting in Python

Rule	Correct Example
Use split() to separate words	words = sentence.split()
Use len() to count words	word_count = len(words)
Remove extra spaces using strip()	sentence = sentence.strip()

Syntax Table

SL	Concept	Syntax/Example	Description
1	Get user input	sentence = input("Enter a sentence: ")	Takes a sentence from the user.
2	Split sentence into words	words = sentence.split()	Uses split() to create a list of words.

3	Count words using `len()`	`word_count = len(words)`	Uses `len()` to determine the number of words.
4	Remove extra spaces	`sentence.strip()`	Cleans up unnecessary spaces at the beginning and end.
5	Print result	`print("Word count:", word_count)`	Displays the calculated word count.

Real-Life Project: Word Counter

Project Code:

```
1.  def count_words(sentence):
2.      sentence = sentence.strip()
3.      words = sentence.split()
4.      return len(words)

5.  sentence = input("Enter a sentence: ")
6.  print("Word count:", count_words(sentence))
```

Project Code Explanation Table

Line	Code Section	Description
1	`def count_words(sentenc e):`	Defines a function to count words in a sentence.
2	`sentence = sentence.strip()`	Removes unnecessary spaces at the start and end of the sentence.
3	`words = sentence.split()`	Splits the sentence into a list of words.
4	`return len(words)`	Returns the number of words in the sentence.
5	`sentence = input("Enter a sentence: ")`	Takes user input as a sentence.
6	`print("Word count:", count_words(sentenc e))`	Calls the function and prints the word count.

Expected Results

- The program asks the user to enter a sentence.
- It counts the number of words in the sentence.
- It prints the word count as output.
- If the user enters an empty string, it prints Word count: 0.

Hands-On Exercise Try improving the Word Counter with these additional features:

1. **Allow users to count words from a paragraph instead of a single sentence.**
2. **Enhance the program to ignore punctuation marks while counting words.**
3. **Create a GUI version using Tkinter for user-friendly interaction.**
4. **Allow users to input text from a file and count words in the document.**
5. **Display the frequency of each word along with the total word count.**

Conclusion This Word Counter project introduces Python concepts such as string manipulation, loops, and built-in functions. By expanding this project, developers can explore more advanced text-processing techniques.

Chapter 46: Check for Anagram Strings

Overview An Anagram Checker is a program that determines whether two given strings are anagrams of each other. Two words are considered anagrams if they contain the same characters in the same frequency but in a different order (e.g., "listen" and "silent").

This chapter covers the step-by-step implementation of checking anagram strings, handling user input, using built-in functions, and implementing a manual character count comparison.

Key Concepts of Anagram Checker in Python

- **String Manipulation:**
  - Sorting strings and comparing them.
  - Removing spaces and converting to lowercase.
- **Using Built-in Functions:**
  - The `sorted()` function sorts characters of the string.
  - The `Counter()` function from the `collections` module counts character frequency.
- **Manual Computation:**
  - Iterating through characters and counting occurrences.

Example Anagram Checks

String 1	String 2	Anagram?
listen	silent	Yes
triangle	integral	Yes
apple	paple	Yes
hello	world	No

Basic Rules for Anagram Checking in Python

Rule	Correct Example
Use `sorted()` to compare sorted versions of both words	`sorted(str1) == sorted(str2)`
Use `Counter()` from `collections` for character count comparison	`Counter(str1) == Counter(str2)`
Convert strings to lowercase and remove spaces before comparison	`str1.replace(" ", "").lower()`

Syntax Table

SL	Concept	Syntax/Example	Description
1	Get user input	`str1 = input("Enter first string: ")`	Takes first string from user.
2	Convert to lowercase and remove spaces	`str1 = str1.replace(" ", "").lower()`	Prepares the string for comparison.
3	Sort and compare strings	`sorted(str1) == sorted(str2)`	Uses sorting to check for anagram condition.
4	Use Counter() from collections	`Counter(str1) == Counter(str2)`	Counts character frequency for comparison.
5	Print result	`print("Anagram!" if result else "Not an Anagram!")`	Displays the result.

Real-Life Project: Anagram Checker

Project Code:

```
1.  from collections import Counter

2.  def is_anagram(str1, str2):
3.      str1 = str1.replace(" ", "").lower()
4.      str2 = str2.replace(" ", "").lower()
5.      return Counter(str1) == Counter(str2)

6.  str1 = input("Enter first string: ")
7.  str2 = input("Enter second string: ")
8.  if is_anagram(str1, str2):
9.      print("The strings are anagrams.")
10. else:
11.     print("The strings are not anagrams.")
```

Project Code Explanation Table

Line	Code Section	Description
1	`from collections import Counter`	Imports the Counter class for character frequency comparison.
2-5	`def is_anagram(str1, str2):`	Defines a function to check if two strings are anagrams.
3-4	`str1.replace(" ", "").lower()`	Removes spaces and converts strings to lowercase.
5	`return Counter(str1) == Counter(str2)`	Compares character frequency using Counter().
6	`str1 = input("Enter first string: ")`	Takes the first string input.
7	`str2 = input("Enter second string: ")`	Takes the second string input.
8-9	`if is_anagram(str1, str2): print("The strings are anagrams.")`	Prints result if strings are anagrams.
10-11	`else: print("The strings are not anagrams.")`	Prints result if strings are not anagrams.

Expected Results

- The program asks the user to enter two strings.
- It removes spaces and converts the strings to lowercase.
- It compares the character frequency of both strings.
- It prints whether the two strings are anagrams or not.

Hands-On Exercise Try improving the Anagram Checker with these additional features:

1. Allow users to enter multiple pairs of strings for checking.
2. Display character frequency counts for both words before comparison.
3. Create a GUI version using Tkinter for interactive input.
4. Allow checking for anagrams from a file input instead of manual entry.
5. Enhance the program to check for multi-word anagrams (e.g., "New York Times" vs. "Monkeys write").

Chapter 47: Simple String Encryption and Decryption

Overview A Simple String Encryption and Decryption program is used to encode and decode messages for basic security. This project helps in understanding character manipulation, ASCII conversions, loops, and basic cryptographic techniques in Python.

This chapter covers the step-by-step implementation of encrypting and decrypting a string using methods such as Caesar cipher and ASCII shifting.

Key Concepts of String Encryption and Decryption in Python

- **Character Manipulation:**
  - Shifting character ASCII values.
  - Using loops to modify each character in a string.
- **Using Built-in Functions:**
  - The ord() function converts a character to its ASCII value.
  - The chr() function converts an ASCII value back to a character.
- **Basic Encryption Methods:**
  - Caesar cipher (shifting characters by a fixed number of positions).
  - XOR encryption for simple bitwise encoding.

Example of Encryption and Decryption

Plain Text	Encrypted (Shift 3)	Decrypted
Hello	Khoor	Hello
Python	Sbwkrq	Python
Encrypt	Hqfubsw	Encrypt

Basic Rules for Encryption and Decryption in Python

Rule	Correct Example
Use ord() and chr() to shift characters	chr(ord(char) + shift)
Ensure characters remain within ASCII bounds	new_char = chr((ord(char) - 97 + shift) % 26 + 97)
Reverse the shift to decrypt	chr(ord(char) - shift)

Syntax Table

SL	Concept	Syntax/Example	Description
1	Get user input	`message = input("Enter text: ")`	Takes text from the user.
2	Encrypt using shift	`encrypted = ''.join(chr(ord(c) + shift) for c in text)`	Shifts each character by `shift` positions.
3	Decrypt using reverse shift	`decrypted = ''.join(chr(ord(c) - shift) for c in text)`	Restores characters by reversing the shift.
4	Handle non-alphabetic characters	`if char.isalpha():`	Ensures only letters are encrypted.
5	Print results	`print("Encrypted text:", encrypted_text)`	Displays encrypted text.

Real-Life Project: String Encryption and Decryption

Project Code:

```
1.  def encrypt(text, shift):
2.      encrypted_text = ""
3.      for char in text:
4.          if char.isalpha():
5.              shift_base = 65 if char.isupper() else 97
6.              encrypted_text += chr((ord(char) - shift_base + shift) % 26 + shift_base)
7.          else:
8.              encrypted_text += char
9.      return encrypted_text

10. def decrypt(text, shift):
11.     decrypted_text = ""
12.     for char in text:
13.         if char.isalpha():
14.             shift_base = 65 if char.isupper() else 97
15.             decrypted_text += chr((ord(char) -
```

```
shift_base - shift) % 26 + shift_base)
16.          else:
17.              decrypted_text += char
18.      return decrypted_text

19. text = input("Enter text: ")
20. shift = int(input("Enter shift value: "))
21. encrypted_text = encrypt(text, shift)
22. print("Encrypted text:", encrypted_text)
23. decrypted_text = decrypt(encrypted_text, shift)
24. print("Decrypted text:", decrypted_text)
```

Project Code Explanation Table

Line	Code Section	Description
1	`def encrypt(text, shift):`	Defines the function to encrypt a text by shifting its characters.
2	`encrypted_text = ""`	Initializes an empty string to store the encrypted text.
3	`for char in text:`	Loops through each character in the input text.
4	`if char.isalpha():`	Checks if the character is an alphabet letter (ignores numbers and symbols).
5	`shift_base = 65 if char.isupper() else 97`	Determines whether the character is uppercase or lowercase and assigns the respective ASCII base value.
6	`encrypted_text += chr((ord(char) - shift_base + shift) % 26 + shift_base)`	Encrypts the character by shifting it within the alphabet.
7-8	`else: encrypted_text += char`	Keeps non-alphabetic characters unchanged.
9	`return encrypted_text`	Returns the final encrypted string.
10	`def decrypt(text,`	Defines the function to decrypt a

	shift):	text by reversing the shift.
11	`decrypted_text = ""`	Initializes an empty string to store the decrypted text.
12	`for char in text:`	Loops through each character in the encrypted text.
13	`if char.isalpha():`	Checks if the character is an alphabet letter before decryption.
14	`shift_base = 65 if char.isupper() else 97`	Determines if the character is uppercase or lowercase.
15	`decrypted_text += chr((ord(char) - shift_base - shift) % 26 + shift_base)`	Reverses the encryption shift to restore the original character.
16-17	`else: decrypted_text += char`	Keeps non-alphabetic characters unchanged.
18	`return decrypted_text`	Returns the final decrypted text.
19	`text = input("Enter text: ")`	Prompts the user to enter the text to encrypt.
20	`shift = int(input("Enter shift value: "))`	Takes the shift value from the user.
21	`encrypted_text = encrypt(text, shift)`	Calls the encrypt function and stores the encrypted text.
22	`print("Encrypted text:", encrypted_text)`	Displays the encrypted text.
23	`decrypted_text = decrypt(encrypted_text, shift)`	Calls the decrypt function and restores the original text.
24	`print("Decrypted text:", decrypted_text)`	Displays the decrypted text.

Expected Results

- The program asks the user to enter a message and a shift value.
- It encrypts the message by shifting characters forward.
- It then decrypts the message by shifting characters backward.
- The program displays both the encrypted and decrypted messages.

Hands-On Exercise Try improving the Encryption and Decryption program with these additional features:

1. **Allow users to choose between different encryption techniques (e.g., XOR, Base64, Vigenère cipher).**
2. **Handle numbers and special characters using a separate encoding scheme.**
3. **Create a GUI version using Tkinter for easier interaction.**
4. **Enable encryption and decryption of entire files instead of just strings.**
5. **Compare the security of different encryption techniques using randomness analysis.**

Conclusion This Simple String Encryption and Decryption project introduces Python concepts such as character manipulation, loops, and ASCII conversions. By expanding this project, developers can explore more advanced cryptographic techniques for secure data handling.

Chapter 48: Number Guessing Game with GUI

Overview A Number Guessing Game with a Graphical User Interface (GUI) is an interactive game where the user guesses a randomly selected number within a given range. The game provides feedback (e.g., "Too High" or "Too Low") until the user correctly guesses the number.

This chapter covers the step-by-step implementation of creating a number guessing game with a GUI using Tkinter in Python.

Key Concepts of Number Guessing Game with GUI in Python

- **Random Number Generation:**
    - Using the random.randint() function to generate a random number.
- **GUI with Tkinter:**
    - Creating an interactive interface with labels, buttons, and input fields.
- **User Input Handling:**
    - Taking the user's guess and validating it.
    - Providing feedback on each guess.

Example Game Flow

User Guess	System Response
10	Too low! Try again.
50	Too high! Try again.
25	Correct! You guessed it!

Basic Rules for Number Guessing Game in Python

Rule	Correct Example
Generate a random number within a range	random.randint(1, 100)
Get user input from a GUI entry box	user_guess = int(entry.get())
Compare guess and provide feedback	if guess > target: print("Too high!")

Syntax Table

SL	Concept	Syntax/Example	Description
1	Import modules	`import tkinter as tk, random`	Imports Tkinter for GUI and random for number generation.
2	Generate random number	`target = random.randint(1, 100)`	Generates a secret number.
3	Create GUI window	`root = tk.Tk()`	Initializes the Tkinter window.
4	Get user input	`entry.get()`	Retrieves user input from the entry field.
5	Provide feedback	`label.config(text="Too High!")`	Updates label text with feedback.

Real-Life Project: Number Guessing Game with GUI

Project Code:

```
1.  import tkinter as tk
2.  import random

3.  target_number = random.randint(1, 100)
4.  attempts = 0

5.  def check_guess():
6.      global attempts
7.      try:
8.          guess = int(entry.get())
9.          attempts += 1
10.         if guess < target_number:
11.             label_feedback.config(text="Too Low!
Try Again.")
12.         elif guess > target_number:
13.             label_feedback.config(text="Too High!
Try Again.")
14.         else:
15.
```

```
label_feedback.config(text=f"Congratulations! You
guessed it in {attempts} attempts.")
16.            entry.config(state='disabled')
17.            button_guess.config(state='disabled')
18.      except ValueError:
19.          label_feedback.config(text="Invalid input!
Enter a number.")

20. root = tk.Tk()
21. root.title("Number Guessing Game")

22. label_instruction = tk.Label(root, text="Guess a
number between 1 and 100")
23. label_instruction.pack()

24. entry = tk.Entry(root)
25. entry.pack()

26. button_guess = tk.Button(root, text="Submit",
command=check_guess)
27. button_guess.pack()

28. label_feedback = tk.Label(root, text="")
29. label_feedback.pack()

30. root.mainloop()
```

Project Code Explanation Table

Line	Code Section	Description
1-2	`import tkinter as tk, random`	Imports necessary libraries for GUI creation and random number generation.
3	`target_number = random.randint(1, 100)`	Generates a random target number between 1 and 100.
4	`attempts = 0`	Initializes an attempt counter to track the number of guesses.

5	`def check_guess():`	Defines a function to check the user's guess against the target number.
6	`global attempts`	Declares `attempts` as a global variable to modify it inside the function.
7-8	`try: guess = int(entry.get())`	Retrieves the user's input from the entry field and converts it to an integer.
9	`attempts += 1`	Increments the attempt counter each time the user submits a guess.
10-11	`if guess < target_number:`	Checks if the guess is lower than the target and updates the feedback label.
12-13	`elif guess > target_number:`	Checks if the guess is higher than the target and updates the feedback label.
14-15	`else:`	If the guess matches the target number, displays a congratulatory message with the number of attempts.
16	`entry.config(state='disabled')`	Disables the entry field after the correct guess.
17	`button_guess.config(state='disabled')`	Disables the submit button after the correct guess.
18-19	`except ValueError:`	Handles invalid (non-numeric) input and displays an error message.
20	`root = tk.Tk()`	Creates the main Tkinter window.
21	`root.title("Number Guessing Game")`	Sets the window title.
22-23	`label_instruction = tk.Label(root, text="Guess a number between 1 and 100")`	Displays game instructions using a label.

24-25	`entry = tk.Entry(root)`	Creates an input field for the user to enter guesses.
26-27	`button_guess = tk.Button(root, text="Submit", command=check_guess )`	Creates a button that calls `check_guess()` when clicked.
28-29	`label_feedback = tk.Label(root, text="")`	Creates a label to display feedback messages.
30	`root.mainloop()`	Starts the Tkinter event loop, keeping the GUI running.

Expected Results

- The program launches a GUI window with an entry field and a submit button.
- The user enters a guess and clicks "Submit".
- The program provides feedback on whether the guess is too high, too low, or correct.
- The game ends when the correct number is guessed, and the input field is disabled.

Hands-On Exercise Try improving the Number Guessing Game with these additional features:

1. **Allow users to restart the game after a correct guess.**
2. **Implement a timer to track how long it takes to guess correctly.**
3. **Add a difficulty level (e.g., Easy: 1-50, Hard: 1-200).**
4. **Improve UI design by using `tkinter.ttk` for better styling.**
5. **Save previous scores and display a leaderboard.**

Conclusion This Number Guessing Game with GUI introduces Python concepts such as event handling, GUI programming with Tkinter, and random number generation. By expanding this project, developers can create more interactive and visually appealing games.

Chapter 49: String to Title Case Converter

Overview A Title Case Converter is a program that transforms a given string so that the first letter of each word is capitalized while the rest remain in lowercase. This project helps in understanding string manipulation, built-in functions, and user input handling in Python.

This chapter covers the step-by-step implementation of converting a string to title case, handling user input, using built-in functions, and implementing manual title case conversion.

Key Concepts of Title Case Conversion in Python

- **Using Built-in Functions:**
  - The `title()` method capitalizes the first letter of each word.
  - The `capitalize()` method capitalizes only the first letter of the sentence.
- **Manual Computation:**
  - Splitting the string into words and capitalizing each word.
  - Handling special cases such as articles and prepositions.

Example Title Case Conversion

Input String	Title Case Output
"hello world"	"Hello World"
"python is fun"	"Python Is Fun"
"tHis is A tEsT"	"This Is A Test"

Basic Rules for Title Case Conversion in Python

Rule	Correct Example
Use `title()` to capitalize words	`string.title()`
Use `split()` and `capitalize()` for manual conversion	`[word.capitalize() for word in string.split()]`
Handle exceptions for articles/prepositions	`word.lower() if word in stopwords else word.capitalize()`

Syntax Table

SL	Concept	Syntax/Example	Description
1	Get user input	`text = input("Enter a string: ")`	Takes input from the user.
2	Convert using `title()`	`title_text = text.title()`	Uses built-in function for title case conversion.
3	Convert manually	`title_text = " ".join([word.capitalize() for word in text.split()])`	Splits, capitalizes, and joins words back together.
4	Handle exceptions	`if word.lower() in stopwords:`	Keeps certain words in lowercase.
5	Print result	`print("Title Case:", title_text)`	Displays the converted string.

Real-Life Project: Title Case Converter

Project Code:

```
1.  def convert_to_title_case(text):
2.      stopwords = {"a", "an", "the", "in", "on",
"at", "to", "with", "for", "but", "or", "and"}
3.      words = text.lower().split()
4.      title_cased_words = [words[0].capitalize()] +
[word if word in stopwords else word.capitalize() for
word in words[1:]]
5.      return " ".join(title_cased_words)

6.  text = input("Enter a string: ")
7.  print("Title Case (Using title()):", text.title())
8.  print("Title Case (Manual Method):",
convert_to_title_case(text))
```

Project Code Explanation Table

Line	Code Section	Description
1	`def convert_to_title_case(text):`	Defines a function to manually convert text to title case.
2	`stopwords = {"a", "an", "the", "in", "on", "at", "to", "with", "for", "but", "or", "and"}`	Defines a set of words that should not be capitalized unless they are the first word.
3	`words = text.lower().split()`	Converts the string to lowercase and splits it into words.
4	`title_cased_words = [words[0].capitalize()] + [word if word in stopwords else word.capitalize() for word in words[1:]]`	Capitalizes the first word and applies title case rules to the remaining words.
5	`return " ".join(title_cased_words)`	Joins the words back into a sentence.
6	`text = input("Enter a string: ")`	Takes user input.
7	`print("Title Case (Using title()):", text.title())`	Uses Python's built-in `title()` method for title case conversion.
8	`print("Title Case (Manual Method):", convert_to_title_case(text))`	Calls the custom function to convert text to title case manually.

Expected Results

- The program asks the user to enter a string.
- It converts the string to title case using both `title()` and manual processing.
- It prints both results.
- Special words (like "a", "an", "the") remain in lowercase unless they appear at the start of the sentence.

Hands-On Exercise Try improving the Title Case Converter with these additional features:

1. **Allow users to choose between built-in and manual conversion methods.**
2. **Enhance the manual method to handle punctuation properly.**
3. **Create a GUI version using `Tkinter` for interactive input.**
4. **Enable batch conversion for multiple sentences at once.**
5. **Save converted text to a file for later use.**

Conclusion This Title Case Converter project introduces Python concepts such as string manipulation, list comprehensions, and user input handling. By expanding this project, developers can create more advanced text-processing applications.

Chapter 50: Days Between Two Dates Calculator

Overview A Days Between Two Dates Calculator is a program that computes the number of days between two given dates. This project helps in understanding date handling, built-in Python libraries, and user input validation.

This chapter covers the step-by-step implementation of calculating the difference between two dates, handling user input, and formatting output.

Key Concepts of Days Between Two Dates Calculation in Python

- **Using Built-in `datetime` Module:**
  - `datetime.strptime()` to convert string dates into `datetime` objects.
  - `timedelta.days` to calculate the number of days between two dates.
- **User Input Handling:**
  - Accepting date inputs in a specific format.
  - Validating input to ensure correct date format.

Example Date Calculations

Start Date	End Date	Days Between
2023-01-01	2023-01-10	9
2022-06-15	2023-06-15	365
2021-12-31	2022-01-01	1

Basic Rules for Date Calculation in Python

Rule	Correct Example
Convert string to date	`date_object = datetime.strptime(date_string, "%Y-%m-%d")`
Find difference between dates	`delta = end_date - start_date`
Extract days from difference	`days_between = delta.days`

Syntax Table

SL	Concept	Syntax/Example	Description
1	Import datetime module	`from datetime import datetime`	Imports necessary module for date handling.
2	Convert string to date	`date_object = datetime.strptime( "2023-01-01", "%Y-%m-%d")`	Converts a date string to a datetime object.
3	Compute date difference	`delta = end_date - start_date`	Finds the difference between two dates.
4	Extract number of days	`days_between = delta.days`	Retrieves the total days from the difference.
5	Print result	`print("Days Between:", days_between)`	Displays the calculated days.

Real-Life Project: Days Between Two Dates Calculator

Project Code:

```
1.  from datetime import datetime
2.  def days_between_dates(start, end):
3.      try:
4.          start_date = datetime.strptime(start, "%Y-%m-%d")
5.          end_date = datetime.strptime(end, "%Y-%m-%d")
6.          delta = end_date - start_date
7.          return delta.days
8.      except ValueError:
9.          return "Invalid date format! Use YYYY-MM-DD."
10. start_date = input("Enter the start date (YYYY-MM-DD): ")
11. end_date = input("Enter the end date (YYYY-MM-DD): ")
12. result = days_between_dates(start_date, end_date)
13. print("Days Between:", result)
```

Project Code Explanation Table

Line	Code Section	Description
1	`from datetime import datetime`	Imports the `datetime` module for date handling.
2	`def days_between_dates(start, end):`	Defines a function to compute days between two dates.
3	`try:`	Handles exceptions in case of invalid date input.
4-5	`datetime.strptime(start, "%Y-%m-%d")`	Converts the input date strings into `datetime` objects.
6	`delta = end_date - start_date`	Finds the difference between the two dates.
7	`return delta.days`	Returns the number of days between the two dates.
8-9	`except ValueError:`	Catches errors if the user enters an incorrectly formatted date.
10-11	`start_date = input(...)`	Takes user input for the start and end dates.
12	`result = days_between_dates(start_date, end_date)`	Calls the function to calculate the difference.
13	`print("Days Between:", result)`	Displays the calculated number of days.

Expected Results

- The program asks the user to enter two dates in YYYY-MM-DD format.
- It computes the difference in days between the two dates.
- It prints the result.
- If the user enters an invalid date format, an error message is displayed.

Chapter 51: Fibonacci Series Using Recursion

Overview The Fibonacci series is a sequence of numbers where each number is the sum of the two preceding ones, starting from 0 and 1. This project demonstrates the implementation of the Fibonacci series using recursion in Python.

This chapter covers the step-by-step implementation of the Fibonacci series using recursion, handling user input, and optimizing performance.

Key Concepts of Fibonacci Series Using Recursion in Python

- **Recursive Function:**
    - A function that calls itself to solve smaller instances of a problem.
    - Base cases to stop infinite recursion.
- **Mathematical Definition:**
    - $F(n)=F(n-1)+F(n-2)$ $F(n) = F(n-1) + F(n-2)$ where $F(0)=0, F(1)=1$ $F(0) = 0, F(1) = 1$
- **Performance Considerations:**
    - Recursive calls can be inefficient for large numbers.
    - Using memoization to store computed values for faster execution.

Example Fibonacci Sequence

Input (n)	Output (First n Fibonacci Numbers)
5	0, 1, 1, 2, 3
8	0, 1, 1, 2, 3, 5, 8, 13
10	0, 1, 1, 2, 3, 5, 8, 13, 21, 34

Basic Rules for Fibonacci Series in Python

Rule	Correct Example
Base case for recursion	`if n == 0 or n == 1: return n`
Recursive call	`return fibonacci(n-1) + fibonacci(n-2)`
Use memoization to optimize	`cache[n] = fibonacci(n-1) + fibonacci(n-2)`

Syntax Table

SL	Concept	Syntax/Example	Description
1	Define recursive function	`def fibonacci(n):`	Defines a function to compute Fibonacci numbers recursively.
2	Base condition	`if n == 0 or n == 1: return n`	Stops recursion at base cases.
3	Recursive call	`return fibonacci(n-1) + fibonacci(n-2)`	Computes Fibonacci numbers recursively.
4	Get user input	`num = int(input("Enter a number: "))`	Takes user input for the number of terms.
5	Print result	`print(fibonacci(n))`	Displays the Fibonacci sequence.

Real-Life Project: Fibonacci Series Using Recursion

Project Code:

```
1.  def fibonacci(n):
2.      if n == 0:
3.          return 0
4.      elif n == 1:
5.          return 1
6.      else:
7.          return fibonacci(n-1) + fibonacci(n-2)

8.  num = int(input("Enter the number of terms: "))
9.  print("Fibonacci Series:", [fibonacci(i) for i in range(num)])
```

Project Code Explanation Table

Line	Code Section	Description
1	`def fibonacci(n):`	Defines a recursive function to compute Fibonacci numbers.
2	`if n == 0:`	Base case: returns 0 when n is 0.
3	`return 0`	Returns 0 as the first Fibonacci number.
4	`elif n == 1:`	Base case: returns 1 when n is 1.
5	`return 1`	Returns 1 as the second Fibonacci number.
6-7	`else: return fibonacci(n-1) + fibonacci(n-2)`	Computes the Fibonacci number by summing the previous two numbers.
8	`num = int(input("Enter the number of terms: "))`	Takes user input for the number of terms.
9	`print("Fibonacci Series:", [fibonacci(i) for i in range(num)])`	Computes and prints the Fibonacci sequence up to num terms.

Expected Results

- The program asks the user to enter the number of Fibonacci terms.
- It recursively calculates and prints the Fibonacci sequence up to the specified term.
- If the user enters a large number, execution may be slow due to redundant recursive calls.

Chapter 52: Countdown Timer Using Tkinter

Overview A Countdown Timer with a Graphical User Interface (GUI) is a program that counts down from a specified time and updates dynamically. This project helps in understanding event-driven programming, time handling, and GUI development using Tkinter in Python.

This chapter covers the step-by-step implementation of a countdown timer with a Tkinter GUI, handling user input, updating the timer dynamically, and providing a start/reset functionality.

Key Concepts of Countdown Timer Using Tkinter in Python

- **Using Tkinter for GUI Development:**
  - Creating labels, buttons, and input fields.
  - Updating the GUI dynamically.
- **Using `time` and `after()` for Timer Execution:**
  - The `after()` method to update the countdown at one-second intervals.
  - Formatting time values for display.
- **User Input Handling:**
  - Accepting and validating user input for countdown time.
  - Restarting or resetting the timer.

Example Countdown Timer Execution

User Input	Timer Countdown
10 seconds	10 → 9 → 8 … 1 → "Time's Up!"
5 seconds	5 → 4 → 3 → 2 → 1 → "Time's Up!"

Basic Rules for Countdown Timer in Python

Rule	Correct Example
Use `after()` for real-time countdown	`root.after(1000, update_timer)`
Convert user input to integer	`time_left = int(entry.get())`
Stop countdown at zero	`if time_left <= 0:` `label.config(text="Time's Up!")`

Syntax Table

SL	Concept	Syntax/Example	Description
1	Import modules	`import tkinter as tk`	Imports Tkinter for GUI creation.
2	Create GUI window	`root = tk.Tk()`	Initializes the main Tkinter window.
3	Get user input	`entry.get()`	Retrieves user input from the entry field.
4	Update timer every second	`root.after(1000, update_timer)`	Calls the update function every second.
5	Stop timer when zero	`if time_left <= 0: label.config(text="Time's Up!")`	Displays message when countdown reaches zero.

Real-Life Project: Countdown Timer with Tkinter

Project Code:

```
1.  import tkinter as tk
2.  from tkinter import messagebox

3.  def start_timer():
4.      global time_left
5.      try:
6.          time_left = int(entry.get())
7.          update_timer()
8.      except ValueError:
9.          messagebox.showerror("Invalid Input",
    "Please enter a valid number.")

10. def update_timer():
11.     global time_left
12.     if time_left > 0:
13.         label.config(text=f"Time Left: {time_left}
    sec")
14.         time_left -= 1
15.         root.after(1000, update_timer)
16.     else:
17.         label.config(text="Time's Up!")
```

```
18. def reset_timer():
19.     global time_left
20.     time_left = 0
21.     label.config(text="Enter Time and Press Start")

22. root = tk.Tk()
23. root.title("Countdown Timer")

24. label = tk.Label(root, text="Enter Time in
Seconds", font=("Arial", 14))
25. label.pack()

26. entry = tk.Entry(root)
27. entry.pack()

28. start_button = tk.Button(root, text="Start",
command=start_timer)
29. start_button.pack()

30. reset_button = tk.Button(root, text="Reset",
command=reset_timer)
31. reset_button.pack()

32. root.mainloop()
```

Project Code Explanation Table

Line	Code Section	Description
1-2	import tkinter as tk, messagebox	Imports necessary libraries for GUI and alerts.
3-9	def start_timer():	Defines a function to start the countdown.
6	time_left = int(entry.get())	Retrieves and converts user input to an integer.

7	`update_timer()`	Calls the function to start updating the timer.
8-9	`except ValueError:`	Displays an error message if input is invalid.
10-17	`def update_timer():`	Defines a function to update the timer every second.
12-15	`if time_left > 0:`	Updates the label and decrements the timer.
16-17	`else:`	Stops countdown and displays "Time's Up!".
18-21	`def reset_timer():`	Defines a function to reset the timer.
22-23	`root = tk.Tk()`	Creates the main Tkinter window.
24-25	`label = tk.Label(root, text="Enter Time in Seconds")`	Creates a label to display instructions.
26-27	`entry = tk.Entry(root)`	Creates an entry box for user input.
28-29	`start_button = tk.Button(root, text="Start", command=start_timer)`	Creates a button to start the countdown.
30-31	`reset_button = tk.Button(root, text="Reset", command=reset_timer)`	Creates a button to reset the timer.
32	`root.mainloop()`	Runs the Tkinter event loop to keep the GUI active.

Expected Results
- The program launches a GUI window with an entry field and buttons.
- The user enters a time in seconds and clicks "Start".

- The countdown timer updates dynamically every second.
- When the timer reaches zero, "Time's Up!" is displayed.
- The user can reset the timer using the "Reset" button.

Hands-On Exercise Try improving the Countdown Timer with these additional features:

1. **Allow users to pause and resume the countdown.**
2. **Add sound notifications when the timer reaches zero.**
3. **Create a GUI version with a progress bar showing remaining time.**
4. **Enable a countdown that automatically starts when the program runs.**
5. **Allow users to enter time in minutes and seconds instead of just seconds.**

Conclusion This Countdown Timer with Tkinter project introduces Python concepts such as event-driven programming, real-time updates, and GUI development. By expanding this project, developers can create more advanced and user-friendly timers for various applications.

Chapter 53: Check if a Year is Leap Year

Overview A Leap Year Checker is a program that determines whether a given year is a leap year or not. A leap year is a year that is evenly divisible by 4, except for years that are both divisible by 100 and not divisible by 400. This project helps in understanding conditional statements and logical operations in Python.

This chapter covers the step-by-step implementation of checking for leap years, handling user input, and validating the year.

Key Concepts of Leap Year Checker in Python

- **Leap Year Conditions:**
  - A year is a leap year if it is divisible by 4.
  - However, if the year is also divisible by 100, it must be divisible by 400 to be a leap year.

- **Using Conditional Statements:**
  - Implementing if-elif-else conditions to check leap year rules.

Example Leap Year Checks

Year	Leap Year?
2020	Yes
2023	No
1900	No
2000	Yes

Basic Rules for Leap Year Calculation in Python

Rule	Correct Example
Year is divisible by 4	year % 4 == 0
Year is divisible by 100 but not 400	year % 100 == 0 and year % 400 != 0
Use if-elif-else for decision-making	if (condition):

Syntax Table

SL	Concept	Syntax/Example	Description
1	Get user input	year = int(input("Enter a year: "))	Takes user input and converts it to an integer.

2	Check divisibility by 4	`if year % 4 == 0:`	Checks if the year is divisible by 4.
3	Check special rule for century years	`if year % 100 == 0 and year % 400 != 0:`	Ensures century years are only leap years if divisible by 400.
4	Print result	`print("Leap Year")`	Displays whether the year is a leap year or not.

Real-Life Project: Leap Year Checker

Project Code:

```
1.  def is_leap_year(year):
2.      if year % 4 == 0:
3.          if year % 100 == 0:
4.              if year % 400 == 0:
5.                  return True
6.              else:
7.                  return False
8.          else:
9.              return True
10.     else:
11.         return False

12. year = int(input("Enter a year: "))
13. if is_leap_year(year):
14.     print(f"{year} is a Leap Year.")
15. else:
16.     print(f"{year} is NOT a Leap Year.")
```

Project Code Explanation Table

Line	Code Section	Description
1	`def is_leap_year(year):`	Defines a function to check if a year is a leap year.
2	`if year % 4 == 0:`	Checks if the year is divisible by 4.
3	`if year % 100 == 0:`	Checks if the year is a century year.

4-5	`if year % 400 == 0:`	Confirms if a century year is also divisible by 400.
6-7	`else: return False`	If a century year is not divisible by 400, it's not a leap year.
8-9	`else: return True`	Non-century years divisible by 4 are leap years.
10-11	`else: return False`	Years not divisible by 4 are not leap years.
12	`year = int(input("Enter a year: "))`	Takes user input and converts it to an integer.
13-16	`if is_leap_year(year):`	Calls the function and prints whether the year is a leap year.

Expected Results

- The program asks the user to enter a year.
- It checks if the entered year satisfies leap year conditions.
- It prints whether the year is a leap year or not.

Hands-On Exercise Try improving the Leap Year Checker with these additional features:

1. **Allow users to check a range of years instead of just one.**
2. **Create a GUI version using `Tkinter` to enter the year and display the result.**
3. **Allow the user to check leap years in both the past and future.**
4. **Modify the program to print all leap years in the last century.**
5. **Store checked years in a list and allow users to view previously checked years.**

Conclusion This Leap Year Checker project introduces Python concepts such as conditional statements, logical operations, and user input handling. By expanding this project, developers can create more advanced date-related applications.

Chapter 54: Find All Divisors of a Number

Overview A program to find all divisors of a number is useful in mathematics and number theory applications. A divisor of a number is any integer that divides it without leaving a remainder. This project helps in understanding loops, conditional statements, and efficient algorithms in Python.

This chapter covers the step-by-step implementation of finding all divisors of a given number, handling user input, and optimizing performance.

Key Concepts of Finding Divisors in Python

- **Definition of Divisors:**
    - A number n is divisible by d if $n \bmod d = 0$ $n \bmod d = 0$.
    - The divisors of n include all numbers between 1 and n that divide n evenly.
- **Using Loops and Conditional Statements:**
    - Iterating through numbers from 1 to n and checking divisibility.
    - Using efficient algorithms to reduce computation time.

Example Divisor Calculations

Number	Divisors
12	1, 2, 3, 4, 6, 12
15	1, 3, 5, 15
25	1, 5, 25
36	1, 2, 3, 4, 6, 9, 12, 18, 36

Basic Rules for Finding Divisors in Python

Rule	Correct Example
Use modulus to check divisibility	`if n % i == 0:`
Loop through numbers up to n	`for i in range(1, n+1):`
Optimize by looping up to sqrt(n)	`for i in range(1, int(n**0.5) + 1):`

Syntax Table

SL	Concept	Syntax/Example	Description
1	Get user input	`num = int(input("Enter a number: "))`	Takes user input as an integer.
2	Use a loop to find divisors	`for i in range(1, num + 1):`	Iterates through possible divisors.
3	Check divisibility	`if num % i == 0:`	Identifies numbers that divide num evenly.
4	Print divisors	`print(divisors)`	Displays the list of divisors.

Real-Life Project: Finding Divisors of a Number

Project Code:

```
1.  def find_divisors(n):
2.      divisors = []
3.      for i in range(1, int(n**0.5) + 1):
4.          if n % i == 0:
5.              divisors.append(i)
6.              if i != n // i:
7.                  divisors.append(n // i)
8.      return sorted(divisors)

9.  num = int(input("Enter a number: "))
10. print(f"Divisors of {num}:", find_divisors(num))
```

Project Code Explanation Table

Line	Code Section	Description
1	`def find_divisors(n):`	Defines a function to find all divisors of a number.
2	`divisors = []`	Initializes an empty list to store divisors.
3	`for i in range(1, int(n**0.5) + 1):`	Loops from 1 to the square root of n for efficiency.
4	`if n % i == 0:`	Checks if i is a divisor of n.
5	`divisors.append(i)`	Adds i to the list of divisors.

6-7	`if i != n // i:`	Adds the complementary divisor to the list if different from `i`.
8	`return sorted(divisors)`	Sorts and returns the list of divisors.
9	`num = int(input("Enter a number: "))`	Takes user input as an integer.
10	`print(f"Divisors of {num}:", find_divisors(num))`	Calls the function and prints the divisors.

Expected Results

- The program asks the user to enter a number.
- It calculates and prints all divisors of the given number.
- If the number is prime, it prints only 1 and the number itself.

Hands-On Exercise Try improving the Find Divisors program with these additional features:

1. **Allow users to check divisors for multiple numbers in a single run.**
2. **Enhance the program to identify prime numbers.**
3. **Create a GUI version using `Tkinter` for interactive input.**
4. **Display the sum of all divisors as an additional feature.**
5. **Allow users to find the greatest common divisor (GCD) of two numbers.**

Conclusion This Find Divisors project introduces Python concepts such as loops, conditionals, and mathematical operations. By expanding this project, developers can explore more advanced number-theory applications like factorization and prime detection.

Chapter 55: Factorial Calculator Using Recursion

Overview A Factorial Calculator computes the factorial of a given number using recursion. The factorial of a number nn is defined as:

$$n! = n \times (n-1) \times (n-2) \times ... \times 1 \quad n! = n \mid times \ (n-1) \mid times \ (n-2) \mid times ... \mid times \ 1$$

with the base case:

$$0! = 1 \quad 0! = 1$$

This project helps in understanding recursion, base cases, and function calls in Python.

This chapter covers the step-by-step implementation of computing the factorial using recursion, handling user input, and optimizing performance.

Key Concepts of Factorial Calculation Using Recursion in Python

- **Mathematical Definition:**
  - $n! = n \times (n-1)! \quad n! = n \mid times \ (n-1)!$
  - Base case: $0! = 1 \quad 0! = 1$
- **Recursive Function:**
  - A function that calls itself to compute smaller subproblems.
- **Performance Considerations:**
  - Recursive calls consume memory due to function stack usage.

Example Factorial Calculations

Input (n)	Factorial (n!)
3	6
5	120
7	5040
10	3,628,800

Basic Rules for Factorial Calculation in Python

Rule	Correct Example
Base case for recursion	`if n == 0: return 1`
Recursive call	`return n * factorial(n-1)`
Ensure valid input	`if n < 0: print("Invalid input")`

Syntax Table

SL	Concept	Syntax/Example	Description
1	Define recursive function	`def factorial(n):`	Defines a function to compute factorial recursively.
2	Base condition	`if n == 0:` `return 1`	Stops recursion when n is 0.
3	Recursive call	`return n * factorial(n-1)`	Calls the function recursively to compute factorial.
4	Get user input	`num = int(input("Enter a number: "))`	Takes user input as an integer.
5	Print result	`print("Factorial:", factorial(n))`	Displays the factorial result.

Real-Life Project: Factorial Calculator Using Recursion

Project Code:

```
1.  def factorial(n):
2.      if n == 0:
3.          return 1
4.      else:
5.          return n * factorial(n-1)

6.  num = int(input("Enter a number: "))
7.  if num < 0:
8.      print("Factorial is not defined for negative numbers.")
9.  else:
10.     print(f"Factorial of {num} is: {factorial(num)}")
```

Project Code Explanation Table

Line	Code Section	Description
1	`def factorial(n):`	Defines a recursive function to compute factorial.
2	`if n == 0:`	Base case: returns 1 when n is 0.
3	`return 1`	Returns 1 for 0!.
4-5	`else: return n * factorial(n-1)`	Recursively calls the function to compute factorial.
6	`num = int(input("Enter a number: "))`	Takes user input and converts it to an integer.
7-8	`if num < 0:`	Checks if the number is negative and prints an error message.
9-10	`else: print(f"Factorial of {num} is: {factorial(num)}")`	Calls the function and prints the factorial result.

Expected Results

- The program asks the user to enter a number.
- It recursively calculates and prints the factorial of the entered number.
- If the user enters a negative number, an error message is displayed.

Hands-On Exercise Try improving the Factorial Calculator with these additional features:

1. **Use memoization to store previously computed values for optimization.**
2. **Implement an iterative version of the factorial function.**
3. **Create a GUI version using `Tkinter` for interactive input.**
4. **Extend the program to compute double factorial (n!!).**

Conclusion This Factorial Calculator using Recursion project introduces Python concepts such as recursion, base cases, and function calls. By expanding this project, developers can explore optimization techniques like memoization and iterative approaches to improve performance.

Chapter 56: Sum of Even Numbers in a List

Overview A program to calculate the sum of even numbers in a list is a fundamental exercise in Python that helps understand loops, conditionals, and list comprehensions.

This chapter covers the step-by-step implementation of summing even numbers in a list, handling user input, and using efficient techniques such as list comprehensions.

Key Concepts of Summing Even Numbers in Python

- **Definition of Even Numbers:**
    - A number is even if it is divisible by 2: $n \bmod 2 = 0$ $n \mid \bmod\ 2 = 0$.

- **Using Loops and Conditional Statements:**
    - Iterating through the list and checking for even numbers.
    - Using built-in functions to optimize performance.

Example Sum of Even Numbers

Input List	Even Numbers	Sum
[1, 2, 3, 4, 5]	[2, 4]	6
[10, 15, 20, 25, 30]	[10, 20, 30]	60
[7, 9, 11]	[]	0

Basic Rules for Finding the Sum of Even Numbers in Python

Rule	Correct Example
Check if a number is even	`if num % 2 == 0:`
Use a loop to iterate through the list	`for num in numbers:`
Use list comprehension for optimization	`sum(num for num in numbers if num % 2 == 0)`

Syntax Table

SL	Concept	Syntax/Example	Description
1	Get user input	`numbers = list(map(int, input().split()))`	Takes a list of numbers as input.
2	Use a loop to find even numbers	`for num in numbers:`	Iterates through the list.

3	Check if a number is even	`if num % 2 == 0:`	Filters even numbers.
4	Sum even numbers	`even_sum += num`	Adds even numbers to the sum.
5	Use list comprehension	`sum_even = sum(num for num in numbers if num % 2 == 0)`	Optimized approach.

Real-Life Project: Sum of Even Numbers in a List

Project Code:

```
1.  def sum_even_numbers(numbers):
2.      even_sum = 0
3.      for num in numbers:
4.          if num % 2 == 0:
5.              even_sum += num
6.      return even_sum

7.  numbers = list(map(int, input("Enter numbers
separated by space: ").split()))
8.  print("Sum of Even Numbers:",
sum_even_numbers(numbers))
```

Project Code Explanation Table

Line	Code Section	Description
1	`def sum_even_numbers(numbers):`	Defines a function to compute the sum of even numbers.
2	`even_sum = 0`	Initializes a variable to store the sum of even numbers.
3	`for num in numbers:`	Loops through each number in the list.
4	`if num % 2 == 0:`	Checks if the number is even.
5	`even_sum += num`	Adds even numbers to the sum.

6	`return even_sum`	Returns the sum of even numbers.
7	`numbers = list(map(int, input("Enter numbers separated by space: ").split()))`	Takes user input as a list of integers.
8	`print("Sum of Even Numbers:", sum_even_numbers(numbers))`	Calls the function and prints the sum of even numbers.

Expected Results

- The program asks the user to enter a list of numbers.
- It filters out the even numbers and computes their sum.
- It prints the total sum of even numbers from the list.
- If there are no even numbers, it returns 0.

Hands-On Exercise Try improving the Sum of Even Numbers program with these additional features:

1. **Modify the program to sum only odd numbers.**
2. **Enhance the program to count how many even numbers exist in the list.**
3. **Create a GUI version using Tkinter for user-friendly input.**
4. **Allow users to enter numbers from a file instead of manual input.**
5. **Optimize performance using built-in functions like filter() and sum().**

Conclusion This Sum of Even Numbers project introduces Python concepts such as loops, conditionals, and list operations. By expanding this project, developers can explore more advanced list-processing techniques and optimizations.

Chapter 57: Basic Phonebook Application

Overview A Basic Phonebook Application allows users to store, search, update, and delete contact information. This project helps in understanding data structures such as dictionaries, user input handling, and file storage in Python.

This chapter covers the step-by-step implementation of a simple phonebook using Python, handling user input, storing contact details, and performing CRUD (Create, Read, Update, Delete) operations.

Key Concepts of Phonebook Application in Python

- **Using Dictionaries to Store Contacts:**
  - Contacts are stored as key-value pairs (Name -> Phone Number).
- **Performing CRUD Operations:**
  - Adding, retrieving, updating, and deleting contacts.
- **User Input Handling:**
  - Accepting user choices for different actions.
  - Validating and formatting phone numbers.

Example Phonebook Operations

Operation	Input	Output
Add Contact	"John, 1234567890"	Contact Added
Search Contact	"John"	1234567890
Update Contact	"John, 9876543210"	Contact Updated
Delete Contact	"John"	Contact Deleted

Basic Rules for Phonebook Application in Python

Rule	Correct Example
Use dictionaries to store contacts	`phonebook = {"Alice": "9876543210"}`
Check if a contact exists before updating/deleting	`if name in phonebook:`
Handle invalid inputs with error messages	`if not number.isdigit():` `print("Invalid number")`

Syntax Table

SL	Concept	Syntax/Example	Description
1	Define dictionary	phonebook = {}	Creates an empty dictionary to store contacts.
2	Add contact	phonebook[name] = number	Stores a contact in the dictionary.
3	Search contact	if name in phonebook: print(phonebook[name])	Retrieves a contact by name.
4	Update contact	phonebook[name] = new_number	Updates an existing contact.
5	Delete contact	del phonebook[name]	Removes a contact from the dictionary.

Real-Life Project: Basic Phonebook Application

Project Code:

```
1.  phonebook = {}

2.  def add_contact(name, number):
3.      phonebook[name] = number
4.      print(f"Contact {name} added successfully.")

5.  def search_contact(name):
6.      if name in phonebook:
7.          print(f"{name}: {phonebook[name]}")
8.      else:
9.          print("Contact not found.")

10. def update_contact(name, new_number):
11.     if name in phonebook:
12.         phonebook[name] = new_number
13.         print(f"Contact {name} updated successfully.")
14.     else:
15.         print("Contact not found.")
```

```python
16. def delete_contact(name):
17.     if name in phonebook:
18.         del phonebook[name]
19.         print(f"Contact {name} deleted
successfully.")
20.     else:
21.         print("Contact not found.")


22. while True:
23.     print("\nPhonebook Menu:")
24.     print("1. Add Contact")
25.     print("2. Search Contact")
26.     print("3. Update Contact")
27.     print("4. Delete Contact")
28.     print("5. Exit")

29.     choice = input("Enter your choice: ")
30.     if choice == "1":
31.         name = input("Enter name: ")
32.         number = input("Enter number: ")
33.         add_contact(name, number)
34.     elif choice == "2":
35.         name = input("Enter name to search: ")
36.         search_contact(name)
37.     elif choice == "3":
38.         name = input("Enter name to update: ")
39.         new_number = input("Enter new number: ")
40.         update_contact(name, new_number)
41.     elif choice == "4":
42.         name = input("Enter name to delete: ")
43.         delete_contact(name)
44.     elif choice == "5":
45.         print("Exiting Phonebook.")
46.         break
47.     else:
48.         print("Invalid choice. Please try again.")
```

Project Code Explanation Table

Line	Code Section	Description
1	`phonebook = {}`	Initializes an empty dictionary for storing contacts.
2-4	`def add_contact(name, number):`	Defines a function to add a contact.
5-9	`def search_contact(name):`	Defines a function to search for a contact.
10-15	`def update_contact(name, new_number):`	Defines a function to update an existing contact.
16-21	`def delete_contact(name):`	Defines a function to delete a contact.
22-28	`while True:`	Creates a menu loop for user interaction.
29-48	Menu Options	Implements choices for adding, searching, updating, deleting, and exiting the program.

Expected Results

- The program presents a menu with options for managing contacts.
- The user can add, search, update, and delete contacts.
- If a contact doesn't exist, an appropriate message is displayed.
- The program continues running until the user chooses to exit.

Hands-On Exercise Try improving the Basic Phonebook Application with these additional features:

1. **Allow saving and loading contacts from a file for persistence.**
2. **Implement input validation for phone numbers (e.g., ensuring they contain only digits).**
3. **Create a GUI version using Tkinter for user-friendly interaction.**
4. **Enhance the program to allow searching for partial names.**
5. **Allow users to export the phonebook to a CSV file.**

Chapter 58: Check if a String is a Pangram

Overview A Pangram Checker is a program that determines whether a given sentence contains all the letters of the English alphabet at least once. A common example of a pangram is:

"The quick brown fox jumps over the lazy dog."

This project helps in understanding string manipulation, sets, loops, and conditionals in Python.

This chapter covers the step-by-step implementation of checking if a given string is a pangram, handling user input, and using efficient techniques.

Key Concepts of Pangram Checker in Python

- **Definition of Pangram:**
    - A sentence that contains every letter of the alphabet at least once.
- **Using Sets to Check Uniqueness:**
    - A set stores unique characters, making it useful for pangram detection.
- **Efficient Algorithms:**
    - Using `set(string.ascii_lowercase)` to compare characters quickly.

Example Pangram Checks

Input String	Pangram?
"The quick brown fox jumps over the lazy dog."	Yes
"Hello, World!"	No
"Pack my box with five dozen liquor jugs."	Yes

Basic Rules for Pangram Checker in Python

Rule	Correct Example
Convert string to lowercase	`text.lower()`
Remove spaces and punctuation	`text.replace(" ", "").replace(".", "")`
Use sets to track unique letters	`set(text) == set(ascii_lowercase)`

Syntax Table

SL	Concept	Syntax/Example	Description
1	Import string module	`import string`	Provides ascii_lowercase for easy comparison.
2	Convert text to lowercase	`text.lower()`	Ensures uniform character comparison.
3	Remove non-alphabetic characters	`text = ''.join(filter(str.isalpha, text))`	Removes spaces and punctuation.
4	Check for pangram	`set(text) == set(string.ascii_lowercase)`	Compares character set with the alphabet.

Real-Life Project: Pangram Checker

Project Code:

```
1.   import string

2.   def is_pangram(text):
3.        text = text.lower()
4.        text = ''.join(filter(str.isalpha, text))
5.        return set(text) == set(string.ascii_lowercase)

6.   user_input = input("Enter a sentence: ")
7.   if is_pangram(user_input):
8.        print("The sentence is a pangram.")
9.   else:
10.       print("The sentence is NOT a pangram.")
```

Project Code Explanation Table

Line	Code Section	Description
1	`import string`	Imports string module for alphabet reference.
2	`def is_pangram(text):`	Defines a function to check if a string is a pangram.

3	`text = text.lower()`	Converts text to lowercase for uniformity.
4	`text = ''.join(filter(str.i salpha, text))`	Removes spaces and punctuation.
5	`return set(text) == set(string.ascii_low ercase)`	Checks if the set of characters in text matches the alphabet.
6	`user_input = input("Enter a sentence: ")`	Takes user input.
7-10	`if is_pangram(user_inpu t):`	Calls the function and prints whether the sentence is a pangram.

Expected Results

- The program asks the user to enter a sentence.
- It processes the text and determines if it is a pangram.
- It prints a message stating whether the sentence contains all letters of the alphabet.

Hands-On Exercise Try improving the Pangram Checker with these additional features:

1. Allow users to enter multiple sentences to check.
2. Ignore numbers and special characters while checking for pangrams.
3. Create a GUI version using Tkinter for user-friendly input.
4. Enhance the program to highlight missing letters if not a pangram.
5. Enable checking pangrams in different languages by modifying the character set.

Conclusion This Pangram Checker project introduces Python concepts such as string manipulation, sets, and conditionals. By expanding this project, developers can explore more advanced text-processing applications.

Chapter 59: Calculate BMI (Body Mass Index)

Overview A BMI (Body Mass Index) Calculator is a program that calculates a person's BMI based on their weight and height. The BMI is used to categorize individuals into different health ranges such as underweight, normal weight, overweight, and obesity.

This chapter covers the step-by-step implementation of BMI calculation using Python, handling user input, and categorizing BMI values.

Key Concepts of BMI Calculation in Python

- **Mathematical Formula for BMI:**
- $BMI = weight\ (kg) \div [height\ (m) \times height\ (m)]$
- **Health Categories Based on BMI:**
  - BMI < 18.5 → Underweight
  - 18.5 ≤ BMI < 24.9 → Normal weight
  - 25.0 ≤ BMI < 29.9 → Overweight
  - BMI ≥ 30 → Obesity
- **Using Conditionals to Classify BMI:**
  - `if-elif-else` statements to determine BMI category.

Example BMI Calculations

Weight (kg)	Height (m)	BMI	Category
50	1.65	18.3	Underweight
70	1.75	22.9	Normal weight
85	1.80	26.2	Overweight
100	1.70	34.6	Obesity

Basic Rules for BMI Calculation in Python

Rule	Correct Example
Convert height to meters	`height = height / 100` if entered in cm
Apply BMI formula	`bmi = weight / (height ** 2)`
Use conditionals to classify BMI	`if bmi < 18.5:`

Syntax Table

SL	Concept	Syntax/Example	Description
1	Get user input	`weight = float(input("Enter weight in kg: "))`	Takes weight input from user.
2	Convert height if needed	`height = float(input("Enter height in meters: "))`	Ensures height is in meters.
3	Calculate BMI	`bmi = weight / (height ** 2)`	Uses formula to compute BMI.
4	Classify BMI	`if bmi < 18.5:`	Determines BMI category.
5	Print result	`print("Your BMI is:", bmi)`	Displays calculated BMI.

Real-Life Project: BMI Calculator

Project Code:

```
1.  def calculate_bmi(weight, height):
2.      bmi = weight / (height ** 2)
3.      if bmi < 18.5:
4.          category = "Underweight"
5.      elif 18.5 <= bmi < 24.9:
6.          category = "Normal weight"
7.      elif 25 <= bmi < 29.9:
8.          category = "Overweight"
9.      else:
10.         category = "Obesity"
11.     return bmi, category

12. weight = float(input("Enter weight in kg: "))
13. height = float(input("Enter height in meters: "))
14. bmi, category = calculate_bmi(weight, height)
15. print(f"Your BMI is {bmi:.2f}, Category: {category}")
```

Project Code Explanation Table

Line	Code Section	Description
1	`def calculate_bmi(weight, height):`	Defines a function to compute BMI.
2	`bmi = weight / (height ** 2)`	Applies the BMI formula.
3-10	Conditional checks	Determines BMI category based on ranges.
11	`return bmi, category`	Returns BMI value and category.
12-13	Get user input	Takes weight and height input from user.
14	Call function	Computes BMI using user inputs.
15	Print result	Displays BMI value and classification.

Expected Results

- The program asks the user to enter weight and height.
- It calculates the BMI using the formula.
- It classifies the BMI into a health category.
- It prints the BMI value and category.

Hands-On Exercise Try improving the BMI Calculator with these additional features:

1. **Allow users to input height in centimeters and convert it to meters.**
2. **Enhance the program to accept weight in pounds and convert to kilograms.**
3. **Create a GUI version using Tkinter for interactive input.**
4. **Provide health advice based on BMI category.**
5. **Save BMI history for multiple entries and display previous calculations.**

Conclusion This BMI Calculator project introduces Python concepts such as mathematical operations, conditionals, and user input handling. By expanding this project, developers can create more advanced health and fitness tracking applications.

Chapter 60: Count the Number of Digits in a Number

Overview A program to count the number of digits in a number helps in understanding loops, mathematical operations, and string manipulations in Python. This project can be useful in various number-processing applications such as validating user input, formatting numerical data, and working with large integers.

This chapter covers the step-by-step implementation of counting digits in a number, handling user input, and using different approaches to achieve the solution.

Key Concepts of Counting Digits in Python

- **Mathematical Approach:**
    - Use a loop to divide the number by 10 repeatedly until it reaches 0.
- **String Conversion Approach:**
    - Convert the number to a string and count the characters.
- **Using Logarithm:**
    - Apply logarithm base 10 to determine the number of digits.

Example Digit Count Calculations

Input Number	Number of Digits
12345	5
987654321	9
1000	4
7	1

Basic Rules for Counting Digits in Python

Rule	Correct Example
Convert number to string and use `len()`	`len(str(num))`
Use a loop to divide the number	`while num > 0: num //= 10`
Use logarithm for efficiency	`math.floor(math.log10(num)) + 1`

Syntax Table

SL	Concept	Syntax/Example	Description
1	Get user input	`num = int(input("Enter a number: "))`	Takes user input as an integer.
2	Convert number to string	`len(str(num))`	Counts digits using string conversion.

3	Loop to count digits	`while num > 0:`
		`count += 1; num`
		`//= 10`
			Uses a loop to repeatedly divide by 10.

4	Logarithmic method	`math.floor(math.log10(num)) + 1`	Computes digits efficiently using logarithm.
5	Print result	`print("Number of digits:", count)`	Displays the number of digits.

Real-Life Project: Count the Number of Digits in a Number

Project Code:

```
1.   import math

2.   def count_digits_math(num):
3.       return len(str(num))

4.   def count_digits_loop(num):
5.       count = 0
6.       while num > 0:
7.           count += 1
8.           num //= 10
9.       return count

10.  def count_digits_log(num):
11.      if num == 0:
12.          return 1
13.      return math.floor(math.log10(num)) + 1

14.  num = int(input("Enter a number: "))
15.  print("Using string conversion:",
```

```
count_digits_math(num))
16. print("Using loop method:", count_digits_loop(num))
17. print("Using logarithm method:",
count_digits_log(num))
```

Project Code Explanation Table

Line	Code Section	Description
1	`import math`	Imports the math module for logarithm calculations.
2-3	`def count_digits_math(num):`	Uses string conversion to count digits.
4-9	`def count_digits_loop(num):`	Uses a loop to count digits by dividing the number.
10-13	`def count_digits_log(num):`	Uses logarithm to compute the number of digits.
14	`num = int(input("Enter a number: "))`	Takes user input as an integer.
15	`print("Using string conversion:", count_digits_math(num))`	Displays digit count using string method.
16	`print("Using loop method:", count_digits_loop(num))`	Displays digit count using loop method.
17	`print("Using logarithm method:", count_digits_log(num))`	Displays digit count using logarithmic method.

Expected Results

- The program asks the user to enter a number.
- It calculates and prints the number of digits using different methods.
- If the user enters 0, it correctly returns 1 digit.

Hands-On Exercise Try improving the Digit Counter with these additional features:

1. **Modify the program to count digits in negative numbers.**
2. **Allow users to count digits in decimal numbers by ignoring the decimal point.**

3. Create a GUI version using `Tkinter` for interactive input.
4. Allow users to count digits in a list of numbers instead of just one.
5. Implement performance comparisons between methods for large numbers.

Conclusion This Digit Counter project introduces Python concepts such as loops, conditionals, mathematical operations, and string manipulations. By expanding this project, developers can explore more efficient ways to process numbers in real-world applications.

Chapter 61: Sum of All Elements in a List

Overview A program to calculate the sum of all elements in a list is a fundamental exercise in Python that helps understand loops, list operations, and built-in functions. Summing elements in a list is commonly used in data analysis, statistics, and financial applications.

This chapter covers the step-by-step implementation of summing elements in a list, handling user input, and using different approaches for efficiency.

Key Concepts of Summing Elements in a List Using Python

- **Using Loops to Sum Elements:**
  - Iterating through the list and adding each element to a total sum.
- **Using Built-in Functions:**
  - Using Python's sum() function for direct summation.
- **List Comprehensions for Optimization:**
  - Utilizing list comprehensions to filter and sum specific values.

Example List Summation

Input List	Sum of Elements
[1, 2, 3, 4, 5]	15
[10, 20, 30, 40]	100
[-5, 10, -15, 20]	10

Basic Rules for Summing Elements in a List Using Python

Rule	Correct Example
Use a loop to iterate through the list	`for num in numbers: total += num`
Use Python's built-in sum() function	`total = sum(numbers)`
Handle empty lists correctly	`if not numbers: return 0`

Syntax Table

SL	Concept	Syntax/Example	Description
1	Get user input	`numbers = list(map(int, input().split()))`	Takes a list of numbers as input.
2	Use a loop to sum elements	`for num in numbers:` `total += num`	Iterates through the list and sums elements.
3	Use the sum() function	`total = sum(numbers)`	Efficiently sums all elements.
4	Handle empty lists	`if len(numbers) == 0: return 0`	Returns 0 for an empty list.
5	Print the result	`print("Sum:", total)`	Displays the total sum.

Real-Life Project: Sum of All Elements in a List

Project Code:

```
1.  def sum_elements_loop(numbers):
2.      total = 0
3.      for num in numbers:
4.          total += num
5.      return total

6.  def sum_elements_builtin(numbers):
7.      return sum(numbers)

8.  numbers = list(map(int, input("Enter numbers
separated by space: ").split()))
9.  print("Using loop method:",
sum_elements_loop(numbers))
10. print("Using built-in function:",
sum_elements_builtin(numbers))
```

Project Code Explanation Table

Line	Code Section	Description
1-5	```def sum_elements_loop(numbers):```	Uses a loop to sum elements in a list.
6-7	```def sum_elements_builtin(numbers):```	Uses Python's built-in sum() function to compute the sum.
8	```numbers = list(map(int, input().split()))```	Takes user input and converts it into a list of integers.
9	```print("Using loop method:", sum_elements_loop(numbers))```	Displays the sum using a loop.
10	```print("Using built-in function:", sum_elements_builtin(numbers))```	Displays the sum using the sum() function.

Expected Results

- The program asks the user to enter a list of numbers.
- It calculates and prints the sum of all numbers using both a loop and the built-in sum() function.
- If the user enters an empty list, it returns 0.

Hands-On Exercise Try improving the Sum of All Elements in a List program with these additional features:

1. **Modify the program to calculate the sum of only even or odd numbers.**
2. **Allow users to enter numbers from a file instead of manual input.**
3. **Create a GUI version using Tkinter for interactive input.**
4. **Handle floating-point numbers instead of just integers.**

Conclusion This Sum of All Elements in a List project introduces Python concepts such as loops, conditionals, and list operations. By expanding this project, developers can explore more advanced list-processing techniques and optimizations.

Chapter 62: Print Prime Numbers from 1 to N

Overview A program to print all prime numbers from 1 to N is a fundamental exercise in Python that helps in understanding loops, conditional statements, and number theory. A prime number is a natural number greater than 1 that has only two divisors: 1 and itself.

This chapter covers the step-by-step implementation of finding prime numbers within a given range, handling user input, and optimizing performance.

Key Concepts of Printing Prime Numbers Using Python

- **Definition of Prime Numbers:**
    - A number is prime if it is only divisible by 1 and itself.
- **Using Loops and Conditional Statements:**
    - Iterating through numbers and checking divisibility.
- **Optimization Techniques:**
    - Checking divisibility up to the square root of the number.
    - Skipping even numbers after 2 to reduce iterations.

Example Prime Number Calculations

Input N	Prime Numbers
10	2, 3, 5, 7
20	2, 3, 5, 7, 11, 13, 17, 19
30	2, 3, 5, 7, 11, 13, 17, 19, 23, 29

Basic Rules for Finding Prime Numbers in Python

Rule	Correct Example
A number is prime if it is not divisible by any number from 2 to √N	`if num % i == 0:`
The number 2 is the only even prime number	`if num == 2:` `return True`
Skip checking even numbers after 2 to improve efficiency	`for i in range(3,` `sqrt(n) + 1, 2):`

Syntax Table

SL	Concept	Syntax/Example	Description
1	Get user input	`N = int(input("Enter a number: "))`	Takes an integer input from the user.
2	Loop through numbers	`for num in range(2, N + 1):`	Iterates through numbers up to N.
3	Check if a number is prime	`if num % i == 0:`	Determines if a number is divisible by another.
4	Use square root optimization	`for i in range(2, int(math.sqrt(num)) + 1):`	Improves efficiency by reducing iterations.
5	Print prime numbers	`print(prime_numbers )`	Displays the list of prime numbers.

Real-Life Project: Print Prime Numbers from 1 to N

Project Code:

```
1.   import math

2.   def is_prime(num):
3.       if num < 2:
4.           return False
5.       for i in range(2, int(math.sqrt(num)) + 1):
6.           if num % i == 0:
7.               return False
8.       return True

9.   def prime_numbers_upto_n(N):
10.      primes = [num for num in range(2, N + 1) if
is_prime(num)]
11.      return primes

12. N = int(input("Enter the value of N: "))
13. print("Prime numbers up to", N, ":",
prime_numbers_upto_n(N))
```

Project Code Explanation Table

Line	Code Section	Description
1	`import math`	Imports the math module for square root calculation.
2-8	`def is_prime(num):`	Defines a function to check if a number is prime.
3-4	`if num < 2: return False`	Returns False for numbers less than 2.
5-7	`for i in range(2, int(math.sqrt(num)) + 1):`	Checks divisibility up to the square root of the number.
8	`return True`	Returns True if no divisor is found.
9-11	`def prime_numbers_upto_n(N):`	Defines a function to generate prime numbers up to N.
10	`primes = [num for num in range(2, N + 1) if is_prime(num)]`	Uses list comprehension to filter prime numbers.
12	`N = int(input("Enter the value of N: "))`	Takes user input for the range limit.
13	`print("Prime numbers up to", N, ":", prime_numbers_upto_n(N))`	Prints the list of prime numbers.

Expected Results

- The program asks the user to enter an integer value for N.
- It calculates and prints all prime numbers from 1 to N.
- The program efficiently finds primes using square root optimization.

Hands-On Exercise Try improving the Prime Number Finder with these additional features:

1. **Modify the program to find the first N prime numbers instead of a range.**
2. **Implement an optimized version using the Sieve of Eratosthenes algorithm.**
3. **Create a GUI version using `Tkinter` for interactive input.**
4. **Allow users to check if a single number is prime.**

Chapter 63: Convert Kilometers to Miles

Overview A Kilometers to Miles Converter is a simple program that converts a distance given in kilometers to miles. This project helps in understanding mathematical calculations, user input handling, and formatting output in Python.

This chapter covers the step-by-step implementation of converting kilometers to miles, handling user input, and using different methods for accurate results.

Key Concepts of Converting Kilometers to Miles in Python

- **Mathematical Formula for Conversion:**
  - $Miles = Kilometers \times 0.621371$
- **User Input Handling:**
  - Accepting the distance in kilometers from the user.
  - Converting the input to a float for precise calculations.
- **Formatting Output:**
  - Rounding off the result for better readability.

Example Kilometers to Miles Conversion

Kilometers	Miles
1	0.62
5	3.11
10	6.21
42.195	26.22 (Marathon distance)

Basic Rules for Conversion in Python

Rule	Correct Example
Multiply kilometers by 0.621371	`miles = km * 0.621371`
Use `float` for precise input handling	`km = float(input("Enter kilometers: "))`
Format the output for readability	`print(f"{miles:.2f}")`

Syntax Table

SL	Concept	Syntax/Example	Description
1	Get user input	`km = float(input("Enter kilometers: "))`	Takes distance input from user.
2	Convert kilometers to miles	`miles = km * 0.621371`	Applies the conversion formula.
3	Print the result	`print(f"Miles: {miles:.2f}")`	Displays the converted value with two decimal places.

Real-Life Project: Convert Kilometers to Miles

Project Code:

```
1.  def km_to_miles(km):
2.      return km * 0.621371

3.  km = float(input("Enter distance in kilometers: "))
4.  miles = km_to_miles(km)
5.  print(f"{km} kilometers is equal to {miles:.2f} miles.")
```

Project Code Explanation Table

Line	Code Section	Description
1-2	`def km_to_miles(km):`	Defines a function to convert kilometers to miles.
3	`km = float(input("Enter distance in kilometers: "))`	Takes user input and converts it to float.
4	`miles = km_to_miles(km)`	Calls the function to perform the conversion.
5	`print(f"{km} kilometers is equal to {miles:.2f} miles.")`	Prints the result with formatted output.

Expected Results

- The program asks the user to enter a distance in kilometers.
- It calculates and prints the equivalent distance in miles.
- The output is formatted to two decimal places for readability.

Hands-On Exercise Try improving the Kilometers to Miles Converter with these additional features:

1. **Allow users to convert miles to kilometers as well.**
2. **Create a GUI version using `Tkinter` for interactive input.**
3. **Handle invalid inputs gracefully using exception handling.**
4. **Allow users to input multiple values at once and display all conversions.**
5. **Save conversion history to a file for later reference.**

Conclusion This Kilometers to Miles Converter project introduces Python concepts such as mathematical calculations, user input handling, and output formatting. By expanding this project, developers can create more advanced unit conversion tools for various applications.

Chapter 64: Generate Multiplication Table of a Given Number

Overview A program to generate a multiplication table of a given number helps in understanding loops, mathematical operations, and formatted output in Python. Multiplication tables are widely used in mathematics and education for quick calculations.

This chapter covers the step-by-step implementation of generating a multiplication table, handling user input, and formatting output for readability.

Key Concepts of Multiplication Table Generation in Python

- **Using Loops to Generate Table:**
  - Iterating through a range to multiply the given number.
- **Formatted Output:**
  - Aligning the output neatly using f-strings or `format()`.
- **Customizable Range:**
  - Allowing users to define the range of the table.

Example Multiplication Table

Number	Multiplier	Result
5	1	5
5	2	10
5	3	15
5	...	...
5	10	50

Basic Rules for Generating Multiplication Table in Python

Rule	Correct Example
Use a loop to iterate through multipliers	`for i in range(1, 11):`
Multiply the given number by the iterator	`result = num * i`
Print output in formatted style	`print(f"{num} x {i} = {result}")`

Syntax Table

SL	Concept	Syntax/Example	Description
1	Get user input	`num = int(input("Enter a number: "))`	Takes the base number for multiplication.
2	Loop through multipliers	`for i in range(1, 11):`	Iterates from 1 to 10.
3	Perform multiplication	`result = num * i`	Computes the multiplication result.
4	Print formatted output	`print(f"{num} x {i} = {result}")`	Displays the result clearly.

Real-Life Project: Multiplication Table Generator

Project Code:

```
1.   def multiplication_table(num, limit=10):
2.       for i in range(1, limit + 1):
3.           print(f"{num} x {i} = {num * i}")

4.   num = int(input("Enter a number: "))
5.   limit = int(input("Enter the range of the table: "))
6.   multiplication_table(num, limit)
```

Project Code Explanation Table

Line	Code Section	Description
1	`def multiplication_table(num, limit=10):`	Defines a function to generate a multiplication table.
2-3	`for i in range(1, limit + 1):`	Loops through the defined range and prints the result.
4	`num = int(input("Enter a number: "))`	Takes user input for the base number.
5	`limit = int(input("Enter the range of the table: "))`	Allows the user to set a custom range.

6	multiplication_table(num, limit)	Calls the function to print the multiplication table.

Expected Results

- The program asks the user to enter a number and a range.
- It prints the multiplication table up to the specified range.
- The output is formatted neatly for readability.

Hands-On Exercise Try improving the Multiplication Table Generator with these additional features:

1. **Allow users to generate tables for multiple numbers in one run.**
2. **Create a GUI version using Tkinter for interactive input.**
3. **Save the generated table to a file for later reference.**
4. **Enhance the program to format output in a table-like structure.**
5. **Implement a feature to generate tables in reverse order.**

Conclusion This Multiplication Table Generator project introduces Python concepts such as loops, mathematical operations, and formatted output. By expanding this project, developers can create more interactive and user-friendly learning tools for educational purposes.

Chapter 65: Count Consonants in a String

Overview A program to count the number of consonants in a string is a fundamental exercise in Python that helps in understanding string manipulation, loops, conditionals, and character filtering. This project is useful in text analysis and natural language processing (NLP) applications. This chapter covers the step-by-step implementation of counting consonants in a given string, handling user input, and using different approaches for efficiency.

Key Concepts of Counting Consonants in Python

- **Definition of Consonants:**
    - A consonant is any letter in the English alphabet that is not a vowel (a, e, i, o, u).
- **Using Loops and Conditionals:**
    - Iterating through each character and checking if it is a consonant.
- **Using String Methods:**
    - Using built-in functions like `isalpha()` to filter alphabetic characters.

Example Consonant Count Calculations

Input String	Consonant Count
"Python Programming"	11
"Hello, World!"	7
"Data Science"	7

Basic Rules for Counting Consonants in Python

Rule	Correct Example
Convert string to lowercase	`text.lower()`
Check if a character is alphabetic	`char.isalpha()`
Exclude vowels from the count	`if char not in "aeiou":`

Syntax Table

SL	Concept	Syntax/Example	Description
1	Get user input	`text = input("Enter a string: ")`	Takes string input from user.
2	Convert text to lowercase	`text.lower()`	Ensures uniform character comparison.
3	Iterate through characters	`for char in text:`	Loops through each character in the string.
4	Check if character is a consonant	`if char.isalpha() and char not in "aeiou":`	Filters out vowels and non-alphabetic characters.
5	Count consonants	`consonant_count += 1`	Increments count when a consonant is found.

Real-Life Project: Count Consonants in a String

Project Code:

```
1.  def count_consonants(text):
2.      consonants = "bcdfghjklmnpqrstvwxyz"
3.      count = 0
4.      text = text.lower()
5.      for char in text:
6.          if char in consonants:
7.              count += 1
8.      return count

9.  text = input("Enter a string: ")
10. print("Number of consonants:",
count_consonants(text))
```

Project Code Explanation Table

Line	Code Section	Description
1	`def count_consonants(text):`	Defines a function to count consonants.
2	`consonants = "bcdfghjklmnpqrstvwxyz"`	Defines a string of consonants for comparison.
3	`count = 0`	Initializes the counter for consonants.
4	`text = text.lower()`	Converts text to lowercase for uniform comparison.
5-7	`for char in text:`	Iterates through each character and checks if it is a consonant.
8	`return count`	Returns the total number of consonants.
9	`text = input("Enter a string: ")`	Takes user input.
10	`print("Number of consonants:", count_consonants(text))`	Calls the function and prints the result.

Expected Results

- The program asks the user to enter a string.
- It processes the string and counts the number of consonants.
- It prints the total count of consonants found in the string.

Hands-On Exercise Try improving the Consonant Counter with these additional features:

1. Allow the program to count vowels and consonants separately.
2. Create a GUI version using Tkinter for interactive input.
3. Modify the program to ignore special characters and numbers.
4. Enable case-insensitive consonant counting.
5. Allow batch processing of multiple strings at once.

Chapter 66: Check if a Word is a Palindrome

Overview A Palindrome Checker is a program that determines whether a given word reads the same forward and backward. Palindromes are widely used in linguistics, mathematics, and computer science applications such as DNA sequencing and data structures.

This chapter covers the step-by-step implementation of checking if a word is a palindrome, handling user input, and using different approaches for efficiency.

Key Concepts of Palindrome Checking in Python

- **Definition of a Palindrome:**
  - A word is a palindrome if it remains the same when reversed (e.g., "madam", "racecar").
- **Using String Slicing:**
  - Reversing a string using [::-1].
- **Using Loops and Conditionals:**
  - Iterating through characters to compare them.

Example Palindrome Checks

Input Word	Palindrome?
"radar"	Yes
"hello"	No
"racecar"	Yes
"Python"	No

Basic Rules for Palindrome Checking in Python

Rule	Correct Example
Convert the word to lowercase	`word.lower()`
Reverse the word using slicing	`word[::-1]`
Compare original and reversed word	`if word == word[::-1]:`

Syntax Table

SL	Concept	Syntax/Example	Description
1	Get user input	`word = input("Enter a word: ")`	Takes user input as a string.

2	Convert to lowercase	`word.lower()`	Ensures case insensitivity.
3	Reverse the string	`word[::-1]`	Reverses the input string.
4	Compare original and reversed word	`if word == word[::-1]:`	Checks if the word is a palindrome.
5	Print result	`print("It is a palindrome.")`	Displays the output.

Real-Life Project: Palindrome Checker

Project Code:

```
1.  def is_palindrome(word):
2.      word = word.lower()
3.      return word == word[::-1]

4.  word = input("Enter a word: ")
5.  if is_palindrome(word):
6.      print(f"'{word}' is a palindrome.")
7.  else:
8.      print(f"'{word}' is NOT a palindrome.")
```

Project Code Explanation Table

Line	Code Section	Description
1	`def is_palindrome(word):`	Defines a function to check if a word is a palindrome.
2	`word = word.lower()`	Converts the word to lowercase for case insensitivity.
3	`return word == word[::-1]`	Compares the original and reversed word.
4	`word = input("Enter a word: ")`	Takes user input.
5-8	`if is_palindrome(word):`	Calls the function and prints whether the word is a palindrome.

Expected Results

- The program asks the user to enter a word.
- It processes the word and checks if it is a palindrome.
- It prints a message indicating whether the word is a palindrome.

Hands-On Exercise Try improving the Palindrome Checker with these additional features:

1. **Allow users to check full sentences for palindromes (ignoring spaces and punctuation).**
2. **Create a GUI version using Tkinter for interactive input.**
3. **Modify the program to check if a number is a palindrome.**
4. **Enable case-insensitive and whitespace-agnostic palindrome checking.**
5. **Allow batch processing of multiple words at once.**

Conclusion This Palindrome Checker project introduces Python concepts such as string manipulation, slicing, and conditionals. By expanding this project, developers can explore more advanced text-processing applications in language processing and data validation.

Chapter 67: Convert Time to Seconds

Overview A Time to Seconds Converter is a simple program that converts a given time (hours, minutes, and seconds) into total seconds. This project helps in understanding mathematical calculations, user input handling, and time-related operations in Python.

This chapter covers the step-by-step implementation of converting time to seconds, handling user input, and formatting output for better readability.

Key Concepts of Time Conversion in Python

- **Mathematical Formula for Conversion:**
  - $TotalSeconds = (Hours \times 3600) + (Minutes \times 60) + Seconds$
- **User Input Handling:**
  - Accepting time in hours, minutes, and seconds from the user.
  - Converting inputs to integers for calculations.
- **Formatting Output:**
  - Displaying the total seconds in a user-friendly manner.

Example Time Conversions

Hours	Minutes	Seconds	Total Seconds
1	0	0	3600
0	30	0	1800
2	15	10	8110
0	0	45	45

Basic Rules for Time Conversion in Python

Rule	Correct Example
Multiply hours by 3600	`seconds = hours * 3600`
Multiply minutes by 60	`seconds += minutes * 60`
Sum up all seconds	`total_seconds = hours * 3600 + minutes * 60 + seconds`

Syntax Table

S L	Concept	Syntax/Example	Description
1	Get user input	`hours = int(input("Enter hours: "))`	Takes input for hours.
2	Convert minutes to seconds	`seconds = minutes * 60`	Converts minutes into seconds.
3	Convert hours to seconds	`seconds = hours * 3600`	Converts hours into seconds.
4	Sum all values	`total_seconds = hours * 3600 + minutes * 60 + seconds`	Computes the final total.
5	Print formatted output	`print("Total seconds:", total_seconds)`	Displays the result.

Real-Life Project: Convert Time to Seconds

Project Code:

```
1.  def time_to_seconds(hours, minutes, seconds):
2.      total_seconds = (hours * 3600) + (minutes * 60)
+ seconds
3.      return total_seconds

4.  hours = int(input("Enter hours: "))
5.  minutes = int(input("Enter minutes: "))
6.  seconds = int(input("Enter seconds: "))
7.  total = time_to_seconds(hours, minutes, seconds)
8.  print(f"Total time in seconds: {total}")
```

Project Code Explanation Table

Line	Code Section	Description
1-3	`def time_to_seconds(hours, minutes, seconds):`	Defines a function to convert time to seconds.

2	`total_seconds = (hours * 3600) + (minutes * 60) + seconds`	Computes the total seconds.
4-6	`hours = int(input("Enter hours: "))`	Takes user input for hours, minutes, and seconds.
7	`total = time_to_seconds(hours, minutes, seconds)`	Calls the function to perform the conversion.
8	`print(f"Total time in seconds: {total}")`	Prints the total seconds in a formatted output.

Expected Results

- The program asks the user to enter time in hours, minutes, and seconds.
- It calculates and prints the equivalent time in total seconds.
- The output is formatted for readability.

Hands-On Exercise Try improving the Time to Seconds Converter with these additional features:

1. Allow users to input time in different formats (e.g., HH:MM:SS).
2. Create a GUI version using `Tkinter` for interactive input.
3. Handle invalid inputs gracefully using exception handling.
4. Allow users to convert seconds back into hours, minutes, and seconds.
5. Save conversion history to a file for later reference.

Conclusion This Time to Seconds Converter project introduces Python concepts such as mathematical operations, user input handling, and formatted output. By expanding this project, developers can create more advanced time conversion tools for various applications.

Chapter 68: Remove Duplicate Elements from a List

Overview A program to remove duplicate elements from a list is a fundamental exercise in Python that helps in understanding data structures, loops, and built-in functions. Removing duplicates is useful in data processing, filtering unique records, and improving efficiency in various applications.

This chapter covers the step-by-step implementation of removing duplicate elements from a list, handling user input, and using different approaches for efficiency.

Key Concepts of Removing Duplicates in Python

- **Using Sets to Remove Duplicates:**
    - A set automatically removes duplicate elements.
- **Using Loops and Conditionals:**
    - Iterating through the list and adding unique elements to a new list.
- **Using List Comprehension for Optimization:**
    - Using `dict.fromkeys()` to preserve order and remove duplicates.

Example Duplicate Removal

Input List	Unique Elements
[1, 2, 2, 3, 4, 4, 5]	[1, 2, 3, 4, 5]
[10, 20, 30, 10, 40, 50, 20]	[10, 20, 30, 40, 50]
["apple", "banana", "apple", "orange"]	["apple", "banana", "orange"]

Basic Rules for Removing Duplicates in Python

Rule	Correct Example
Use sets to remove duplicates	`unique_list = list(set(numbers))`
Use loops to filter unique elements	`if num not in unique_list: unique_list.append(num)`
Use `dict.fromkeys()` to preserve order	`unique_list = list(dict.fromkeys(numbers))`

Syntax Table

S L	Concept	Syntax/Example	Description
1	Get user input	`numbers = list(map(int, input().split()))`	Takes a list of numbers as input.
2	Use a set to remove duplicates	`unique_list = list(set(numbers))`	Removes duplicates but does not preserve order.
3	Use a loop to filter unique elements	`for num in numbers: if num not in unique_list: unique_list.append(num)`	Removes duplicates while preserving order.
4	Use `dict.fromkeys()` for ordered removal	`unique_list = list(dict.fromkeys(numbers))`	Preserves order while removing duplicates.
5	Print the result	`print("Unique list:", unique_list)`	Displays the list without duplicates.

Real-Life Project: Remove Duplicate Elements from a List

Project Code:

```
1.  def remove_duplicates_set(numbers):
2.      return list(set(numbers))

3.  def remove_duplicates_loop(numbers):
4.      unique_list = []
5.      for num in numbers:
6.          if num not in unique_list:
7.              unique_list.append(num)
8.      return unique_list

9.  def remove_duplicates_dict(numbers):
10.     return list(dict.fromkeys(numbers))

11. numbers = list(map(int, input("Enter numbers
```

```
separated by space: ").split()))
12. print("Using set method:",
remove_duplicates_set(numbers))
13. print("Using loop method:",
remove_duplicates_loop(numbers))
14. print("Using dictionary method:",
remove_duplicates_dict(numbers))
```

Project Code Explanation Table

Line	Code Section	Description
1-2	`def remove_duplicates_set(numbers):`	Uses a set to remove duplicates quickly.
3-8	`def remove_duplicates_loop(numbers):`	Uses a loop to filter unique elements manually.
9-10	`def remove_duplicates_dict(numbers):`	Uses `dict.fromkeys()` to remove duplicates while preserving order.
11	`numbers = list(map(int, input().split()))`	Takes user input as a list of integers.
12	`print("Using set method:", remove_duplicates_set(numbers))`	Displays unique elements using the set method.
13	`print("Using loop method:", remove_duplicates_loop(numbers))`	Displays unique elements using the loop method.
14	`print("Using dictionary method:", remove_duplicates_dict(numbers))`	Displays unique elements using the dictionary method.

Expected Results

- The program asks the user to enter a list of numbers.
- It removes duplicates using three different methods.
- It prints the unique elements in each method's output.

Hands-On Exercise Try improving the Duplicate Removal program with these additional features:

1. **Modify the program to remove duplicates from a list of words instead of numbers.**
2. **Create a GUI version using Tkinter for interactive input.**
3. **Allow users to choose which method they want to use for removing duplicates.**
4. **Enhance the program to handle mixed data types in the list.**
5. **Save the unique list to a file for later reference.**

Conclusion This Remove Duplicates project introduces Python concepts such as sets, loops, and dictionary operations. By expanding this project, developers can explore more advanced data processing techniques and optimizations.

Chapter 69: Find the Largest Element in a List

Overview A program to find the largest element in a list is a fundamental exercise in Python that helps in understanding loops, conditional statements, and built-in functions. This operation is widely used in data analysis, sorting, and performance optimization tasks.

This chapter covers the step-by-step implementation of finding the largest element in a list, handling user input, and using different approaches for efficiency.

Key Concepts of Finding the Largest Element in Python

- **Using Loops to Find the Maximum:**
  - Iterating through the list and keeping track of the largest element.
- **Using Built-in Functions:**
  - Utilizing Python's max() function for direct computation.
- **Handling Edge Cases:**
  - Handling empty lists and lists with negative numbers.

Example Largest Element Searches

Input List	Largest Element
[1, 5, 3, 9, 2]	9
[10, 20, 30, 40, 50]	50
[-5, -2, -9, -1, -7]	-1

Basic Rules for Finding the Largest Element in Python

Rule	Correct Example
Use max() function for quick computation	`largest = max(numbers)`
Use a loop to find the maximum manually	`if num > largest: largest = num`
Handle empty lists gracefully	`if not numbers:` `print("List is empty")`

Syntax Table

SL	Concept	Syntax/Example	Description
1	Get user input	`numbers = list(map(int, input().split()))`	Takes a list of numbers as input.
2	Use max() function	`largest = max(numbers)`	Finds the largest element quickly.

3	Loop through list to find maximum	`for num in numbers:`
		`if num > largest:`
		`largest = num`
			Finds the maximum manually.

4	Handle empty list	`if len(numbers) == 0: print("List is empty")`	Handles cases where the list has no elements.
5	Print the result	`print("Largest element:", largest)`	Displays the largest element.

Real-Life Project: Find the Largest Element in a List

Project Code:

```
1.  def find_largest_loop(numbers):
2.      if not numbers:
3.          return "List is empty"
4.      largest = numbers[0]
5.      for num in numbers:
6.          if num > largest:
7.              largest = num
8.      return largest

9.  def find_largest_builtin(numbers):
10.     return max(numbers) if numbers else "List is empty"

11. numbers = list(map(int, input("Enter numbers separated by space: ").split()))
12. print("Using loop method:", find_largest_loop(numbers))
13. print("Using built-in function:", find_largest_builtin(numbers))
```

Project Code Explanation Table

Line	Code Section	Description

1-8	`def`
	`find_largest_loop(numbers)`
	`:`
		Uses a loop to find the largest element manually.

2-3	`if not numbers:`	Checks if the list is empty.
4	`largest = numbers[0]`	Initializes the first element as the largest.
5-7	`for num in numbers:`	Iterates through the list to find the maximum.

9-10	`def`
	`find_largest_builtin(numbe`
	`rs):`
		Uses the max() function to find the largest element.

11	`numbers = list(map(int,` `input().split()))`	Takes user input as a list of integers.

12	`print("Using loop`
	`method:",`
	`find_largest_loop(numbers)`
	`)`
		Displays the largest element using the loop method.

13	`print("Using built-in`
	`function:",`
	`find_largest_builtin(numbe`
	`rs))`
		Displays the largest element using the built-in function.

Expected Results

- The program asks the user to enter a list of numbers.
- It calculates and prints the largest number using both the loop and built-in method.
- It handles cases where the list is empty by displaying an appropriate message.

Hands-On Exercise Try improving the Find Largest Element program with these additional features:

1. **Modify the program to find the smallest element in the list.**
2. **Create a GUI version using Tkinter for interactive input.**
3. **Handle mixed data types (integers and floats) in the list.**
4. **Allow users to find the largest number in multiple lists at once.**

Chapter 70: Check if a String is a Number

Overview A program to check if a given string is a number is a useful exercise in Python that helps in understanding string manipulations, type conversions, and exception handling. This operation is often used in form validation, user input handling, and data processing applications.

This chapter covers the step-by-step implementation of checking if a string is a number, handling different numeric formats, and using different methods for efficiency.

Key Concepts of Checking if a String is a Number in Python

- **Using `isdigit()` for Integer Check:**
  - The `isdigit()` method returns True if all characters in the string are digits.
- **Using `float()` for Numeric Check:**
  - Converting a string to `float` helps identify decimal numbers.
- **Handling Negative Numbers and Decimal Points:**
  - Checking if a string contains - or . appropriately.

Example String Number Checks

Input String	Is Number?
"123"	Yes
"45.67"	Yes
"-98.5"	Yes
"Hello123"	No
"12a34"	No

Basic Rules for Checking if a String is a Number in Python

Rule	Correct Example
Use `isdigit()` for integers only	`if text.isdigit():`
Use `float()` with `try-except` to check numbers	`try: float(text)`
Handle negative and decimal values	`if text.replace('.', '').replace('-', '').isdigit():`

Syntax Table

SL	Concept	Syntax/Example	Description
1	Get user input	`text = input("Enter a string: ")`	Takes a string input.
2	Check for integers	`text.isdigit()`	Returns True if all characters are digits.
3	Use `float()` conversion	`float(text)`	Converts text to float if possible.
4	Handle exceptions	`try: float(text) except ValueError:`	Catches errors for non-numeric values.
5	Print the result	`print("It is a number.")`	Displays the result.

Real-Life Project: Check if a String is a Number

Project Code:

```
1.  def is_number(text):
2.      try:
3.          float(text)
4.          return True
5.      except ValueError:
6.          return False

7.  text = input("Enter a string: ")
8.  if is_number(text):
9.      print(f"'{text}' is a number.")
10. else:
11.     print(f"'{text}' is NOT a number.")
```

Project Code Explanation Table

Line	Code Section	Description
1	`def is_number(text):`	Defines a function to check if a string is a number.
2-4	`try: float(text)`	Tries to convert the string to a float.
5-6	`except ValueError:`	Returns False if the conversion fails.

7	`text = input("Enter a string: ")`	Takes user input.
8-11	`if is_number(text):`	Calls the function and prints whether the string is a number.

Expected Results

- The program asks the user to enter a string.
- It processes the string and checks if it represents a valid number.
- It prints whether the input is a number or not.

Hands-On Exercise Try improving the String Number Checker with these additional features:

1. Allow checking for hexadecimal numbers (e.g., 0x1A3F).
2. Create a GUI version using `Tkinter` for interactive input.
3. Modify the program to check if the number is an integer or a float.
4. Enhance the program to handle scientific notation (e.g., 1.23e4).
5. Allow batch processing of multiple strings at once.

Conclusion This String Number Checker project introduces Python concepts such as string manipulation, type conversion, and exception handling. By expanding this project, developers can explore more advanced text validation and numeric processing applications.

Chapter 71: Python Quiz Game

Overview A Python Quiz Game is an interactive application where users answer multiple-choice or true/false questions. This project helps in understanding lists, dictionaries, loops, conditionals, and user input handling in Python.

This chapter covers the step-by-step implementation of a quiz game, storing questions and answers, scoring, and enhancing user interaction.

Key Concepts of Python Quiz Game in Python

- **Using Dictionaries to Store Questions and Answers:**
    - A dictionary can be used to store questions as keys and correct answers as values.
- **Using Loops for Repeated Questions:**
    - Iterating through questions to present them to the user.
- **Scoring System:**
    - Keeping track of correct and incorrect answers to calculate a final score.

Example Quiz Structure

Question	Options	Correct Answer
What is the output of `print(2 * 3)`?	a) 6, b) 8, c) 5, d) 3	a
What data type is `True` in Python?	a) int, b) bool, c) string, d) float	b
Which keyword is used to define a function in Python?	a) define, b) def, c) func, d) function	b

Basic Rules for Python Quiz Game in Python

Rule	Correct Example
Use dictionaries to store questions and answers	`quiz = {"Question": "Answer"}`
Use a loop to iterate through questions	`for question in quiz:`
Compare user input with the correct answer	`if user_answer == correct_answer:`
Keep track of the score	`score += 1`

Syntax Table

SL	Concept	Syntax/Example	Description
1	Define a dictionary for questions	`quiz = {"What is 2+2?": "4"}`	Stores quiz questions and answers.
2	Loop through questions	`for question in quiz:`	Iterates through the quiz dictionary.
3	Get user input	`answer = input(question + " ")`	Takes user input as an answer.
4	Compare user answer with correct answer	`if answer == quiz[question]:`	Checks correctness.
5	Keep track of score	`score += 1`	Increments score for correct answers.

Real-Life Project: Python Quiz Game

Project Code:

```
1.  def quiz_game():
2.      questions = {
3.          "What is the capital of France?": "a",
4.          "Which language is used for web development?\n a) Python\n b) JavaScript\n c) Java\n d) C++\n": "b",
5.          "What does CPU stand for?\n a) Central Processing Unit\n b) Computer Personal Unit\n c) Central Personal Unit\n d) Computer Processing Unit\n": "a",
6.      }
7.      score = 0
8.      for question, correct_answer in questions.items():
9.          user_answer = input(question + "\nYour answer: ").lower()
10.         if user_answer == correct_answer:
11.             print("Correct!\n")
12.             score += 1
13.         else:
```

```
14.              print("Wrong answer!\n")
15.          print(f"You scored {score}/{len(questions)}")

16. quiz_game()
```

Project Code Explanation Table

Line	Code Section	Description
1	def quiz_game():	Defines the function for the quiz game.
2-6	questions = {...}	Creates a dictionary with quiz questions and correct answers.
7	score = 0	Initializes the score variable.
8	for question, correct_answer in questions.items():	Iterates through each question.
9	user_answer = input(question + "\nYour answer: ").lower()	Gets user input and converts it to lowercase.
10-12	if user_answer == correct_answer:	Checks if the answer is correct and updates the score.
13-14	else:	Prints "Wrong answer!" if the response is incorrect.
15	print(f"You scored {score}/{len(questions)}")	Displays the final score.
16	quiz_game()	Calls the quiz function to start the game.

Expected Results

- The program presents the user with a series of multiple-choice questions.
- The user enters an answer, and the program provides feedback on correctness.
- At the end, the program displays the final score.

Hands-On Exercise Try improving the Python Quiz Game with these additional features:

1. **Add more questions with different difficulty levels.**
2. **Create a GUI version using `Tkinter` for an interactive experience.**
3. **Enhance the program to keep track of high scores.**
4. **Implement a timer to limit the time for each question.**
5. **Allow users to select quiz categories before starting.**

Conclusion This Python Quiz Game project introduces Python concepts such as loops, dictionaries, user input handling, and scoring logic. By expanding this project, developers can create a more interactive and engaging educational tool.

Chapter 72: Palindrome Number Finder

Overview A Palindrome Number Finder is a program that determines whether a given number reads the same forward and backward. Palindromes are commonly used in mathematical computations and problem-solving scenarios.

This chapter covers the step-by-step implementation of checking if a number is a palindrome, handling user input, and using different approaches for efficiency.

Key Concepts of Palindrome Number Finder in Python

- **Definition of a Palindrome Number:**
  - A number is a palindrome if it remains the same when reversed (e.g., 121, 454, 9889).
- **Using String Conversion:**
  - Convert the number to a string and compare it with its reversed version.
- **Using Mathematical Approach:**
  - Reverse the number mathematically without converting it to a string.

Example Palindrome Number Checks

Input Number	Palindrome?
121	Yes
123	No
9889	Yes
45654	Yes

Basic Rules for Palindrome Number Finder in Python

Rule	Correct Example
Convert the number to a string and reverse it	`str(num)[::-1]`
Compare original and reversed number	`if str(num) == str(num)[::-1]:`
Use mathematical method to reverse number	`while num > 0:`

Syntax Table

SL	Concept	Syntax/Example	Description
1	Get user input	`num = int(input("Enter a number: "))`	Takes user input as an integer.
2	Convert to string	`str(num)`	Converts the number to a string for comparison.
3	Reverse the string	`str(num)[::-1]`	Reverses the number as a string.
4	Compare original and reversed number	`if str(num) == str(num)[::-1]:`	Checks if the number is a palindrome.
5	Print result	`print("It is a palindrome.")`	Displays the output.

Real-Life Project: Palindrome Number Finder

Project Code:

```
1.  def is_palindrome_number(num):
2.      return str(num) == str(num)[::-1]

3.  num = int(input("Enter a number: "))
4.  if is_palindrome_number(num):
5.      print(f"{num} is a palindrome number.")
6.  else:
7.      print(f"{num} is NOT a palindrome number.")
```

Project Code Explanation Table

Line	Code Section	Description
1	`def is_palindrome_number(num):`	Defines a function to check if a number is a palindrome.
2	`return str(num) == str(num)[::-1]`	Compares the original and reversed number.

3	`num = int(input("Enter a number: "))`	Takes user input as an integer.
4-7	`if is_palindrome_nu mber(num):`	Calls the function and prints whether the number is a palindrome.

Expected Results

- The program asks the user to enter a number.
- It processes the number and checks if it is a palindrome.
- It prints a message indicating whether the number is a palindrome.

Hands-On Exercise Try improving the Palindrome Number Finder with these additional features:

1. **Use a mathematical approach without converting the number to a string.**
2. **Create a GUI version using Tkinter for interactive input.**
3. **Modify the program to check for palindrome numbers within a given range.**
4. **Enable case-insensitive handling for numbers with leading zeros.**
5. **Allow batch processing of multiple numbers at once.**

Conclusion This Palindrome Number Finder project introduces Python concepts such as string manipulation, loops, and conditionals. By expanding this project, developers can explore more advanced number-processing applications in mathematical computations and data validation.

Chapter 73: Create a Simple Quiz App

Overview A Simple Quiz App is an interactive application where users answer multiple-choice questions. This project helps in understanding lists, dictionaries, loops, conditionals, and user input handling in Python. This chapter covers the step-by-step implementation of a quiz app, storing questions and answers, scoring, and enhancing user interaction.

Key Concepts of a Simple Quiz App in Python

- **Using Dictionaries to Store Questions and Answers:**
    - A dictionary can store questions as keys and correct answers as values.
- **Using Loops for Repeated Questions:**
    - Iterating through questions to present them to the user.
- **Scoring System:**
    - Keeping track of correct and incorrect answers to calculate a final score.

Example Quiz Structure

Question	Options	Correct Answer
What is the output of `print(2 * 3)`?	a) 6, b) 8, c) 5, d) 3	a
What data type is `True` in Python?	a) int, b) bool, c) string, d) float	b
Which keyword is used to define a function in Python?	a) define, b) def, c) func, d) function	b

Basic Rules for a Quiz App in Python

Rule	Correct Example
Use dictionaries to store questions and answers	`quiz = {"Question": "Answer"}`
Use a loop to iterate through questions	`for question in quiz:`
Compare user input with the correct answer	`if user_answer == correct_answer:`
Keep track of the score	`score += 1`

Syntax Table

SL	Concept	Syntax/Example	Description
1	Define a dictionary for questions	`quiz = {"What is 2+2?": "4"}`	Stores quiz questions and answers.
2	Loop through questions	`for question in quiz:`	Iterates through the quiz dictionary.
3	Get user input	`answer = input(question + " ")`	Takes user input as an answer.
4	Compare user answer with correct answer	`if answer == quiz[question]:`	Checks correctness.
5	Keep track of score	`score += 1`	Increments score for correct answers.

Real-Life Project: Simple Quiz App

Project Code:

```
1.  def quiz_game():
2.      questions = {
3.          "What is the capital of France?": "a",
4.          "Which language is used for web
development?\n a) Python\n b) JavaScript\n c) Java\n d)
C++\n": "b",
5.          "What does CPU stand for?\n a) Central
Processing Unit\n b) Computer Personal Unit\n c)
Central Personal Unit\n d) Computer Processing Unit\n":
"a",
6.      }
7.      score = 0
8.      for question, correct_answer in
questions.items():
9.          user_answer = input(question + "\nYour
answer: ").lower()
10.         if user_answer == correct_answer:
11.             print("Correct!\n")
12.             score += 1
13.         else:
```

```
14.              print("Wrong answer!\n")
15.        print(f"You scored {score}/{len(questions)}")

16. quiz_game()
```

Project Code Explanation Table

Line	Code Section	Description
1	`def quiz_game():`	Defines the function for the quiz app.
2-6	`questions = {...}`	Creates a dictionary with quiz questions and correct answers.
7	`score = 0`	Initializes the score variable.
8	`for question, correct_answer in questions.items():`	Iterates through each question.
9	`user_answer = input(question + "\nYour answer: ").lower()`	Gets user input and converts it to lowercase.
10-12	`if user_answer == correct_answer:`	Checks if the answer is correct and updates the score.
13-14	`else:`	Prints "Wrong answer!" if the response is incorrect.
15	`print(f"You scored {score}/{len(questions)}")`	Displays the final score.
16	`quiz_game()`	Calls the quiz function to start the game.

Expected Results

- The program presents the user with a series of multiple-choice questions.
- The user enters an answer, and the program provides feedback on correctness.
- At the end, the program displays the final score.

Hands-On Exercise Try improving the Simple Quiz App with these additional features:

1. **Add more questions with different difficulty levels.**
2. **Create a GUI version using Tkinter for an interactive experience.**
3. **Enhance the program to keep track of high scores.**
4. **Implement a timer to limit the time for each question.**
5. **Allow users to select quiz categories before starting.**

Conclusion This Simple Quiz App project introduces Python concepts such as loops, dictionaries, user input handling, and scoring logic. By expanding this project, developers can create a more interactive and engaging educational tool.

Chapter 74: Create a Simple Text Editor

Overview A Simple Text Editor is an interactive application that allows users to write, save, and open text files. This project helps in understanding GUI programming using Tkinter, file handling, and event-driven programming in Python.

This chapter covers the step-by-step implementation of a text editor, handling user input, integrating basic file operations, and improving the interface.

Key Concepts of a Simple Text Editor in Python

- **Using Tkinter for GUI Development:**
    - Creating a text area using Tkinter's Text widget.
- **File Handling for Saving and Opening Files:**
    - Using Python's open() function to read and write files.
- **Menu Bar for File Operations:**
    - Creating a menu bar for Open, Save, and Exit options.

Example Text Editor Functions

Feature	Functionality
Open File	Loads a text file into the editor.
Save File	Saves the content to a text file.
Exit Application	Closes the editor safely.

Basic Rules for a Simple Text Editor in Python

Rule	Correct Example
Use Tkinter to create a text widget	Text(root, wrap='word')
Use open() to read files	file.read()
Use write() to save content	file.write(data)
Handle errors gracefully	try: open(filename) except: print("Error")

Syntax Table

SL	Concept	Syntax/Example	Description
1	Create Tkinter window	root = Tk()	Initializes the main window.

2	Add text widget	Text(root, wrap='word')	Adds a text editor area.
3	Open a file	with open(filename, 'r') as file:	Reads content from a file.
4	Save a file	with open(filename, 'w') as file:	Writes content to a file.
5	Create menu bar	menu = Menu(root)	Adds a menu bar for file operations.

Real-Life Project: Simple Text Editor

Project Code:

```
1.  from tkinter import *
2.  from tkinter import filedialog

3.  def open_file():
4.      file =
filedialog.askopenfilename(defaultextension=".txt",
filetypes=[("Text Files", "*.txt"), ("All Files",
"*.*")])
5.      if file:
6.          text_area.delete(1.0, END)
7.          with open(file, "r") as f:
8.              text_area.insert(INSERT, f.read())

9.  def save_file():
10.     file =
filedialog.asksaveasfilename(defaultextension=".txt",
filetypes=[("Text Files", "*.txt"), ("All Files",
"*.*")])
11.     if file:
12.         with open(file, "w") as f:
13.             f.write(text_area.get(1.0, END))

14. root = Tk()
15. root.title("Simple Text Editor")
16. root.geometry("500x500")
```

```
17. text_area = Text(root, wrap='word')
18. text_area.pack(expand=YES, fill=BOTH)

19. menu_bar = Menu(root)
20. file_menu = Menu(menu_bar, tearoff=0)
21. file_menu.add_command(label="Open",
command=open_file)
22. file_menu.add_command(label="Save",
command=save_file)
23. file_menu.add_separator()
24. file_menu.add_command(label="Exit",
command=root.quit)
25. menu_bar.add_cascade(label="File", menu=file_menu)
26. root.config(menu=menu_bar)

27. root.mainloop()
```

Project Code Explanation Table

Line	Code Section	Description
1-2	`from tkinter import *`, `from tkinter import filedialog`	Imports Tkinter and file dialog for GUI and file handling.
3-8	`def open_file():`	Defines a function to open a file and insert its content into the text area.
4	`file = filedialog.askopenfilename(...)`	Opens a file selection dialog for the user.
5	`if file:`	Ensures that a file is selected before proceeding.
6	`text_area.delete(1.0, END)`	Clears the text area before inserting new content.
7-8	`with open(file, "r") as f:`	Reads the content of the selected file and inserts it into the text area.

9-13	`def save_file():`	Defines a function to save the content of the text area into a file.
10	`file = filedialog.asksaveas filename(...)`	Opens a save dialog for the user to choose a file location.
11	`if file:`	Ensures that a file is selected before saving.
12-13	`with open(file, "w") as f:`	Saves the content of the text area into the chosen file.

14-16	`root = Tk(),`
	`root.title(...),`
	`root.geometry(...)`
		Initializes the Tkinter window and sets its properties.

17-18	`text_area =`
	`Text(root,`
	`wrap='word')`
		Creates a text area where users can write and edit text.

19-26	`menu_bar =`
	`Menu(root), file_menu`
	`= Menu(...)`
		Creates a menu bar with options for opening, saving, and exiting.

21-22	`file_menu.add_comman d(...)`	Adds commands for opening and saving files.
23	`file_menu.add_separa tor()`	Adds a separator in the menu for better visual organization.
24	`file_menu.add_comman d(label="Exit",` `command=root.quit)`	Adds an exit command to close the editor.
25-26	`menu_bar.add_cascade (...),` `root.config(menu=men u_bar)`	Configures the menu bar in the application window.
27	`root.mainloop()`	Starts the Tkinter event loop to run the application.

Expected Results

- The program opens a simple text editor.
- Users can write text and save it to a file.
- Users can open and edit existing text files.

Hands-On Exercise Try improving the Simple Text Editor with these additional features:

1. **Add functionality to open multiple file formats (e.g., `.csv`, `.log`).**
2. **Create a toolbar for quick access to Save, Open, and Exit functions.**
3. **Enable text formatting options like bold, italic, and underline.**
4. **Implement a 'Find and Replace' feature for editing text.**
5. **Allow users to change fonts and colors.**

Conclusion This Simple Text Editor project introduces Python concepts such as Tkinter GUI development, file handling, and event-driven programming. By expanding this project, developers can create more advanced text editing applications.

Chapter 75: Calculator Using GUI

Overview A GUI-based calculator is an interactive application that allows users to perform basic arithmetic operations like addition, subtraction, multiplication, and division. This project helps in understanding GUI programming using Tkinter, event handling, and user interface design in Python.

This chapter covers the step-by-step implementation of a GUI calculator, handling user input, creating buttons for operations, and displaying results.

Key Concepts of a GUI Calculator in Python

- **Using Tkinter for GUI Development:**
  - Creating a graphical interface with buttons, labels, and an entry field.
- **Event Handling for Button Clicks:**
  - Associating button clicks with arithmetic operations.
- **Displaying Results Dynamically:**
  - Updating the entry field with user input and calculation results.

Example Calculator Operations

Input Expression	Result
5 + 3	8
12 - 7	5
6 × 4	24
10 ÷ 2	5

Basic Rules for a GUI Calculator in Python

Rule	Correct Example
Use Tkinter to create an entry field	`Entry(root, textvariable=expression)`
Use buttons for numeric and operator input	`Button(root, text="+", command=lambda: click("+"))`
Use `eval()` to perform calculations	`result = eval(expression)`
Handle errors gracefully	`try: eval(expression) except: print("Error")`

Syntax Table

SL	Concept	Syntax/Example	Description
1	Create Tkinter window	`root = Tk()`	Initializes the main window.
2	Add an entry field	`Entry(root, textvariable=expression)`	Creates an input field for numbers.
3	Create buttons	`Button(root, text="+", command=lambda: click("+"))`	Adds a button for addition.
4	Evaluate expression	`result = eval(expression.get())`	Computes the mathematical result.
5	Clear the entry field	`expression.set("")`	Clears the input field.

Real-Life Project: GUI Calculator

Project Code:

```python
1.  from tkinter import *

2.  def click(button_value):
3.      current_text = expression.get()
4.      expression.set(current_text + button_value)

5.  def clear():
6.      expression.set("")

7.  def evaluate():
8.      try:
9.          result = eval(expression.get())
10.         expression.set(result)
11.     except:
12.         expression.set("Error")

13. root = Tk()
14. root.title("Simple Calculator")
15. root.geometry("300x400")
```

```
16. expression = StringVar()
17. entry_field = Entry(root, textvariable=expression,
font=("Arial", 20))
18. entry_field.grid(row=0, column=0, columnspan=4)

19. buttons = [
20.      '7', '8', '9', '/',
21.      '4', '5', '6', '*',
22.      '1', '2', '3', '-',
23.      '0', 'C', '=', '+'
24. ]

25. row, col = 1, 0
26. for button in buttons:
27.      Button(root, text=button, width=5, height=2,
font=("Arial", 18),
28.             command=lambda btn=button: click(btn) if
btn not in ['C', '='] else (clear() if btn == 'C' else
evaluate())).grid(row=row, column=col)
29.      col += 1
30.      if col > 3:
31.          col = 0
32.          row += 1

33. root.mainloop()
```

Project Code Explanation Table

Line	Code Section	Description
1	`from tkinter import *`	Imports Tkinter for GUI development.
2-4	`def click(button _value):`	Updates the entry field with clicked button value.
5-6	`def clear():`	Clears the entry field when 'C' is pressed.
7-12	`def evaluate():`	Computes the entered mathematical expression.

13-15	`root = Tk()`	Initializes the Tkinter window and sets its title and size.
16-18	`expression = StringVar()`	Defines a variable to hold the expression entered by the user.
19-24	`buttons = [...]`	Defines button labels for the calculator.
25-32	`for button in buttons:`	Creates buttons dynamically and assigns them functions.
33	`root.mainloop()`	Runs the Tkinter main event loop to keep the application running.

Expected Results
- The program opens a GUI-based calculator.
- Users can enter numbers and perform basic arithmetic operations.
- The calculator evaluates the expression and displays the result.

Hands-On Exercise Try improving the GUI Calculator with these additional features:

1. Add support for square root and power functions.
2. Create a scientific calculator with trigonometric functions.
3. Enable keyboard input for entering numbers and operations.
4. Modify the layout to enhance user experience.
5. Implement a memory function to store previous calculations.

Conclusion This GUI Calculator project introduces Python concepts such as Tkinter GUI development, event handling, and mathematical evaluations. By expanding this project, developers can create more advanced and user-friendly calculator applications.

Chapter 76: Reverse a Number

Overview Reversing a number is a fundamental exercise in Python that helps in understanding mathematical operations, loops, and string manipulation. This operation is widely used in number processing, encryption techniques, and data transformations.

This chapter covers the step-by-step implementation of reversing a number using different approaches, handling user input, and ensuring efficiency.

Key Concepts of Reversing a Number in Python

- **Using Mathematical Operations:**
  - Extracting digits and reversing their order using modulus and division.
- **Using String Manipulation:**
  - Converting the number to a string and reversing it using slicing.
- **Handling Edge Cases:**
  - Handling negative numbers and leading zeros properly.

Example Number Reversals

Input Number	Reversed Number
12345	54321
9087	7809
-456	-654
100	1

Basic Rules for Reversing a Number in Python

Rule	Correct Example
Convert the number to a string and reverse it	`str(num)[::-1]`
Use mathematical operations for reversing	`rev_num = rev_num * 10 + num % 10`
Handle negative numbers correctly	`if num < 0: reverse = -reverse`

Syntax Table

S.L	Concept	Syntax/Example	Description
1	Get user input	`num = int(input("Enter a number: "))`	Takes user input as an integer.
2	Convert to string	`str(num)`	Converts the number to a string for manipulation.
3	Reverse the string	`str(num)[::-1]`	Reverses the number using slicing.
4	Convert back to integer	`int(reversed_string)`	Converts the reversed string back to an integer.
5	Use a loop for reversal	`while num > 0: rev = rev * 10 + num % 10`	Uses arithmetic operations to reverse a number.

Real-Life Project: Reverse a Number

Project Code:

```
1.  def reverse_number(num):
2.      negative = num < 0
3.      num = abs(num)
4.      reversed_num = int(str(num)[::-1])
5.      return -reversed_num if negative else
reversed_num

6.  num = int(input("Enter a number: "))
7.  print("Reversed number:", reverse_number(num))
```

Project Code Explanation Table

Line	Code Section	Description
1	`def reverse_number(num):`	Defines a function to reverse a number.
2	`negative = num < 0`	Checks if the number is negative.
3	`num = abs(num)`	Converts negative numbers to positive for processing.

4	`reversed_num = int(str(num)[::-1])`	Converts the number to a string, reverses it, and converts it back to an integer.
5	`return - reversed_num if negative else reversed_num`	Restores the negative sign if applicable.
6	`num = int(input("Enter a number: "))`	Takes user input as an integer.
7	`print("Reversed number:", reverse_number(num) )`	Calls the function and displays the reversed number.

Expected Results

- The program asks the user to enter a number.
- It processes the number and reverses its digits.
- It prints the reversed number, handling negative numbers correctly.

Hands-On Exercise Try improving the Number Reversal program with these additional features:

1. **Use a loop instead of string manipulation for reversing the number.**
2. **Create a GUI version using Tkinter for interactive input.**
3. **Modify the program to reverse floating-point numbers.**
4. **Enable batch processing of multiple numbers at once.**
5. **Ensure that the program handles leading zeros correctly.**

Conclusion This Number Reversal project introduces Python concepts such as string manipulation, loops, and conditionals. By expanding this project, developers can explore more advanced number-processing applications in mathematical computations and data analysis.

Chapter 77: Simple Email Validation

Overview Email validation is an essential process used to verify if an email address follows the correct format. This project helps in understanding string manipulation, regular expressions, and user input validation in Python.

This chapter covers the step-by-step implementation of validating an email address, handling user input, and ensuring correctness using different approaches.

Key Concepts of Email Validation in Python

- **Using String Methods:**
  - Checking if an email contains '@' and a domain.
- **Using Regular Expressions (re module):**
  - Using regex patterns to match valid email formats.
- **Handling Edge Cases:**
  - Ensuring the email has valid characters and a correct domain structure.

Example Email Validation

Input Email	Valid?
user@example.com	Yes
hello@domain	No
test.email@org.net	Yes
user@.com	No

Basic Rules for Email Validation in Python

Rule	Correct Example
An email must contain '@'	`if "@" in email:`
A domain must follow '@'	`if email.split("@")[1]:`
Use regex for precise matching	`re.match(r"^[a-zA-Z0-9._%+-]+@[a-zA-Z0-9.-]+\.[a-zA-Z]{2,}$", email)`

Syntax Table

S L	Concept	Syntax/Example	Description
1	Get user input	`email = input("Enter an email: ")`	Takes user input as a string.
2	Check for '@'	`if "@" in email:`	Ensures '@' is present in the email.
3	Use regex for validation	`re.match(pattern, email)`	Uses regex to validate the format.
4	Print validation result	`print("Valid email" if valid else "Invalid email")`	Displays whether the email is valid or not.

Real-Life Project: Simple Email Validator

Project Code:

```
1.  import re

2.  def is_valid_email(email):
3.      pattern = r"^[a-zA-Z0-9._%+-]+@[a-zA-Z0-9.-]+\.[a-zA-Z]{2,}$"
4.      return re.match(pattern, email)

5.  email = input("Enter an email: ")
6.  if is_valid_email(email):
7.      print(f"'{email}' is a valid email address.")
8.  else:
9.      print(f"'{email}' is NOT a valid email address.")
```

Project Code Explanation Table

Line	Code Section	Description
1	`import re`	Imports the regex module for pattern matching.
2-4	`def is_valid_email(email):`	Defines a function to validate an email.
3	`pattern = r"^[a-zA-Z0-`	Defines the regex pattern

	9._%+-]+@[a-zA-Z0-9.-]+\.[a-zA-Z]{2,}$"	for validation.
4	`return re.match(pattern, email)`	Checks if the email matches the pattern.
5	`email = input("Enter an email: ")`	Takes user input for an email.
6-9	`if is_valid_email(email):`	Calls the function and prints whether the email is valid.

Expected Results

- The program asks the user to enter an email address.
- It validates the format using regex.
- It prints whether the email is valid or not.

Hands-On Exercise Try improving the Email Validator with these additional features:

1. **Allow the program to check for popular email domain extensions (e.g., .com, .net, .org).**
2. **Create a GUI version using Tkinter for interactive input.**
3. **Modify the program to detect temporary or disposable email addresses.**
4. **Enable batch processing of multiple emails at once.**
5. **Enhance error messages to specify why an email is invalid.**

Conclusion This Email Validation project introduces Python concepts such as string manipulation, regex validation, and user input handling. By expanding this project, developers can explore more advanced text validation applications in data processing and user authentication.

Chapter 78: Convert Hours to Minutes

Overview Converting hours to minutes is a fundamental exercise in Python that helps in understanding mathematical operations, user input handling, and simple calculations. This operation is widely used in time-related applications, scheduling systems, and data conversions.

This chapter covers the step-by-step implementation of converting hours to minutes, handling user input, and ensuring efficiency.

Key Concepts of Converting Hours to Minutes in Python

- **Using Mathematical Operations:**
    - The formula for converting hours to minutes is:
      $$Minutes = Hours \times 60 \quad Minutes = Hours \mid 60$$
- **Handling User Input:**
    - Taking input from users and ensuring data type consistency.
- **Displaying the Result in a Readable Format:**
    - Using formatted output for clarity.

Example Time Conversions

Hours	Minutes
1	60
2.5	150
4	240
0.75	45

Basic Rules for Converting Hours to Minutes in Python

Rule	Correct Example
Multiply hours by 60	`minutes = hours * 60`
Use `float` for precise input handling	`hours = float(input("Enter hours: "))`
Format the output for readability	`print(f"{hours} hours = {minutes} minutes")`

Syntax Table

SL	Concept	Syntax/Example	Description
1	Get user input	`hours = float(input("Enter hours: "))`	Takes time input from user.
2	Convert hours to minutes	`minutes = hours * 60`	Applies the conversion formula.
3	Print the result	`print(f"Minutes: {minutes}")`	Displays the converted value.

Real-Life Project: Convert Hours to Minutes

Project Code:

```
1.  def hours_to_minutes(hours):
2.      return hours * 60

3.  hours = float(input("Enter hours: "))
4.  minutes = hours_to_minutes(hours)
5.  print(f"{hours} hours is equal to {minutes} minutes.")
```

Project Code Explanation Table

Line	Code Section	Description
1-2	`def hours_to_minutes(hours):`	Defines a function to convert hours to minutes.
3	`hours = float(input("Enter hours: "))`	Takes user input and converts it to float.
4	`minutes = hours_to_minutes(hours)`	Calls the function to perform the conversion.
5	`print(f"{hours} hours is equal to {minutes} minutes.")`	Prints the result with formatted output.

Expected Results

- The program asks the user to enter a time in hours.
- It calculates and prints the equivalent time in minutes.
- The output is formatted to ensure readability.

Hands-On Exercise Try improving the Hours to Minutes Converter with these additional features:

1. Allow users to convert minutes back to hours as well.
2. Create a GUI version using `Tkinter` for interactive input.
3. Handle invalid inputs gracefully using exception handling.
4. Allow users to input multiple values at once and display all conversions.
5. Save conversion history to a file for later reference.

Conclusion This Hours to Minutes Converter project introduces Python concepts such as mathematical calculations, user input handling, and output formatting. By expanding this project, developers can create more advanced time conversion tools for various applications.

Chapter 79: Text to Speech Application

Overview A Text to Speech (TTS) application converts written text into spoken words. This project helps in understanding Python libraries such as pyttsx3 for text-to-speech conversion. TTS applications are widely used in assistive technologies, audiobooks, and automation systems.

This chapter covers the step-by-step implementation of a TTS application, handling user input, and generating speech output using Python.

Key Concepts of a Text to Speech Application in Python

- **Using the pyttsx3 Library:**
  - A text-to-speech conversion library that supports multiple voices and speech rate control.
- **Handling User Input:**
  - Accepting text input and processing it for speech output.
- **Generating Speech Output:**
  - Using the TTS engine to generate spoken output.

Example Text-to-Speech Conversions

Input Text	Spoken Output
"Hello, World!"	Reads "Hello, World!" aloud
"Python is amazing!"	Reads "Python is amazing!" aloud
"This is a text-to-speech converter."	Reads the sentence aloud

Basic Rules for a Text-to-Speech Application in Python

Rule	Correct Example
Initialize the TTS engine	`engine = pyttsx3.init()`
Set speech rate	`engine.setProperty('rate', 150)`
Select voice	`voices = engine.getProperty('voices')`
Convert text to speech	`engine.say("Hello, world!")`

Syntax Table

SL	Concept	Syntax/Example	Description
1	Import the library	`import pyttsx3`	Loads the text-to-speech module.
2	Initialize the engine	`engine = pyttsx3.init()`	Creates a TTS engine instance.

3	Set speech rate	`engine.setProperty('rate', 150)`	Adjusts the speech speed.
4	Set voice type	`engine.setProperty('voice', voices[0].id)`	Selects a male or female voice.
5	Convert text to speech	`engine.say(text)`	Processes the text and prepares speech output.
6	Execute speech	`engine.runAndWait()`	Plays the generated speech.

Real-Life Project: Text to Speech Converter

Project Code:

```
1.  import pyttsx3

2.  def text_to_speech(text):
3.      engine = pyttsx3.init()
4.      engine.setProperty('rate', 150)
5.      voices = engine.getProperty('voices')
6.      engine.setProperty('voice', voices[0].id)  #
Selects default voice
7.      engine.say(text)
8.      engine.runAndWait()

9.  user_text = input("Enter text to convert to speech:
")
10. text_to_speech(user_text)
```

Project Code Explanation Table

Line	Code Section	Description
1	`import pyttsx3`	Imports the text-to-speech library.
2	`def text_to_speech(text):`	Defines a function to convert text to speech.
3	`engine = pyttsx3.init()`	Initializes the TTS engine.
4	`engine.setProperty('rate', 150)`	Sets the speech speed.

5	`voices = engine.getProperty('voices')`	Retrieves available voices.
6	`engine.setProperty('voice', voices[0].id)`	Selects the default voice.
7	`engine.say(text)`	Processes the given text for speech conversion.
8	`engine.runAndWait()`	Plays the generated speech.
9	`user_text = input("Enter text to convert to speech: ")`	Takes user input.
10	`text_to_speech(user_text)`	Calls the function to convert and play speech.

Expected Results

- The program asks the user to enter a text string.
- It processes the text and generates spoken output.
- The text is read aloud using the selected voice.

Hands-On Exercise Try improving the Text to Speech Converter with these additional features:

1. **Allow users to select different voices (male/female).**
2. **Create a GUI version using Tkinter for interactive input.**
3. **Enable saving speech output as an audio file.**
4. **Allow users to adjust the speech rate dynamically.**
5. **Support multi-language speech conversion.**

Conclusion This Text to Speech project introduces Python concepts such as GUI development, audio processing, and user interaction. By expanding this project, developers can create more advanced speech-based applications for accessibility and automation.

Chapter 80: Word Count from a File

Overview A Word Count application is used to determine the number of words in a text file. This project helps in understanding file handling, string manipulation, and text analysis in Python.

This chapter covers the step-by-step implementation of reading a file, counting words, and displaying the result efficiently.

Key Concepts of Word Count in Python

- **Using File Handling to Read Data:**
  - Opening and reading a text file using Python's built-in functions.
- **Splitting Text into Words:**
  - Using split() to break the text into words.
- **Counting Words Efficiently:**
  - Using loops or len() function to count words accurately.

Example Word Count Results

File Content	Word Count
"Python is fun."	3
"This is a simple text file."	6
"Hello, world! Welcome to Python."	5

Basic Rules for Word Count in Python

Rule	Correct Example
Use open() to read a file	with open('file.txt', 'r') as file:
Read file contents	text = file.read()
Split text into words	words = text.split()
Count words	word_count = len(words)

Syntax Table

SL	Concept	Syntax/Example	Description
1	Open a file	with open('file.txt', 'r') as file:	Opens a text file in read mode.
2	Read file contents	text = file.read()	Reads the content of the file.
3	Split text	words = text.split()	Breaks the text into a

	into words		list of words.
4	Count words	`word_count = len(words)`	Counts the number of words.
5	Print the result	`print(f'Total words: {word_count}')`	Displays the word count.

Real-Life Project: Word Count from a File

Project Code:

```
1.  def count_words(filename):
2.      try:
3.          with open(filename, 'r') as file:
4.              text = file.read()
5.              words = text.split()
6.              return len(words)
7.      except FileNotFoundError:
8.          return "File not found."

9.  filename = input("Enter the file name: ")
10. word_count = count_words(filename)
11. print(f"Total words in {filename}: {word_count}")
```

Project Code Explanation Table

Line	Code Section	Description
1	`def count_words(filename):`	Defines a function to count words in a file.
2-3	`try: with open(filename, 'r') as file:`	Tries to open the file in read mode.
4	`text = file.read()`	Reads the entire content of the file.
5	`words = text.split()`	Splits the text into words.
6	`return len(words)`	Returns the word count.
7-8	`except FileNotFoundError:`	Handles cases where the file does not exist.
9	`filename = input("Enter the file name: ")`	Takes the filename as user input.
10	`word_count = count_words(filename)`	Calls the function to count words.

	print(f"Total words in {filename}: {word_count}")	Displays the result.
11		

Expected Results

- The program asks the user to enter a file name.
- It reads the file and counts the number of words.
- It prints the total word count.
- If the file does not exist, it displays an error message.

Hands-On Exercise Try improving the Word Count program with these additional features:

1. **Ignore punctuation and special characters when counting words.**
2. **Create a GUI version using Tkinter for interactive file selection.**
3. **Allow users to count words from multiple files at once.**
4. **Generate a word frequency report to show the most common words.**
5. **Save the word count results to a new file.**

Conclusion This Word Count project introduces Python concepts such as file handling, string manipulation, and error handling. By expanding this project, developers can build more advanced text processing tools for analyzing documents, reports, and large datasets.

Chapter 81: Phone Number Validator

Overview A Phone Number Validator is a program that verifies whether a given phone number follows the correct format. This project helps in understanding string manipulation, regular expressions, and input validation in Python.

This chapter covers the step-by-step implementation of validating phone numbers, handling different formats, and ensuring accuracy using Python.

Key Concepts of Phone Number Validation in Python

- **Using Regular Expressions (re module):**
  - Defining patterns to validate phone numbers.
- **Handling Different Phone Number Formats:**
  - Supporting various formats like (123) 456-7890, 123-456-7890, +1 123 456 7890.
- **Detecting Invalid Numbers:**
  - Ensuring numbers have valid digits and length constraints.

Example Phone Number Validations

Input Phone Number	Valid?
9876543210	Yes
+1 234-567-8901	Yes
123-45-6789	No
(999) 999-9999	Yes
abc1234567	No

Basic Rules for Phone Number Validation in Python

Rule	Correct Example
Use regex for precise matching	`re.match(r"^[0-9]{10}$", number)`
Accept country codes with +	`re.match(r"^\+?[0-9]{1,3}[0-9]{10}$", number)`
Remove non-digit characters for validation	`re.sub(r"\D", "", number)`

Syntax Table

SL	Concept	Syntax/Example	Description
1	Import regex module	`import re`	Loads the regex module for pattern matching.
2	Define validation pattern	`pattern = r"^\+?[0-9]{1,3}[-.\s]?[0-9]{10}$"`	Specifies the valid phone number format.
3	Match user input	`if re.match(pattern, phone_number):`	Checks if the input matches the pattern.
4	Remove special characters	`clean_number = re.sub(r"\D", "", phone_number)`	Cleans non-numeric characters for processing.
5	Print validation result	`print("Valid phone number")`	Displays whether the phone number is valid or not.

Real-Life Project: Phone Number Validator

Project Code:

```
1.  import re

2.  def is_valid_phone_number(phone_number):
3.      pattern = r"^\+?[0-9]{1,3}[-.\s]?[0-9]{10}$"
4.      return re.match(pattern, phone_number)

5.  phone_number = input("Enter a phone number: ")
6.  if is_valid_phone_number(phone_number):
7.      print(f"'{phone_number}' is a valid phone
number.")
8.  else:
9.      print(f"'{phone_number}' is NOT a valid phone
number.")
```

Project Code Explanation Table

Line	Code Section	Description
1	`import re`	Imports the regex module for pattern matching.
2-4	`def is_valid_phone_numbe r(phone_number):`	Defines a function to validate phone numbers.
3	`pattern = r"^\+?[0-9]{1,3}[-.\s]?[0-9]{10}$"`	Defines the regex pattern for validation.
4	`return re.match(pattern, phone_number)`	Checks if the phone number matches the pattern.
5	`phone_number = input("Enter a phone number: ")`	Takes user input for a phone number.
6-9	`if is_valid_phone_numbe r(phone_number):`	Calls the function and prints whether the phone number is valid.

Expected Results

- The program asks the user to enter a phone number.
- It validates the format using regex.
- It prints whether the phone number is valid or not.

Hands-On Exercise Try improving the Phone Number Validator with these additional features:

1. **Allow the program to format valid phone numbers into a standard structure.**
2. **Create a GUI version using `Tkinter` for interactive input.**
3. **Modify the program to detect specific country codes.**
4. **Enable batch processing of multiple phone numbers at once.**

Conclusion This Phone Number Validator project introduces Python concepts such as string manipulation, regex validation, and user input handling. By expanding this project, developers can explore more advanced text validation applications in data processing and user authentication.

Chapter 82: Convert Celsius to Fahrenheit

Overview Temperature conversion from Celsius to Fahrenheit is a simple yet essential operation in programming. This project helps in understanding mathematical operations, user input handling, and formatted output in Python. The conversion formula is widely used in weather applications and scientific calculations.

This chapter covers the step-by-step implementation of converting Celsius to Fahrenheit, handling user input, and displaying results efficiently.

Key Concepts of Celsius to Fahrenheit Conversion in Python

- **Using Mathematical Operations:**
  - The formula for conversion is:
  - *Celsius= ((Fahrenheit−32)×5)/6*
- **Handling User Input:**
  - Accepting temperature values in Celsius and ensuring data type consistency.
- **Displaying the Result in a Readable Format:**
  - Using formatted output for clarity.

Example Temperature Conversions

Celsius	Fahrenheit
0	32.0
25	77.0
37	98.6
-10	14.0

Basic Rules for Celsius to Fahrenheit Conversion in Python

Rule	Correct Example
Multiply Celsius by 9/5 and add 32	`fahrenheit = (celsius * 9/5) + 32`
Use `float` for precise input handling	`celsius = float(input("Enter Celsius: "))`
Format the output for readability	`print(f"{celsius}°C = {fahrenheit}°F")`

Syntax Table

SL	Concept	Syntax/Example	Description
1	Get user input	`celsius = float(input("Enter Celsius: "))`	Takes temperature input from the user.
2	Apply conversion formula	`fahrenheit = (celsius * 9/5) + 32`	Computes the Fahrenheit equivalent.
3	Print the result	`print(f"{celsius}°C = {fahrenheit}°F")`	Displays the converted temperature.

Real-Life Project: Convert Celsius to Fahrenheit

Project Code:

```
1. def celsius_to_fahrenheit(celsius):
2.     return (celsius * 9/5) + 32

3. celsius = float(input("Enter Celsius temperature: "))
4. fahrenheit = celsius_to_fahrenheit(celsius)
5. print(f"{celsius}°C is equal to {fahrenheit}°F")
```

Project Code Explanation Table

Line	Code Section	Description
1-2	`def celsius_to_fahrenheit(celsius):`	Defines a function to convert Celsius to Fahrenheit.
3	`celsius = float(input("Enter Celsius temperature: "))`	Takes user input and converts it to float.
4	`fahrenheit = celsius_to_fahrenheit(celsius)`	Calls the function to perform the conversion.
5	`print(f"{celsius}°C is equal to {fahrenheit}°F")`	Prints the result with formatted output.

Expected Results

- The program asks the user to enter a temperature in Celsius.
- It calculates and prints the equivalent temperature in Fahrenheit.
- The output is formatted for clarity and accuracy.

Hands-On Exercise Try improving the Celsius to Fahrenheit Converter with these additional features:

1. **Allow users to convert Fahrenheit back to Celsius as well.**
2. **Create a GUI version using `Tkinter` for interactive input.**
3. **Handle invalid inputs gracefully using exception handling.**
4. **Allow users to input multiple values at once and display all conversions.**
5. **Save conversion history to a file for later reference.**

Conclusion This Celsius to Fahrenheit Converter project introduces Python concepts such as mathematical calculations, user input handling, and output formatting. By expanding this project, developers can create more advanced temperature conversion tools for various applications.

Chapter 83: Write a Program to Create a Folder

Overview Creating a folder (directory) using Python is an essential skill in file handling. This operation is commonly used in organizing files, saving application-generated content, and automating file system management. This chapter covers the step-by-step implementation of creating a folder, handling errors, and verifying folder existence before creation.

Key Concepts of Creating a Folder in Python

- **Using os and pathlib Modules:**
  - os.mkdir() and pathlib.Path.mkdir() are two common methods to create directories.
- **Handling File System Errors:**
  - Checking if a folder exists before attempting to create one to avoid errors.
- **Creating Nested Directories:**
  - Using os.makedirs() to create multiple levels of directories at once.

Example Folder Creation

Folder Name	Creation Method
MyFolder	os.mkdir("MyFolder")
Projects/Python	os.makedirs("Projects/Python")
Documents/NewFolder	Path("Documents/NewFolder").mkdir(parents=True, exist_ok=True)

Basic Rules for Creating a Folder in Python

Rule	Correct Example
Use os.mkdir() for a single folder	os.mkdir("MyFolder")
Use os.makedirs() for nested folders	os.makedirs("Parent/Child")
Use pathlib.Path.mkdir() for flexibility	Path("Folder").mkdir(parents=True, exist_ok=True)

Check if a folder exists before creating it	`if not os.path.exists("Folder"): os.mkdir("Folder")`	

Syntax Table

SL	Concept	Syntax/Example	Description
1	Import required module	`import os`	Loads the OS module for file system operations.
2	Create a single folder	`os.mkdir("MyFolder")`	Creates a folder in the current directory.
3	Create nested folders	`os.makedirs("Parent /Child")`	Creates parent and child directories if they don't exist.
4	Check if folder exists before creating	`if not os.path.exists("Fol der"): os.mkdir("Folder")`	Prevents errors by verifying existence.
5	Use pathlib for folder creation	`Path("NewFolder").m kdir(parents=True, exist_ok=True)`	Creates a folder using an alternative method.

Real-Life Project: Create a Folder
Project Code:

```
1.  import os

2.  def create_folder(folder_name):
3.      if not os.path.exists(folder_name):
4.          os.mkdir(folder_name)
5.          print(f"Folder '{folder_name}' created
successfully.")
6.      else:
7.          print(f"Folder '{folder_name}' already
exists.")
8.  folder_name = input("Enter the folder name to
create: ")
9.  create_folder(folder_name)
```

Project Code Explanation Table

Line	Code Section	Description
1	`import os`	Imports the OS module for file operations.
2	`def create_folder(folder_name ):`	Defines a function to create a folder.
3	`if not os.path.exists(folder_nam e):`	Checks if the folder already exists.
4	`os.mkdir(folder_name)`	Creates the folder if it does not exist.
5	`print(f"Folder '{folder_name}' created successfully.")`	Displays success message.
6-7	`else:`	Handles the case when the folder already exists.
8	`folder_name = input("Enter the folder name to create: ")`	Takes folder name input from the user.
9	`create_folder(folder_name )`	Calls the function to create the folder.

Expected Results

- The program asks the user to enter a folder name.
- It checks if the folder already exists.
- If not, it creates the folder and prints a success message.
- If the folder exists, it notifies the user.

Hands-On Exercise Try improving the Folder Creator with these additional features:

1. Modify the program to create multiple folders at once.
2. Create a GUI version using `Tkinter` for interactive input.
3. Allow users to specify the folder location instead of using the current directory.
4. Enhance error handling for permission issues.
5. Automatically organize files into the created folder.

Chapter 84: Check if a String is a Substring of Another String

Overview Checking if one string is a substring of another is a common operation in text processing and data validation. This concept is used in search engines, authentication systems, and string manipulation tasks. This chapter covers the step-by-step implementation of checking for substrings, handling user input, and using different methods to verify substring presence in Python.

Key Concepts of Substring Checking in Python

- **Using the in Operator:**
  - The simplest way to check if one string exists within another.
- **Using String Methods (find() and index()):**
  - The find() method returns the index of the first occurrence of a substring.
  - The index() method works similarly but raises an exception if the substring is not found.
- **Using Regular Expressions (re module):**
  - Allows pattern-based substring matching.

Example Substring Checks

String	Substring	Exists?
"Hello, world!"	"world"	Yes
"Python programming"	"Java"	No
"abcdefg"	"cde"	Yes

Basic Rules for Checking Substrings in Python

Rule	Correct Example
Use in for simple substring search	`if "apple" in "pineapple":`
Use find() to get the position	`position = text.find("apple")`
Use index() to locate a substring	`position = text.index("apple")`
Use regex for complex pattern matching	`re.search("apple", text)`

Syntax Table

SL	Concept	Syntax/Example	Description
1	Get user input	`text = input("Enter main string: ")`	Takes input from the user.
2	Use in operator	`if substring in text:`	Checks if the substring exists.
3	Use find() method	`position = text.find(substring)`	Finds the position of the substring.
4	Use index() method	`position = text.index(substring)`	Returns the index or raises an error.
5	Use regex for advanced search	`re.search(pattern, text)`	Matches substrings using patterns.

Real-Life Project: Substring Checker

Project Code:

```
1.  def check_substring(main_string, substring):
2.      if substring in main_string:
3.          print(f"'{substring}' is found in the main string.")
4.      else:
5.          print(f"'{substring}' is NOT found in the main string.")

6.  main_string = input("Enter the main string: ")
7.  substring = input("Enter the substring to check: ")
8.  check_substring(main_string, substring)
```

Project Code Explanation Table

Line	Code Section	Description
1	`def check_substring(main_string, substring):`	Defines a function to check if a substring exists.
2	`if substring in`	Checks if the substring is

	main_string:	present in the main string.
3	print(f"'{substring}' is found in the main string.")	Displays a success message if the substring exists.
4-5	else:	Displays a message if the substring is not found.
6	main_string = input("Enter the main string: ")	Takes the main string input from the user.
7	substring = input("Enter the substring to check: ")	Takes the substring input from the user.
8	check_substring(main_st ring, substring)	Calls the function to check for the substring.

Expected Results

- The program asks the user to enter a main string and a substring.
- It checks if the substring exists within the main string.
- It prints a message indicating whether the substring is found or not.

Hands-On Exercise Try improving the Substring Checker with these additional features:

1. **Modify the program to return the position of the substring if found.**
2. **Create a GUI version using Tkinter for interactive input.**
3. **Implement case-insensitive substring checking.**
4. **Enhance error handling for empty input cases.**
5. **Allow users to search for multiple substrings at once.**

Conclusion This Substring Checker project introduces Python concepts such as string manipulation, user input handling, and search operations. By expanding this project, developers can explore more advanced text processing applications in search engines and data validation.

Chapter 85: Count the Number of Occurrences of Each Character

Overview Counting the occurrences of each character in a string is a common operation in text analysis, cryptography, and data processing. This task helps in understanding dictionary usage, loops, and string manipulation in Python.

This chapter covers the step-by-step implementation of counting character occurrences, handling user input, and displaying results effectively.

Key Concepts of Character Frequency Counting in Python

- **Using a Dictionary for Counting:**
    - Storing characters as keys and their counts as values.
- **Iterating Through a String:**
    - Processing each character and updating its count.
- **Using `collections.Counter`:**
    - A built-in method to simplify frequency counting.

Example Character Counting

Input String	Character Count
"banana"	{ 'b': 1, 'a': 3, 'n': 2 }
"hello"	{ 'h': 1, 'e': 1, 'l': 2, 'o': 1 }
"apple"	{ 'a': 1, 'p': 2, 'l': 1, 'e': 1 }

Basic Rules for Character Frequency Counting in Python

Rule	Correct Example
Use a dictionary to store counts	`char_count = {}`
Use a loop to iterate through a string	`for char in text:`
Use Counter for simplified counting	`collections.Counter(text)`
Ignore case differences (optional)	`text.lower()`

Syntax Table

SL	Concept	Syntax/Example	Description
1	Get user input	`text = input("Enter a string: ")`	Takes input from the user.
2	Initialize dictionary	`char_count = {}`	Creates an empty dictionary.
3	Loop through the string	`for char in text:`	Iterates through characters.
4	Update character count	`char_count[char] = char_count.get(char, 0) + 1`	Increments character count.
5	Print frequency result	`print(char_count)`	Displays character occurrences.

Real-Life Project: Character Frequency Counter

Project Code:

```
1.  from collections import Counter

2.  def count_characters(text):
3.      char_count = Counter(text)
4.      return char_count

5.  text = input("Enter a string: ")
6.  result = count_characters(text)
7.  print("Character Frequency:")
8.  for char, count in result.items():
9.      print(f"'{char}': {count}")
```

Project Code Explanation Table

Line	Code Section	Description
1	`from collections import Counter`	Imports Counter for counting characters.
2-4	`def count_characters(text):`	Defines a function to count character occurrences.

3	`char_count = Counter(text)`	Uses Counter to count characters efficiently.
5	`text = input("Enter a string: ")`	Takes user input.
6	`result = count_characters(text)`	Calls the function and stores the result.
7	`print("Character Frequency:")`	Displays output header.
8-9	`for char, count in result.items():`	Iterates through character counts and prints them.

Expected Results

- The program asks the user to enter a string.
- It processes the string and counts the occurrences of each character.
- It prints a list of characters along with their frequency.

Hands-On Exercise Try improving the Character Frequency Counter with these additional features:

1. **Ignore case differences to count uppercase and lowercase letters as the same.**
2. **Create a GUI version using Tkinter for interactive input.**
3. **Ignore spaces and punctuation in character counting.**
4. **Sort the output by character frequency.**
5. **Save the character count results to a file.**

Conclusion This Character Frequency Counter project introduces Python concepts such as dictionaries, loops, and built-in modules like `collections.Counter`. By expanding this project, developers can explore more advanced text processing applications in data analysis and natural language processing.

Chapter 86: Reverse a List

Overview Reversing a list is a fundamental operation in Python that is useful in various applications such as data analysis, sorting, and algorithm optimization. Python provides multiple ways to reverse a list efficiently. This chapter covers different techniques to reverse a list, handling user input, and implementing efficient methods for reversing lists in Python.

Key Concepts of Reversing a List in Python

- **Using the `reverse()` Method:**
  - The built-in method that directly modifies the list.
- **Using Slicing (`[::-1]`):**
  - A simple and readable method to reverse a list.
- **Using `reversed()` Function:**
  - Returns an iterator for a reversed list.

Example List Reversal

Original List	Reversed List
`[1, 2, 3, 4, 5]`	`[5, 4, 3, 2, 1]`
`['a', 'b', 'c']`	`['c', 'b', 'a']`
`[10, 20, 30, 40]`	`[40, 30, 20, 10]`

Basic Rules for Reversing a List in Python

Rule	Correct Example
Use `list.reverse()` for in-place reversal	`my_list.reverse()`
Use slicing for a new reversed list	`reversed_list = my_list[::-1]`
Use `reversed()` for an iterator	`list(reversed(my_list))`

Syntax Table

SL	Concept	Syntax/Example	Description
1	Get user input as a list	`my_list = list(map(int, input().split()))`	Takes a list of numbers as input.

2	Reverse using reverse()	`my_list.reverse()`	Modifies the list in place.
3	Reverse using slicing	`reversed_list = my_list[::-1]`	Creates a new reversed list.
4	Reverse using reversed()	`list(reversed(my_list))`	Returns a reversed iterator.

Real-Life Project: Reverse a List

Project Code:

```
1.  def reverse_list(lst):
2.      return lst[::-1]

3.  my_list = list(map(int, input("Enter numbers
separated by space: ").split()))
4.  reversed_list = reverse_list(my_list)
5.  print("Reversed List:", reversed_list)
```

Project Code Explanation Table

Line	Code Section	Description
1	`def reverse_list(lst):`	Defines a function to reverse a list.
2	`return lst[::-1]`	Uses slicing to reverse the list.
3	`my_list = list(map(int, input().split()))`	Takes user input as a list of integers.
4	`reversed_list = reverse_list(my_list)`	Calls the function to reverse the list.
5	`print("Reversed List:", reversed_list)`	Prints the reversed list.

Expected Results

- The program asks the user to enter a list of numbers.
- It reverses the list and prints the output.
- The reversed list is displayed in the console.

Hands-On Exercise Try improving the List Reversal program with these additional features:

1. **Allow the program to reverse lists with mixed data types (strings, floats).**

Chapter 87: Find the Second Largest Element in a List

Overview Finding the second largest element in a list is a common programming task used in data processing and competitive programming. This exercise helps in understanding list operations, sorting techniques, and conditional logic in Python.

This chapter covers different methods to find the second largest element efficiently, handling edge cases, and ensuring optimized performance.

Key Concepts of Finding the Second Largest Element in Python

- **Sorting and Indexing:**
    - Sorting the list and selecting the second largest element.
- **Using Loops and Conditions:**
    - Iterating through the list to find the two largest numbers.
- **Handling Duplicates and Edge Cases:**
    - Ensuring the list has at least two unique numbers.

Example Second Largest Element Searches

Input List	Second Largest Element
`[10, 20, 4, 45, 99]`	45
`[5, 1, 8, 8, 3]`	5
`[100, 100, 99]`	99
`[7, 7, 7]`	None (No Second Largest)

Basic Rules for Finding the Second Largest Element in Python

Rule	Correct Example
Use `sorted()` to sort and get the second largest	`sorted_list[-2]`
Use a loop to track the two largest elements	`if num > first: second = first; first = num`
Remove duplicates to ensure uniqueness	`list(set(numbers))`
Handle lists with fewer than two unique values	`if len(set(numbers)) < 2: return None`

Syntax Table

SL	Concept	Syntax/Example	Description
1	Get user input as a list	`numbers = list(map(int, input().split()))`	Takes a list of numbers as input.
2	Remove duplicates	`unique_numbers = list(set(numbers))`	Ensures uniqueness before finding second largest.
3	Sort the list	`sorted_numbers = sorted(unique_numb ers)`	Sorts the numbers in ascending order.
4	Find second largest	`second_largest = sorted_numbers[-2]`	Retrieves the second last element.
5	Use a loop to track max values	`if num > first: second = first; first = num`	Finds the two largest values efficiently.

Real-Life Project: Find the Second Largest Element

Project Code:

```
1.  def second_largest(numbers):
2.      unique_numbers = list(set(numbers))
3.      if len(unique_numbers) < 2:
4.          return None
5.      unique_numbers.sort()
6.      return unique_numbers[-2]

7.  numbers = list(map(int, input("Enter numbers
separated by space: ").split()))
8.  result = second_largest(numbers)
9.  if result is None:
10.     print("No second largest element found.")
11. else:
12.     print("Second largest element:", result)
```

Project Code Explanation Table

Line	Code Section	Description
1	`def second_largest(numbers):`	Defines a function to find the second largest number.
2	`unique_numbers = list(set(numbers))`	Removes duplicates to ensure unique values.
3	`if len(unique_numbers) < 2:`	Checks if there are at least two unique numbers.
4	`return None`	Returns None if no second largest element exists.
5	`unique_numbers.sort()`	Sorts the list in ascending order.
6	`return unique_numbers[-2]`	Retrieves the second largest number.
7	`numbers = list(map(int, input().split()))`	Takes user input as a list of integers.
8	`result = second_largest(numbers)`	Calls the function to find the second largest number.
9-10	`if result is None:`	Handles cases where there is no second largest value.
11-12	`print("Second largest element:", result)`	Prints the second largest number if found.

Expected Results

- The program asks the user to enter a list of numbers.
- It processes the list and finds the second largest unique number.
- It prints the result or notifies the user if no second largest element exists.

Hands-On Exercise Try improving the Second Largest Element Finder with these additional features:

1. **Use a loop instead of sorting to improve performance.**
2. **Create a GUI version using Tkinter for interactive input.**

Chapter 88: Create a Digital Clock

Overview A digital clock displays the current time and updates in real-time. This project helps in understanding GUI programming using Tkinter and working with the time module in Python.

This chapter covers the step-by-step implementation of a digital clock, updating time dynamically, and enhancing the interface using Tkinter.

Key Concepts of a Digital Clock in Python

- **Using Tkinter for GUI Development:**
  - Creating a GUI window and placing a label to display the time.
- **Using the time Module:**
  - Fetching the current time using strftime.
- **Updating Time in Real-Time:**
  - Using the after() method in Tkinter to refresh the time every second.

Example Digital Clock Display

Time Format	Example
12-hour	02:30:15 PM
24-hour	14:30:15

Basic Rules for Creating a Digital Clock in Python

Rule	Correct Example
Use time.strftime() to get current time	current_time = time.strftime('%H:%M:%S')
Use Tkinter.Label() to display time	Label(root, text=current_time)
Use after(1000, update_time) for updates	clock_label.after(1000, update_time)

Syntax Table

SL	Concept	Syntax/Example	Description
1	Import necessary modules	import time, tkinter as tk	Loads the required modules.
2	Create a Tkinter window	root = tk.Tk()	Initializes the main window.

3	Create a label for time display	`clock_label = tk.Label(root, text="")`	Sets up a label to show time.
4	Fetch current time	`current_time = time.strftime('%H:%M:%S')`	Retrieves formatted time.
5	Schedule updates	`clock_label.after(1000, update_time)`	Updates time every second.

Real-Life Project: Digital Clock

Project Code:

```
1.  import time
2.  import tkinter as tk

3.  def update_time():
4.      current_time = time.strftime('%H:%M:%S %p')
5.      clock_label.config(text=current_time)
6.      clock_label.after(1000, update_time)

7.  root = tk.Tk()
8.  root.title("Digital Clock")
9.  root.geometry("300x100")

10. clock_label = tk.Label(root, font=("Arial", 30),
bg="black", fg="white")
11. clock_label.pack(pady=20)

12. update_time()

13. root.mainloop()
```

Project Code Explanation Table

Line	Code Section	Description
1-2	`import time, tkinter as tk`	Imports necessary modules.
3-6	`def update_time():`	Defines a function to update the clock every second.

4	`current_time = time.strftime('%H:%M: %S %p')`	Fetches the current time in 12-hour format.
5	`clock_label.config(te xt=current_time)`	Updates the label text with the current time.
6	`clock_label.after(100 0, update_time)`	Calls the function every second for updates.
7-9	`root = tk.Tk()`	Initializes the main application window.
10-11	`clock_label = tk.Label(...)`	Creates and configures a label for displaying time.
12	`update_time()`	Calls the function to start updating the clock.
13	`root.mainloop()`	Runs the Tkinter event loop.

Expected Results

- The program opens a GUI window displaying the current time.
- The clock updates every second automatically.
- The time is formatted as HH:MM:SS AM/PM.

Hands-On Exercise Try improving the Digital Clock with these additional features:

1. **Allow users to switch between 12-hour and 24-hour formats.**
2. **Customize the clock interface with different fonts and colors.**
3. **Display the date along with the time.**
4. **Create an alarm feature that alerts users at a set time.**
5. **Implement a stopwatch feature using Tkinter buttons.**

Conclusion This Digital Clock project introduces Python concepts such as GUI development, event handling, and time manipulation. By expanding this project, developers can create more advanced time-related applications for daily use.

Chapter 89: Number System Conversion

Overview Number system conversion is an essential concept in computer science and programming. This project helps in converting numbers between different bases such as binary, octal, decimal, and hexadecimal using Python's built-in functions.

This chapter covers various techniques to convert numbers between different number systems, handling user input, and displaying results effectively.

Key Concepts of Number System Conversion in Python

- **Using Built-in Functions:**
  - `bin()`, `oct()`, `hex()`, and `int()` for conversion.
- **Converting Between Number Systems:**
  - Decimal to Binary, Octal, Hexadecimal.
  - Binary, Octal, Hexadecimal to Decimal.
- **Handling User Input and Displaying Results:**
  - Ensuring proper format and valid number entry.

Example Number Conversions

Input Number	Base	Converted Value
25	Binary	11001
1101	Decimal (from Binary)	13
45	Octal	55
A3	Decimal (from Hex)	163

Basic Rules for Number System Conversion in Python

Rule	Correct Example
Convert Decimal to Binary	`bin(25)` → `'0b11001'`
Convert Decimal to Octal	`oct(45)` → `'0o55'`
Convert Decimal to Hexadecimal	`hex(255)` → `'0xff'`
Convert Binary to Decimal	`int('1010', 2)` → 10
Convert Octal to Decimal	`int('55', 8)` → 45
Convert Hexadecimal to Decimal	`int('A3', 16)` → 163

Syntax Table

SL	Concept	Syntax/Example	Description
1	Convert Decimal to Binary	`bin(10)`	Returns binary equivalent of a decimal number.
2	Convert Decimal to Octal	`oct(45)`	Returns octal equivalent of a decimal number.
3	Convert Decimal to Hexadecimal	`hex(255)`	Returns hexadecimal equivalent of a decimal number.
4	Convert Binary to Decimal	`int('1101', 2)`	Converts a binary string to decimal.
5	Convert Octal to Decimal	`int('55', 8)`	Converts an octal string to decimal.
6	Convert Hexadecimal to Decimal	`int('A3', 16)`	Converts a hexadecimal string to decimal.

Real-Life Project: Number System Converter

Project Code:

```python
1.  def convert_number(number, from_base, to_base):
2.      decimal_number = int(number, from_base)
3.      if to_base == 2:
4.          return bin(decimal_number)[2:]
5.      elif to_base == 8:
6.          return oct(decimal_number)[2:]
7.      elif to_base == 16:
8.          return hex(decimal_number)[2:].upper()
9.      else:
10.         return str(decimal_number)

11. number = input("Enter the number: ")
12. from_base = int(input("Enter the base of the input
number (2, 8, 10, 16): "))
13. to_base = int(input("Enter the base to convert to
(2, 8, 10, 16): "))
14. result = convert_number(number, from_base, to_base)
15. print(f"Converted value: {result}")
```

Project Code Explanation Table

Line	Code Section	Description
1	`def convert_number(number, from_base, to_base):`	Defines a function to convert between number systems.
2	`decimal_number = int(number, from_base)`	Converts the input number to decimal.
3-4	`if to_base == 2:`	Converts decimal to binary.
5-6	`elif to_base == 8:`	Converts decimal to octal.
7-8	`elif to_base == 16:`	Converts decimal to hexadecimal.
9-10	`else:`	Returns decimal as a string.
11	`number = input("Enter the number: ")`	Takes user input for the number to convert.
12	`from_base = int(input("Enter the base of the input number (2, 8, 10, 16): "))`	Takes the base of the input number.
13	`to_base = int(input("Enter the base to convert to (2, 8, 10, 16): "))`	Takes the base for conversion.
14	`result = convert_number(number, from_base, to_base)`	Calls the function to convert the number.
15	`print(f"Converted value: {result}")`	Displays the converted result.

Expected Results

- The program asks the user to enter a number and its base.
- It asks for the base to which the number should be converted.
- It performs the conversion and displays the result.

Hands-On Exercise Try improving the Number System Converter with these additional features:

1. **Enhance the program to validate user input before conversion.**

Chapter 90: Guess the Number Game

Overview The "Guess the Number" game is a simple interactive game where the user attempts to guess a randomly generated number. This project helps in understanding random number generation, loops, conditional statements, and user input handling in Python.

This chapter covers the step-by-step implementation of the game, setting a range for guessing, providing feedback to the player, and implementing attempts tracking.

Key Concepts of the Guess the Number Game in Python

- **Using the random Module:**
    - Generating a random number within a defined range.
- **Handling User Input:**
    - Taking guesses from the user and validating input.
- **Using Loops and Conditional Statements:**
    - Providing feedback on whether the guess is too high or too low.

Example Game Flow

User Guess	Feedback
50	Too low!
75	Too high!
62	Correct! You won!

Basic Rules for the Guess the Number Game in Python

Rule	Correct Example
Generate a random number	`random.randint(1, 100)`
Take user input	`guess = int(input("Enter your guess: "))`
Compare guess with target	`if guess > target:`
Provide feedback to the user	`print("Too high!")`

Syntax Table

SL	Concept	Syntax/Example	Description
1	Import random module	`import random`	Loads the module to generate random numbers.
2	Generate a random number	`random.randint(1, 100)`	Generates a random number between 1 and 100.
3	Get user input	`guess = int(input("Enter your guess: "))`	Takes a number input from the user.
4	Use a loop for multiple attempts	`while guess != target:`	Keeps asking for input until the correct guess.
5	Provide hints	`if guess > target: print("Too high!")`	Gives feedback based on the user's guess.

Real-Life Project: Guess the Number Game

Project Code:

```
1.  import random

2.  def guess_the_number():
3.      target = random.randint(1, 100)
4.      attempts = 0

5.      while True:
6.          try:
7.              guess = int(input("Guess a number between 1 and 100: "))
8.              attempts += 1
9.              if guess < target:
10.                 print("Too low! Try again.")
11.             elif guess > target:
12.                 print("Too high! Try again.")
13.             else:
```

```
14.                      print(f"Congratulations! You
guessed the number {target} in {attempts} attempts.")
15.                      break
16.          except ValueError:
17.              print("Invalid input! Please enter a
number.")

18. guess_the_number()
```

Project Code Explanation Table

Line	Code Section	Description
1	`import random`	Imports the random module for generating numbers.
2	`def guess_the_num ber():`	Defines the function for the game.
3	`target = random.randin t(1, 100)`	Generates a random target number.
4	`attempts = 0`	Initializes attempt counter.
5	`while True:`	Starts an infinite loop until the correct number is guessed.
6-7	`try: guess = int(input(... ))`	Takes user input and converts it to an integer.
8	`attempts += 1`	Increments the attempts counter.
9-10	`if guess < target:`	Prints "Too low!" if the guess is smaller than the target.
11-12	`elif guess > target:`	Prints "Too high!" if the guess is larger than the target.
13-15	`else:`	Congratulates the user and exits the loop when the correct number is guessed.
16-17	`except ValueError:`	Handles invalid inputs and prompts for a valid number.
18	`guess_the_num ber()`	Calls the function to start the game.

Expected Results

- The program generates a random number between 1 and 100.
- The user is prompted to enter a guess.
- The program provides hints if the guess is too high or too low.
- The game continues until the correct number is guessed.
- The number of attempts is displayed at the end.

Hands-On Exercise Try improving the Guess the Number game with these additional features:

1. **Allow users to set the number range (e.g., 1-50, 1-500).**
2. **Create a GUI version using Tkinter for interactive play.**
3. **Implement difficulty levels that limit the number of attempts.**
4. **Store and display high scores (minimum attempts to win).**
5. **Give hints such as "You're close!" when the guess is within 5 of the target.**

Conclusion This Guess the Number project introduces Python concepts such as loops, conditional statements, exception handling, and random number generation. By expanding this project, developers can explore more interactive and challenging versions of the game.

Chapter 91: Python Dictionary Sorting

Overview Sorting a dictionary in Python is a common operation used in data processing and organizing structured information. Python provides various methods to sort dictionaries based on keys or values efficiently. This chapter covers different ways to sort dictionaries, handling user input, and displaying results in an organized manner.

Key Concepts of Dictionary Sorting in Python

- **Sorting by Keys:**
    - Using `sorted(dictionary.keys())` to sort by keys.
- **Sorting by Values:**
    - Using `sorted(dictionary.items(), key=lambda item: item[1])`.
- **Using `operator.itemgetter()`:**
    - Importing the `operator` module for efficient sorting.

Example Dictionary Sorting

Input Dictionary	Sorted by Keys	Sorted by Values
`{'b': 3, 'a': 5, 'c': 1}`	`{'a': 5, 'b': 3, 'c': 1}`	`{'c': 1, 'b': 3, 'a': 5}`
`{'x': 8, 'y': 2, 'z': 10}`	`{'x': 8, 'y': 2, 'z': 10}`	`{'y': 2, 'x': 8, 'z': 10}`

Basic Rules for Sorting a Dictionary in Python

Rule	Correct Example
Sort by keys	`sorted(dictionary.keys())`
Sort by values	`sorted(dictionary.items(), key=lambda item: item[1])`
Use `operator.itemgetter()` for efficiency	`sorted(dictionary.items(), key=itemgetter(1))`
Convert sorted result back to dictionary	`dict(sorted_items)`

Syntax Table

SL	Concept	Syntax/Example	Description
1	Sort by keys	`sorted(dictionary.keys())`	Returns a sorted list of keys.
2	Sort dictionary by keys	`dict(sorted(dictionary.items()))`	Returns a dictionary sorted by keys.
3	Sort by values using lambda	`sorted(dictionary.items(), key=lambda x: x[1])`	Returns sorted dictionary items by values.
4	Use operator.itemgetter()	`sorted(dictionary.items(), key=itemgetter(1))`	Efficiently sorts dictionary items.
5	Convert sorted items back to dictionary	`dict(sorted_items)`	Converts sorted items into a dictionary.

Real-Life Project: Dictionary Sorting

Project Code:

```
1.  from operator import itemgetter

2.  def sort_dict_by_key(dictionary):
3.      return dict(sorted(dictionary.items()))

4.  def sort_dict_by_value(dictionary):
5.      return dict(sorted(dictionary.items(),
    key=itemgetter(1)))

6.  user_dict = {'apple': 3, 'banana': 1, 'cherry': 2}
7.  print("Original Dictionary:", user_dict)
8.  print("Sorted by Keys:",
    sort_dict_by_key(user_dict))
9.  print("Sorted by Values:",
    sort_dict_by_value(user_dict))
```

Project Code Explanation Table

Line	Code Section	Description
1	`from operator import itemgetter`	Imports `itemgetter` for sorting.
2-3	`def sort_dict_by_key(dictionary):`	Defines a function to sort dictionary by keys.
4-5	`def sort_dict_by_value(dictionary):`	Defines a function to sort dictionary by values.
6	`user_dict = {'apple': 3, 'banana': 1, 'cherry': 2}`	Example dictionary.
7	`print("Original Dictionary:", user_dict)`	Displays the original dictionary.
8	`print("Sorted by Keys:", sort_dict_by_key(user_dict))`	Prints dictionary sorted by keys.
9	`print("Sorted by Values:", sort_dict_by_value(user_dict))`	Prints dictionary sorted by values.

Expected Results

- The program prints the original dictionary.
- It sorts the dictionary by keys and prints the result.
- It sorts the dictionary by values and prints the result.

Hands-On Exercise Try improving the Dictionary Sorting program with these additional features:

1. Allow users to input their own dictionary values.
2. Create a GUI version using Tkinter for interactive sorting.
3. Allow users to sort in ascending or descending order.
4. Enhance the program to handle large data sets efficiently.
5. Implement sorting based on custom key functions.

Conclusion This Dictionary Sorting project introduces Python concepts such as dictionaries, sorting techniques, and lambda functions. By expanding this project, developers can explore more efficient ways of organizing data in real-world applications.

Chapter 92: Check for Perfect Number

Overview A perfect number is a positive integer that is equal to the sum of its proper divisors, excluding itself. For example, 6 is a perfect number because its divisors (excluding 6) are 1, 2, and 3, and their sum is 6.

This chapter covers the implementation of a perfect number checker, handling user input, and verifying results efficiently using Python.

Key Concepts of Checking for a Perfect Number in Python

- **Using Loops for Finding Divisors:**
  - Iterating through numbers to find divisors.
- **Using Conditional Statements:**
  - Checking if the sum of divisors equals the original number.
- **Handling User Input and Displaying Results:**
  - Ensuring valid input and proper output formatting.

Example Perfect Number Checks

Number	Perfect?	Sum of Proper Divisors
6	Yes	1 + 2 + 3 = 6
28	Yes	1 + 2 + 4 + 7 + 14 = 28
15	No	1 + 3 + 5 = 9
496	Yes	1 + 2 + 4 + 8 + ... + 248 = 496

Basic Rules for Checking a Perfect Number in Python

Rule	Correct Example
Find divisors using a loop	`for i in range(1, num):`
Sum up the proper divisors	`sum_divisors += i`
Check if the sum equals the number	`if sum_divisors == num:`
Ensure the number is positive	`if num <= 0: return False`

Syntax Table

SL	Concept	Syntax/Example	Description
1	Get user input	`num = int(input("Enter a number: "))`	Takes an integer input.

2	Initialize sum variable	`sum_divisors = 0`	Stores the sum of divisors.
3	Use loop to find divisors	`for i in range(1, num):`	Iterates through numbers to find divisors.
4	Add divisors to sum	`sum_divisors += i`	Sums up proper divisors.
5	Check if number is perfect	`if sum_divisors == num:`	Compares sum to the original number.

Real-Life Project: Perfect Number Checker

Project Code:

```
1.  def is_perfect_number(num):
2.      if num < 1:
3.          return False
4.      sum_divisors = sum(i for i in range(1, num) if
num % i == 0)
5.      return sum_divisors == num

6.  num = int(input("Enter a number: "))
7.  if is_perfect_number(num):
8.      print(f"{num} is a perfect number.")
9.  else:
10.     print(f"{num} is NOT a perfect number.")
```

Project Code Explanation Table

Line	Code Section	Description
1	`def is_perfect_number(num):`	Defines the function to check perfect numbers.
2-3	`if num < 1:`	Ensures the number is positive.
4	`sum_divisors = sum(i for i in range(1, num) if num % i == 0)`	Finds and sums up divisors.
5	`return sum_divisors == num`	Returns True if the number is perfect.

6	`num = int(input("Enter a number: "))`	Takes user input.
7-10	`if is_perfect_number(num):`	Calls the function and prints the result.

Expected Results

- The program asks the user to enter a number.
- It calculates the sum of proper divisors.
- It checks if the sum equals the original number.
- It prints whether the number is perfect or not.

Hands-On Exercise Try improving the Perfect Number Checker with these additional features:

1. **Allow the program to check a range of numbers for perfect numbers.**
2. **Create a GUI version using `Tkinter` for interactive input.**
3. **Optimize performance by iterating only up to num//2.**
4. **Enhance the program to check for near-perfect numbers.**
5. **Store results and display all perfect numbers found within a given range.**

Conclusion This Perfect Number Checker project introduces Python concepts such as loops, conditional statements, and mathematical operations. By expanding this project, developers can explore number theory and its applications in computing and data analysis.

Chapter 93: Create a Random Quote Generator

Overview A Random Quote Generator is a fun and interactive program that displays a randomly selected quote every time it runs. This project helps in understanding the use of lists, random selection, and user interaction in Python.

This chapter covers the step-by-step implementation of a random quote generator, handling user input, and formatting output efficiently.

Key Concepts of a Random Quote Generator in Python

- **Using Lists to Store Quotes:**
    - A collection of predefined quotes for selection.
- **Using the random Module:**
    - Selecting a random quote from the list.
- **Displaying Quotes to the User:**
    - Formatting the output for readability.

Example Random Quotes Output

Run	Random Quote Output
1st	"Believe you can and you're halfway there." - Theodore Roosevelt
2nd	"Success is not final, failure is not fatal: It is the courage to continue that counts." - Winston Churchill
3rd	"Life is 10% what happens to us and 90% how we react to it." - Charles R. Swindoll

Basic Rules for Random Quote Generation in Python

Rule	Correct Example
Store quotes in a list	`quotes = ["Quote 1", "Quote 2"]`
Use `random.choice()` for selection	`random.choice(quotes)`
Print the selected quote	`print(random_quote)`
Allow users to request another quote	`input("Press Enter to get a new quote...")`

Syntax Table

SL	Concept	Syntax/Example	Description
1	Import random module	`import random`	Loads the random selection module.
2	Define a list of quotes	`quotes = ["Quote 1", "Quote 2"]`	Stores multiple quotes.
3	Select a random quote	`random.choice(quotes)`	Picks a quote randomly.
4	Display the quote	`print(random_quote)`	Prints the selected quote.
5	Loop for user interaction	`while input("Get another quote? (y/n)") == 'y':`	Allows multiple quote requests.

Real-Life Project: Random Quote Generator

Project Code:

```
1.  import random

2.  quotes = [
3.      "Believe you can and you're halfway there. -
Theodore Roosevelt",
4.      "Success is not final, failure is not fatal: It
is the courage to continue that counts. - Winston
Churchill",
5.      "Life is 10% what happens to us and 90% how we
react to it. - Charles R. Swindoll",
6.      "Happiness depends upon ourselves. -
Aristotle",
7.      "Do what you can, with what you have, where you
are. - Theodore Roosevelt"
8.  ]

9.  def get_random_quote():
10.     return random.choice(quotes)

11. while True:
12.     print("\nRandom Quote: ")
```

```
13.        print(get_random_quote())
14.        user_input = input("\nWould you like another
quote? (y/n): ")
15.        if user_input.lower() != 'y':
16.           break
```

Project Code Explanation Table

Line	Code Section	Description
1	`import random`	Imports the random module for selecting quotes.
2-8	`quotes = [...]`	Defines a list of inspirational quotes.
9-10	`def get_random_quote():`	Defines a function to return a random quote.
11	`while True:`	Starts a loop to allow multiple quote requests.
12-13	`print(get_random_quote())`	Displays a randomly selected quote.
14	`user_input = input("Would you like another quote? (y/n): ")`	Asks the user if they want another quote.
15-16	`if user_input.lower() != 'y': break`	Exits the loop if the user enters anything other than 'y'.

Expected Results

- The program displays a randomly selected quote each time it runs.
- It prompts the user to request another quote.
- If the user enters 'y', it generates a new quote; otherwise, it exits.

Hands-On Exercise Try improving the Random Quote Generator with these additional features:

1. **Allow users to add their own quotes to the list dynamically.**
2. **Create a GUI version using `Tkinter` for interactive display.**
3. **Store quotes in an external file and load them dynamically.**
4. **Categorize quotes (e.g., motivational, life, success) and let users choose a category.**

Chapter 94: Create a Basic Unit Converter

Overview A unit converter is a useful tool that allows users to convert values from one measurement unit to another. This project helps in understanding mathematical operations, conditional statements, and user input handling in Python.

This chapter covers the step-by-step implementation of a basic unit converter, handling multiple unit types, and displaying accurate conversion results.

Key Concepts of a Unit Converter in Python

- **Using Dictionaries for Conversion Factors:**
  - Storing conversion values for easy lookup.
- **Using Conditional Statements:**
  - Determining the correct conversion based on user input.
- **Handling User Input and Displaying Results:**
  - Ensuring valid input and providing formatted output.

Example Unit Conversions

Input Value	From Unit	To Unit	Converted Value
1	Kilometers	Miles	0.621371
5	Kilograms	Pounds	11.0231
100	Celsius	Fahrenheit	212
60	Minutes	Hours	1

Basic Rules for Unit Conversion in Python

Rule	Correct Example
Use a dictionary to store conversion factors	`conversion_factors = {"km_to_miles": 0.621371}`
Use multiplication for conversion	`miles = km * conversion_factors["km_to_miles"]`
Handle user input dynamically	`input("Enter value to convert: ")`
Use conditionals to select conversions	`if from_unit == "km" and to_unit == "miles":`

Syntax Table

S L	Concept	Syntax/Example	Description
1	Get user input	`value = float(input("Enter value: "))`	Takes input from the user.
2	Use dictionary for conversion factors	`conversion_factors = {"km_to_miles": 0.621371}`	Stores conversion rates.
3	Convert value using multiplication	`converted_value = value * conversion_factors[key]`	Performs conversion calculation.
4	Display result	`print(f"{value} km is {converted_value} miles")`	Prints the converted value.
5	Use if statements for unit selection	`if from_unit == "kg" and to_unit == "lbs":`	Determines the correct conversion.

Real-Life Project: Basic Unit Converter

Project Code:

```
1.  def convert_units(value, from_unit, to_unit):
2.      conversion_factors = {
3.          "km_to_miles": 0.621371,
4.          "miles_to_km": 1.60934,
5.          "kg_to_lbs": 2.20462,
6.          "lbs_to_kg": 0.453592,
7.          "celsius_to_fahrenheit": lambda c: (c * 9/5) + 32,
8.          "fahrenheit_to_celsius": lambda f: (f - 32) * 5/9
9.      }
10.     key = f"{from_unit}_to_{to_unit}"
11.     if key in conversion_factors:
12.         return conversion_factors[key](value) if callable(conversion_factors[key]) else value * conversion_factors[key]
```

```
13.        else:
14.               return "Invalid conversion"

15. value = float(input("Enter value: "))
16. from_unit = input("Enter from unit: ")
17. to_unit = input("Enter to unit: ")
18. result = convert_units(value, from_unit, to_unit)
19. print(f"Converted Value: {result}")
```

Project Code Explanation Table

Line	Code Section	Description
1	`def convert_units(value, from_unit, to_unit):`	Defines the function for conversion.
2-9	`conversion_factors = {...}`	Stores conversion factors in a dictionary.
10	`key = f"{from_unit}_to_{to_unit}"`	Creates a dynamic key for lookup.
11	`if key in conversion_factors:`	Checks if the conversion exists.
12	`return conversion_factors[key](value) if callable(...)`	Uses lambda functions for dynamic conversions.
13-14	`else: return "Invalid conversion"`	Handles invalid conversions.
15-17	`value, from_unit, to_unit = input(...)`	Takes user input.
18	`result = convert_units(value, from_unit, to_unit)`	Calls the function.
19	`print(f"Converted Value: {result}")`	Displays the converted value.

Expected Results

- The program asks the user to enter a value and select units.
- It calculates and prints the converted value.
- It handles different unit types dynamically.

Hands-On Exercise Try improving the Unit Converter with these additional features:

1. **Allow users to add their own conversion factors.**
2. **Create a GUI version using Tkinter for interactive use.**
3. **Enable more unit categories such as time, volume, and speed.**
4. **Store conversion history and allow users to view past conversions.**
5. **Handle edge cases such as zero or negative values gracefully.**

Conclusion This Unit Converter project introduces Python concepts such as dictionaries, lambda functions, and conditional logic. By expanding this project, developers can create more advanced and flexible conversion tools for real-world applications.

Chapter 95: Generate a Random Color

Overview Generating random colors in Python is useful for graphics programming, UI development, and game design. This project helps in understanding the use of the `random` module and how to represent colors in different formats such as RGB and Hex.

This chapter covers the step-by-step implementation of generating random colors, handling different color formats, and displaying results effectively.

Key Concepts of Random Color Generation in Python

- **Using the `random` Module:**
  - Generating random RGB values.
- **Converting RGB to Hexadecimal:**
  - Using Python's string formatting to convert RGB values to Hex.
- **Using `matplotlib` to Display Colors:**
  - Visualizing the generated random colors.

Example Random Colors

RGB Values	Hex Code
(255, 0, 0)	#FF0000
(34, 139, 34)	#228B22
(173, 216, 230)	#ADD8E6

Basic Rules for Random Color Generation in Python

Rule	Correct Example
Generate RGB values	`random.randint(0, 255)`
Convert RGB to Hex	`f"#{r:02X}{g:02X}{b:02X}"`
Use `matplotlib` to display color	`plt.imshow([[color]])`
Ensure RGB values are within range	`0 <= r, g, b <= 255`

Syntax Table

SL	Concept	Syntax/Example	Description
1	Import random module	`import random`	Loads the module for generating random numbers.
2	Generate random RGB values	`r, g, b = random.randint( 0, 255)`	Generates random color components.
3	Convert RGB to Hex	`hex_color = f"#{r:02X}{g:02X}{b:02X}"`	Converts RGB to Hex format.
4	Display color using matplotlib	`plt.imshow([[color]])`	Shows the generated color visually.
5	Return both RGB and Hex values	`return rgb, hex_color`	Provides color in both formats.

Real-Life Project: Random Color Generator

Project Code:

```
1.  import random
2.  import matplotlib.pyplot as plt

3.  def generate_random_color():
4.      r = random.randint(0, 255)
5.      g = random.randint(0, 255)
6.      b = random.randint(0, 255)
7.      hex_color = f"#{r:02X}{g:02X}{b:02X}"
8.      return (r, g, b), hex_color

9.  rgb, hex_color = generate_random_color()
10. print(f"Generated Color - RGB: {rgb}, Hex: {hex_color}")

11. plt.figure(figsize=(2, 2))
12. plt.imshow([[rgb]], aspect='auto')
13. plt.axis('off')
14. plt.show()
```

Project Code Explanation Table

Line	Code Section	Description
1-2	`import random,` `matplotlib.pyplot as plt`	Imports required modules.
3	`def` `generate_random_color():`	Defines a function to generate a random color.
4-6	`r, g, b =` `random.randint(0, 255)`	Generates random RGB values.
7	`hex_color =` `f"#{r:02X}{g:02X}{b:02X}"`	Converts RGB values to Hex.
8	`return (r, g, b),` `hex_color`	Returns both RGB and Hex values.

9-10	`print(f"Generated Color -`
	`RGB: {rgb}, Hex:`
	`{hex_color}")`
		Displays the generated color values.

11-14	`plt.imshow([[rgb]],` `aspect='auto')`	Visualizes the color using `matplotlib`.

Expected Results

- The program generates and prints a random color in RGB and Hex format.
- The generated color is displayed using `matplotlib`.
- The colors change every time the script is run.

Hands-On Exercise Try improving the Random Color Generator with these additional features:

1. **Generate multiple random colors and display them as a palette.**
2. **Allow users to specify the number of colors to generate.**
3. **Create a GUI version using `Tkinter` for interactive use.**
4. **Save the generated color palette as an image file.**
5. **Allow users to specify a preferred color range (e.g., pastel shades, dark colors).**

Conclusion This Random Color Generator project introduces Python concepts such as random number generation, string formatting, and visualization using `matplotlib`. By expanding this project, developers can explore color generation techniques for graphic design and game development applications.

Chapter 96: Simple Python Stopwatch

Overview A stopwatch is a time-tracking tool that helps in measuring elapsed time accurately. This project helps in understanding Python's `time` module, user input handling, and event-based programming. This chapter covers the step-by-step implementation of a simple stopwatch, handling start/stop functionality, and displaying elapsed time efficiently.

Key Concepts of a Python Stopwatch

- **Using the `time` Module:**
    - Tracking the start and stop times.
- **Handling User Input:**
    - Allowing users to start, stop, and reset the stopwatch.
- **Formatting Elapsed Time:**
    - Displaying time in a readable format (HH:MM:SS).

Example Stopwatch Usage

Action	Output
Start	Stopwatch started...
Stop	Elapsed Time: 00:02:15
Reset	Stopwatch reset to 00:00:00

Basic Rules for Implementing a Stopwatch in Python

Rule	Correct Example
Use `time.time()` to get current time	`start_time = time.time()`
Calculate elapsed time	`elapsed = time.time() - start_time`
Format time using `divmod()`	`hours, rem = divmod(seconds, 3600)`
Handle user input for control	`input("Press Enter to stop...")`

Syntax Table

S L	Concept	Syntax/Example	Description
1	Import `time` module	`import time`	Loads the module for time tracking.

2	Get current time	`start_time = time.time()`	Stores the start timestamp.
3	Calculate elapsed time	`elapsed = time.time() - start_time`	Computes time difference.
4	Format time for display	`f"{int(hours):02}:{int(minutes):02}:{int(seconds):02}"`	Converts time to HH:MM:SS.
5	Use loop for real-time updates	`while running: print_elapsed_time()`	Continuously updates the display.

Real-Life Project: Simple Python Stopwatch

Project Code:

```python
1.  import time

2.  def format_time(seconds):
3.      hours, rem = divmod(seconds, 3600)
4.      minutes, seconds = divmod(rem, 60)
5.      return f"{int(hours):02}:{int(minutes):02}:{int(seconds):02}"

6.  def stopwatch():
7.      input("Press Enter to start the stopwatch...")
8.      start_time = time.time()
9.      input("Press Enter to stop the stopwatch...")
10.     elapsed_time = time.time() - start_time
11.     print(f"Elapsed Time: {format_time(elapsed_time)}")

12. stopwatch()
```

Project Code Explanation Table

Line	Code Section	Description
1	`import time`	Imports the `time` module.
2-5	`def format_time(seconds):`	Defines a function to format elapsed time.

3-4	`divmod()`	Converts seconds into hours, minutes, and seconds.
6	`def stopwatch():`	Defines the main stopwatch function.
7	`input("Press Enter to start the stopwatch...")`	Waits for user to start.
8	`start_time = time.time()`	Records the start time.
9	`input("Press Enter to stop the stopwatch...")`	Waits for user to stop.
10	`elapsed_time = time.time() - start_time`	Calculates elapsed time.
11	`print(f"Elapsed Time: {format_time(elapsed_time)}")`	Displays formatted elapsed time.

Expected Results

- The program waits for the user to start the stopwatch.
- It calculates the elapsed time until the user stops it.
- It displays the formatted elapsed time in HH:MM:SS format.

Hands-On Exercise Try improving the Python Stopwatch with these additional features:

1. **Allow users to pause and resume the stopwatch.**
2. **Create a GUI version using `Tkinter` for better user interaction.**
3. **Add a lap-time feature to record multiple time intervals.**
4. **Enable a countdown timer mode for timed activities.**
5. **Display live elapsed time while running instead of only at the end.**

Conclusion This Python Stopwatch project introduces time-based calculations, user interaction handling, and formatting time outputs. By expanding this project, developers can build more advanced timing applications such as countdown timers, alarms, or productivity trackers.

Chapter 97: Sorting a List of Tuples

Overview Sorting a list of tuples is a common operation in data processing and manipulation. Tuples often contain multiple elements, such as (name, age) or (score, student_id), and sorting helps organize the data efficiently. This chapter covers different techniques to sort a list of tuples, including sorting by the first element, sorting by a specific index, and sorting using custom key functions.

Key Concepts of Sorting a List of Tuples in Python

- **Using sorted() Function:**
    - Sorting tuples based on default order (first element).
- **Using lambda for Custom Sorting:**
    - Sorting tuples based on a specific element.
- **Using operator.itemgetter():**
    - A more efficient way to sort by an index.

Example Tuple Sorting

Input List	Sorted by First Element	Sorted by Second Element
[(3, 'Banana'), (1, 'Apple'), (2, 'Cherry')]	[(1, 'Apple'), (2, 'Cherry'), (3, 'Banana')]	[(3, 'Banana'), (1, 'Apple'), (2, 'Cherry')]
[(20, 'Alice'), (18, 'Bob'), (25, 'Charlie')]	[(18, 'Bob'), (20, 'Alice'), (25, 'Charlie')]	[(20, 'Alice'), (18, 'Bob'), (25, 'Charlie')]

Basic Rules for Sorting a List of Tuples in Python

Rule	Correct Example
Use sorted() for basic sorting	sorted(list_of_tuples)
Use lambda to sort by index	sorted(list_of_tuples, key=lambda x: x[1])
Use reverse=True for descending order	sorted(list_of_tuples, reverse=True)
Use operator.itemgetter() for efficiency	sorted(list_of_tuples, key=itemgetter(1))

Syntax Table

S L	Concept	Syntax/Example	Description
1	Sort by first element	`sorted(list_of_tupl es)`	Uses default sorting (by first element).
2	Sort by second element	`sorted(list_of_tupl es, key=lambda x: x[1])`	Uses `lambda` to sort by index.
3	Sort in descending order	`sorted(list_of_tupl es, reverse=True)`	Sorts in descending order.
4	Use `itemgetter()` for efficiency	`sorted(list_of_tupl es, key=itemgetter(1))`	Sorts using `operator.itemge tter()`.

Real-Life Project: Sorting a List of Tuples

Project Code:

```
1.  from operator import itemgetter

2.  def sort_tuples_by_index(tuples_list, index,
descending=False):
3.      return sorted(tuples_list,
key=itemgetter(index), reverse=descending)

4.  tuples_list = [(3, 'Banana'), (1, 'Apple'), (2,
'Cherry')]
5.  print("Original List:", tuples_list)

6.  sorted_by_first = sort_tuples_by_index(tuples_list,
0)
7.  print("Sorted by First Element:", sorted_by_first)

8.  sorted_by_second =
sort_tuples_by_index(tuples_list, 1)
9.  print("Sorted by Second Element:",
sorted_by_second)
```

Project Code Explanation Table

Line	Code Section	Description
1	`from operator import itemgetter`	Imports `itemgetter` for efficient sorting.
2-3	`def sort_tuples_by_index(tuples _list, index, descending=False):`	Defines a function to sort tuples by any index.
4	`tuples_list = [(3, 'Banana'), (1, 'Apple'), (2, 'Cherry')]`	Sample list of tuples.
5	`print("Original List:", tuples_list)`	Prints the original list.
6	`sorted_by_first = sort_tuples_by_index(tuples _list, 0)`	Sorts by first element.
7	`print("Sorted by First Element:", sorted_by_first)`	Displays sorted tuples.
8	`sorted_by_second = sort_tuples_by_index(tuples _list, 1)`	Sorts by second element.
9	`print("Sorted by Second Element:", sorted_by_second)`	Displays sorted tuples.

Expected Results

- The program prints the original list of tuples.
- It sorts the list by the first element and prints the result.
- It sorts the list by the second element and prints the result.

Hands-On Exercise Try improving the Tuple Sorting program with these additional features:

1. **Allow users to enter their own list of tuples.**
2. **Create a GUI version using `Tkinter` for interactive sorting.**
3. **Enable multi-level sorting (e.g., sort by second element, then by first).**
4. **Handle sorting of tuples with different data types (numbers, strings).**

Chapter 98: Extract Numbers from a String

Overview Extracting numbers from a string is a common task in text processing, data extraction, and natural language processing. This project helps in understanding string manipulation, regular expressions, and list operations in Python.

This chapter covers different techniques to extract numbers from a string, including using loops, list comprehensions, and regular expressions.

Key Concepts of Extracting Numbers from a String in Python

- **Using Loops to Identify Digits:**
  - Iterating through a string and extracting numeric characters.
- **Using Regular Expressions (re module):**
  - Using pattern matching to find numbers in a string.
- **Converting Extracted Numbers to Integers:**
  - Converting string numbers into integer or float values.

Example Number Extraction

Input String	Extracted Numbers
"Price is 45 dollars and 30 cents"	`[45, 30]`
"Order #1234 shipped in 2 days"	`[1234, 2]`
"The 5 boxes cost $100 each"	`[5, 100]`

Basic Rules for Extracting Numbers in Python

Rule	Correct Example
Use `isdigit()` to find numeric characters	`if char.isdigit():`
Use regex for efficient extraction	`re.findall(r'\d+', text)`
Convert extracted numbers to integers	`list(map(int, numbers))`
Handle float values properly	`re.findall(r'\d+\.\d+', text)`

Syntax Table

S L	Concept	Syntax/Example	Description
1	Extract numbers using loops	`[char for char in text if char.isdigit()]`	Finds individual digits.
2	Use regex to extract numbers	`re.findall(r'\d+', text)`	Finds whole numbers in a string.
3	Convert extracted values	`list(map(int, numbers))`	Converts extracted strings to integers.
4	Extract decimal numbers	`re.findall(r'\d+\.\d+', text)`	Finds floating-point numbers.
5	Combine regex and mapping	`` `[float(num) for num in re.findall(r'\d+.\d+ ``	`` \d+', text)]` ``

Real-Life Project: Extract Numbers from a String

Project Code:

```
1.  import re

2.  def extract_numbers(text):
3.      numbers = re.findall(r'\d+\.\d+|\d+', text)
4.      return [float(num) if '.' in num else int(num)
for num in numbers]

5.  text = input("Enter a string: ")
6.  extracted_numbers = extract_numbers(text)
7.  print("Extracted Numbers:", extracted_numbers)
```

Project Code Explanation Table

Line	Code Section	Description
1	`import re`	Imports the re module for regex operations.
2	`def extract_numbers(text):`	Defines the function to extract numbers.
3	`` `re.findall(r'\d+.\d+ ``	`` \d+', text)` ``

4	`[float(num) if '.' in num else int(num) for num in numbers]`	Converts extracted values into numeric types.
5	`text = input("Enter a string: ")`	Takes a string input from the user.
6	`extracted_numbers = extract_numbers(text)`	Calls the function to extract numbers.
7	`print("Extracted Numbers:", extracted_numbers)`	Displays the extracted numbers.

Expected Results

- The program asks the user to enter a string containing numbers.
- It extracts all numbers (integers and decimals) from the input.
- It converts them into numeric values and prints the result.

Hands-On Exercise Try improving the Number Extraction program with these additional features:

1. Allow extraction of negative numbers and currency values (e.g., $50.75).
2. Create a GUI version using Tkinter for interactive input.
3. Enable extraction of phone numbers from a text.
4. Handle large numbers with commas (e.g., 1,000,000).
5. Save extracted numbers to a file for later use.

Conclusion This Number Extraction project introduces Python concepts such as string manipulation, regular expressions, and data processing. By expanding this project, developers can create more advanced data extraction tools for real-world applications in finance, text analytics, and automation.

Chapter 99: Check if a Number is a Palindrome

Overview A palindrome number is a number that remains the same when its digits are reversed. For example, 121, 454, and 1221 are palindrome numbers. This project helps in understanding number manipulation, string conversion, and conditional logic in Python.

This chapter covers different techniques to check if a number is a palindrome, handling user input, and displaying results effectively.

Key Concepts of Checking Palindrome Numbers in Python

- **Reversing a Number:**
  - Converting the number to a string and checking its reverse.
- **Using Loops to Reverse a Number:**
  - Extracting digits and constructing the reversed number.
- **Handling User Input and Displaying Results:**
  - Ensuring valid input and providing formatted output.

Example Palindrome Checks

Number	Palindrome?
121	Yes
454	Yes
1221	Yes
123	No
9876	No

Basic Rules for Checking Palindromes in Python

Rule	Correct Example
Convert number to string and compare with its reverse	`str(num) == str(num)[::-1]`
Reverse a number using arithmetic operations	`reversed_num = int(str(num)[::-1])`
Use a loop to construct the reversed number	`while num > 0: reversed_num = reversed_num * 10 + num % 10`

Syntax Table

SL	Concept	Syntax/Example	Description
1	Convert number to string	`str(num)`	Converts the number into a string.
2	Reverse string using slicing	`str(num)[::-1]`	Gets the reversed version of the string.
3	Check for palindrome	`str(num) == str(num)[::-1]`	Compares original and reversed string.
4	Use a loop for reversing number	`while num > 0:`	Iterates over the digits of the number.
5	Construct the reversed number	`reversed_num = reversed_num * 10 + num % 10`	Builds the reversed number step by step.

Real-Life Project: Palindrome Number Checker

Project Code:

```
1.  def is_palindrome(num):
2.      return str(num) == str(num)[::-1]

3.  num = int(input("Enter a number: "))
4.  if is_palindrome(num):
5.      print(f"{num} is a palindrome number.")
6.  else:
7.      print(f"{num} is NOT a palindrome number.")
```

Project Code Explanation Table

Line	Code Section	Description
1	`def is_palindrome(num):`	Defines a function to check if a number is a palindrome.
2	`return str(num) == str(num)[::-1]`	Converts the number to a string and compares it with its reverse.

3	`num = int(input("Enter a number: "))`	Takes user input and converts it to an integer.
4-5	`if is_palindrome(nu m):`	Checks if the number is a palindrome and prints the result.
6-7	`else:`	Displays a message if the number is not a palindrome.

Expected Results

- The program asks the user to enter a number.
- It checks if the number remains the same when reversed.
- It prints whether the number is a palindrome or not.

Hands-On Exercise Try improving the Palindrome Number Checker with these additional features:

1. **Allow the program to check a range of numbers for palindromes.**
2. **Create a GUI version using Tkinter for interactive input.**
3. **Check for negative numbers and handle them appropriately.**
4. **Optimize the logic using a mathematical approach instead of string conversion.**
5. **Enhance the program to count and display the total palindrome numbers within a given range.**

Conclusion This Palindrome Number Checker project introduces Python concepts such as string manipulation, loops, and number operations. By expanding this project, developers can explore number theory and its applications in computing and data validation.

Chapter 100: Create a Python Program to Calculate Factorial

Overview Factorial calculation is a fundamental mathematical operation used in permutations, combinations, and various algorithms. The factorial of a number nn, denoted as $n!n!$, is the product of all positive integers from 1 to nn.

This chapter covers different techniques to compute the factorial of a number, including iterative, recursive, and built-in function approaches.

Key Concepts of Factorial Calculation in Python

- **Using Loops to Compute Factorial:**
  - Iterating through numbers to calculate factorial.
- **Using Recursion for Factorial Calculation:**
  - A function that calls itself to compute factorial.
- **Using Python's `math.factorial()` Function:**
  - A built-in method to compute factorial efficiently.

Example Factorial Calculations

Number (n)	Factorial (n!)
3	6 (3×2×1)
5	120 (5×4×3×2×1)
7	5040 (7×6×5×4×3×2×1)
10	3,628,800

Basic Rules for Calculating Factorial in Python

Rule	Correct Example
Use a loop to calculate factorial	`for i in range(1, n+1):` `fact *= i`
Use recursion for factorial calculation	`def fact(n): return n *` `fact(n-1)`
Use `math.factorial()` for efficiency	`math.factorial(n)`
Handle edge cases like 0! = 1	`if n == 0: return 1`

Syntax Table

SL	Concept	Syntax/Example	Description
1	Calculate factorial using a loop	`for i in range(1, n+1): fact *= i`	Uses iteration to compute factorial.
2	Compute factorial using recursion	`def factorial(n): return n * factorial(n-1) if n > 1 else 1`	Recursively calculates factorial.
3	Use `math.factorial()`	`import math; math.factorial(n)`	Uses Python's built-in function for factorial.
4	Handle base case in recursion	`if n == 1: return 1`	Ensures recursion terminates properly.

Real-Life Project: Factorial Calculator

Project Code:

```
1.  import math

2.  def factorial_iterative(n):
3.      fact = 1
4.      for i in range(1, n + 1):
5.          fact *= i
6.      return fact

7.  def factorial_recursive(n):
8.      return 1 if n == 0 else n *
factorial_recursive(n - 1)

9.  num = int(input("Enter a number: "))
10. print(f"Factorial (Iterative):
{factorial_iterative(num)}")
11. print(f"Factorial (Recursive):
{factorial_recursive(num)}")
12. print(f"Factorial (Using math module):
{math.factorial(num)}")
```

Project Code Explanation Table

Line	Code Section	Description
1	`import math`	Imports the math module for factorial calculation.
2-6	`def factorial_iterative (n):`	Defines an iterative function to compute factorial.
4-5	`for i in range(1, n + 1): fact *= i`	Uses a loop to compute factorial.
7-8	`def factorial_recursive (n):`	Defines a recursive function for factorial.
9	`num = int(input("Enter a number: "))`	Takes user input and converts it to an integer.
10	`factorial_iterative (num)`	Calls the iterative function and prints the result.
11	`factorial_recursive (num)`	Calls the recursive function and prints the result.
12	`math.factorial(num)`	Uses the built-in function and prints the result.

Expected Results

- The program asks the user to enter a number.
- It calculates the factorial using three different methods: iterative, recursive, and the built-in function.
- It prints the calculated factorial for each method.

Hands-On Exercise Try improving the Factorial Calculator with these additional features:

1. Allow the program to compute factorial for a range of numbers.
2. Create a GUI version using `Tkinter` for interactive input.
3. Optimize the recursive function using memoization.
4. Handle large numbers gracefully and prevent recursion depth errors.
5. Display the factorial calculation step-by-step for better understanding.

www.ingramcontent.com/pod-product-compliance
Lightning Source LLC
LaVergne TN
LVHW051428050326
832903LV00030BD/2979